PROBLEMS AND PRACTICE
OF PASTORAL CARE

by the same author

The Teacher and Counselling
The Teacher and Pastoral Care
Study Skills

PROBLEMS AND PRACTICE OF PASTORAL CARE

Edited By:

DOUGLAS HAMBLIN

BASIL BLACKWELL PUBLISHER

© Basil Blackwell Publisher 1981

First published in 1981 by
Basil Blackwell Publisher
108 Cowley Road
Oxford OX4 1JF
England

British Library Cataloguing in Publication Data

Problems and Practice of Pastoral Care
(1) Personnel service in Secondary Education
(2) Hamblin, Douglas

373.1'4   LB 1620.5

ISBN 0 631 12931 6 Paperback
ISBN 0 631 12921 9 Hardback

Typeset in Bembo 10/12pt
by Preface Ltd., Salisbury
Printed in Great Britain by
Billing and Sons Ltd.,
Guildford, London, Oxford, Worcester

Contents

v

Introduction

This book is written by those who have had experience of successful pastoral care which raises the pupil's level of functioning, and helps them achieve success in school. Pastoral care is seen by them as an essential part of efficient secondary school education. It is neither a luxury nor an irrelevance but an essential element in the attainment of the educational objectives of the school.

The emphasis is on active approaches which provide pupils with the skills necessary for achievement. The contributors also give due attention to the social and emotional aspects of education. Teachers will find much that will help them use the tutorial periods to greater effect and develop productive activities. Each contribution stresses in its particular field the need for clearly defined objectives and structures. Implicit in them all is acceptance that the teacher is an important figure in the life of the pupil, and that we as teachers make an important contribution to society. Involvement in pastoral care increases our job satisfaction because it allows us to use our knowledge of adolescent development and the processes through which pupils learn in a way which boosts pupil performance and reduces tensions within the school.

The book falls into three parts. The first is concerned with basic skills and activities. Then follows a section which deals with major problems, including the integration of handicapped pupils into the ordinary secondary school. Finally, the important questions of evaluation, assessment and development are explored.

SECTION ONE: BASIC SKILLS

1

Pastoral Care and Pupil Performance

Douglas Hamblin
(Senior Lecturer in Education, University College of Swansea)

THE NEED FOR OBJECTIVES

First-hand experience during the last ten years has made me increasingly aware of schools where the pastoral system is underfunctioning or making little direct contribution to the attainment of the goals of the school. This did not mean that commitment and involvement were absent. To the contrary: those who held pastoral roles were working extremely hard and displayed deep concern for pupils; but they were largely ineffective because their efforts were unbacked by a structured programme of skills-based guidance for success. They saw themselves as solely concerned with the provision of emotional first aid; as a source of support for pupils under stress; as the equivalent of a social worker or welfare officer or even more vaguely as one whose main task was to 'get to know the pupils'.

There is nothing improper about these activities. What is wrong is that for these heads of year they constituted their specialist role. They are necessary components of pastoral activity, but the undue emphasis upon them led to inefficiency. As I have pointed out elsewhere (Hamblin, 1974), there are different levels of guidance and counselling in the secondary school. The functions listed above more properly belong to the 'immediate level', that is, they form part of the form tutor's role. It is not uncommon to find fairly

3

experienced and senior figures wasting time in routine tasks such as checking registers. This could be carried out more effectively by form tutors.

Criticisms of such approaches to pastoral care are justified. But just as poor teaching of a subject does not allow us to condemn the subject as useless, evidence of inefficiency does not give us licence to indulge in wholesale condemnation of pastoral care. To be effective, the key figures – heads of year or house – have to develop a set of skills which contribute to improved pupil performance and integrate the pastoral and the curricular. The relationship of pastoral care to achievement cannot be stressed too strongly. These skills can only be used effectively when they are employed within a structure of pastoral care which has clear objectives.

An apparently well-designed structure can conceal self-defeating attitudes and actions despite the keenness of those involved. In one school an apparently well-developed system of pastoral care was, in practice, amorphous. The development desired by the head of the school and others within the pastoral team was inhibited because the heads of year and their deputies held extremely limited perceptions of their functions. Despite commitment and concern – perhaps because of it – they could not step outside the frame of reference provided by their beliefs about the nature of pastoral care. They saw it solely in terms of individual relationships with pupils, often embedded in crises, and not also as a long-term process which was essential to improving the performance of all pupils. They provided palliatives, but no positive change. In this school, where the monetary rewards for pastoral work were high, there were no clear long-run objectives.

This discussion is not condemnatory. Instead it draws attention to the need for evaluation. What we face is the product of the regrettable tendency during reorganization to assume that pastoral posts merely required 'the right sort of person' and that the possession of intellect and specialist skills were of small account. Surprisingly, those undertaking the work have subscribed to these derogatory myths. In the school mentioned above it was possible for heads of year and others to examine and redefine their roles in terms of skills. They evolved a tentative set of objectives for each year which were related to the progressive acquisition of study and social skills by pupils. After this, they began to integrate their ideas into a planned programme of guidance. They began to compare notes, inviting evaluation, and overcoming the barriers through which they had insulated themselves against observation and evaluation.

The astonishing thing was that such a planned group effort had not occurred before. Fragmentation and compartmentalization had reduced efficiency. The results of such evaluatory exercises can, if well planned, have a considerable impact and boost development of pastoral work. The way in which relatively brief and inexpensive forms of in-service training can shift pastoral care into making an active contribution to pupil performance can be illustrated by one good girls' comprehensive school. During a day course which was organized into year groups the staff, including the headmistress, developed enough activities and materials in embryonic form to construct what they called a 'pastoral curriculum' for the remaining two and a half terms of the academic year. Obviously, they had already invested a great deal of thought and energy in pastoral care to create the climate in which such co-operation could occur. In the other school, the form tutors were not so fully involved: the heads of year had failed to communicate the objectives of the pastoral system in a way which highlighted their relevance to the teaching task. Obversely, the form tutors felt that the heads of year were 'paid to do pastoral care'.

Objectives take three forms. Long-term objectives specify the broad outcomes of the pastoral effort. We should be able to say what it contributes, and detail the ways in which the school would function less well, if the pastoral system were to be removed. Long-term objectives include the systematic detection of pupils who are at risk, and early – and therefore probably more effective – intervention in truancy and aggressive or disruptive behaviours. They also contribute to a diagnosis of the factors which exacerbate disaffiliation from the school, impede learning and academic performance and provide an understanding of unwittingly self-defeating elements in methods and organization.

The most serious defects tend to be found in the intermediate objectives which specify what is to be done in each year. A head of year should be able to state precisely what is being done in tutorial periods to:

1. Develop positive attitudes to academic tasks and develop effective ways of study for the individual pupil.
2. Induce social competence in interaction with both peers and adults in areas relevant to that age group.

3. Prepare pupils to cope with impending tasks, for example induction in the first year; the transition from school to work or to the sixth form with its new demands in the fifth year.
4. Explore areas of personal development which are problematical for that age group.

If this cannot be done, then the head of year deserves criticism.

Planning is crucial. Each year's activities must be germane to the needs of the pupils. A head of year should make a list of topics organized into modules, indicating the sequence in which they will be tackled. If streaming is a marked feature of the school, then one would expect evidence as to how the materials and activities are to be adapted to allow pupils to benefit from them. The principle of positive discrimination should be applied, namely that for equality of opportunity, the disadvantaged and less able need, not the same, but better education. The provision of skills in tutorial periods is one aspect of this 'better' education. We should not forget, however, that such approaches are equally relevant to the able pupil.

Immediate objectives are the most crucial. It is here that success or failure is determined. Gross *et al.* (1971) have shown that we should, when introducing innovations, carefully consider the likelihood that barriers and frustrations may be present which stem from the management and organization of the school. Senior management may fail to see them, or if they do, they fail to deal with them. Heads of year have to be alert to the possibility of conflicting demands, overload of the form tutor, inefficient spacing of tasks and inadequate resources. Open-minded examination of difficulties, and formulation of them as problems which have to be resolved if pastoral care is to work, is part of the role of head of year. Senior management will then have to face their existence and help the heads of year tackle them.

We must accept that negative attitudes can develop in those who were originally favourable to pastoral activity. Either they begin to feel it yields little result and they abandon it, or it degenerates into a routine performance conducted without zest or variation. Teachers seize on materials with enthusiasm, but this is no guarantee that they will use them efficiently. Questionnaires and activities are handed out to tutor groups, but there is striking absence of planned follow-up. At times their use seems to be a form of propitiation of the head of year or the senior management rather than a tool

6

designed to achieve certain specifiable results. Even more predictably, materials are not properly introduced, so that their relevance remains hidden from the pupil. Pupils are entitled to a clear statement of the objectives of the activity which allow them to orientate themselves to it purposefully.

Materials can be misused because the form tutor misinterprets their purpose – for example, an exercise which should be the preliminary for a structured discussion can be seen as an end in itself. The divide which has been created between the pastoral and the curricular obscures the importance of good teaching as part of pastoral care. Form tutors must work to sharpen the pupil's perceptions of the basic principles of the activity. Above all, they must show pupils the application of what they have learned in the pastoral activity to the classroom, playground and relevant areas of their lives. Poor pastoral work is also poor teaching. The conditions leading to efficient learning in a subject are also those leading to successful pastoral activity. Why? Simply because the only basic difference is that in pastoral care the subject and object of learning are identical – the learner is learning about himself.

Good classroom management, the considered use of materials and a sensitive balance between the experiential and teacher-directed components of the tutor period have to be kept in mind. One weakness of pastoral care has been a tendency to overvalue experiential learning as if it were inherently superior. In so-called discovery or informal learning it is possible for the wrong things to be learned or for existing prejudices and stereotypes to be reinforced. What is learned conflicts with our intentions. Pupils may miss crucial points without the planned intervention of the tutor. Similar materials therefore produce widely differing results and reactions in classroom settings which seem to have much in common.

FUNCTIONS AND SKILLS OF HEAD OF YEAR

The reader may well comment that there seems to be no lack of job specifications for the head of year. But it may not be easy to see that the current divorce of the pastoral and the curricular is at least reinforced by stereotyped job specifications which hold a limited conception of pastoral care. They often imply that pastoral care is an inferior welfare system dealing only with 'problem pupils'; that it is almost solely concerned with the provision of emotional 'first aid' and crises; that it requires few, if any, specialist skills; and that it is composed of a vague process of 'getting to know them', disciplinary and administrative duties, and the provision of encouragement and reassurance.

Little training is available for the key post of head of year. Heads of department do have the support of training in their subject, but initial teacher training does not offer the same foundation to the middle management in pastoral care. Yet without the essential skills, the head of year will contribute little that systematically raises pupil performance.

The first and major skill is that of diagnosis. This requires an analytic style of thought which asks the head of year to evaluate a problem by answering the following questions:

1. WHEN and WHERE do the behaviours which are the object of concern occur?
2. WHY does it occur? (The 'Why' may be less important than the 'When' and 'Where'.)
3. What are the DIFFERENCES between the SITUATIONS in which these behaviours occur and those in which they do not?
4. What CHANGES have to be made in:
   (a) the pupil's behaviour and attitudes;
   (b) the classroom situations?

Once such an elementary analysis has been made, a plan for action can be constructed. Teachers tend to ignore the need for systematic diagnosis. Yet piecemeal or impulsive measures are grossly uneconomical. The style of thought behind pastoral care is basically that found in any intellectual discipline. One must scan the situation, looking at the evidence without immediately imposing one's own meaning on it. Pre-categorizations are death to pastoral care. From the survey of the evidence we derive hypotheses which we then try to confirm or refute.

A key element is the detection of patterns. It is a curious fact that in our large secondary schools eight pupils can often absorb a vast amount of the time of a far larger number of teachers. Yet even with classes, as I argue in Best (1980), systematic observation will reveal simple patterns of behaviour and a set of transactions which support disruptive behaviour. Once detected, they can be interrupted and replaced. Comparison of experiences between those who teach an individual or class within a planned framework reveals habitual sequences of responses. They escape detection because the secondary school teacher has only intermittent experience of the class. What would be obvious in the primary school tends to elude the secondary school teacher. If this is true of classes, it is even more true for the individual. Labelling pupils as 'aggressive' or 'unco-operative' often obscures the triggers to which they respond. Because of lack of training, there is a tendency for the head of year to issue stereotyped prescriptions for improvement or rely somewhat blindly on exhortation and encouragement.

This diagnostic approach can be applied to a key area in pupil performance – underfunctioning. Underfunctioning remains a remarkably cloudy concept. Behind it there seems to be some idea of an objective standard: of some measure which could be used, and of some standard which the pupil should reach. Banks and Finlayson (1973) and Gaudry and Spielberger (1971), amongst others, show that underfunctioning is a complex concept.

The relationship between intelligence and attainment is not a linear one. There is a tendency for high intelligence to be paralleled by high achievement, but this is merely a tendency. A wide range of influences enter into the determination of performance: the personality and sex of the teacher in relation to those of the pupil; family pressures, values and support; the previous learning history of the pupil and the pupil's assessment of the relevance of the subject. More underfunctioning is reported amongst boys than girls. There seems to be no evidence of sex-based differences in intelligence, therefore differences in attainment between boys and girls must be explained by reference to other factors.

We must also take into account the part played by teachers' expectations. But on what are those expectations based? Appearance, vocabulary, rate and type of speech, likeability of the pupil or some standard derived from experience of similar pupils in the past?

The first step is to realize that there is a choice between coercion or exhortation and the professional approach of systematic diagnosis followed by a planned attack on the problem, mobilizing the resources available in the school. In the early stages the problem is given a more precise shape. Does the alleged underfunctioning appear to be pervasive or is it limited to a particular area of schoolwork or a subject? If we assume that it is general underfunctioning, the first step is to get some measure of general ability. This can be provided by the AH 2 (1975) measure of general ability which, if used properly, can provide a reliable estimate. The volume by Jackson and Juniper (1971) will provide a useful guide, although heads of year should request their Institute of Education or local education authority to provide a course of training which deals with appropriate tests and, more crucially, with the interpretation of the results. Consultation with the educational psychologist will be rewarding, for he or she can do much to raise the level of assessment skills in pastoral staff.

We should not place too much reliance upon a solitary score, nor assume that the problem is ended if we apparently find no discrepancy between the test score and the level of performance. Although intelligence tests have been found to be the best single predictor of academic performance, we must also remember that in cases of underfunctioning such tests sometimes reflect current psychological states rather than potential.

When there is some confirmation that a problem exists we must ask *when* and *how* the underfunctioning began. Was it a gradual process or did it occur suddenly? The diagnostic element means that we begin to gather evidence using the simple framework set out earlier. In what situations or subjects does he function, if not well, at a higher level than elsewhere? In what situations is the underfunctioning marked? What part do his friends or family play in this failure? Before working with pupils, the head of year should discover these things:

1. The pupil's reaction to difficulties and frustration.
2. His tendency towards anxiety or aggression. (Both can be found in the same person, the latter being a way of coping with the former.)
3. His general perceptions of teachers and the relevance of school work.
4. Any evidence about the predictions as to eventual success or failure held by the pupil.
5. The special strengths and abilities of the pupil.
6. Some assessment of his study skills.

Much of this information can be garnered quickly through informal consultation with the form tutor, although it is helpful in more difficult cases to hold a group meeting of those who teach the pupil. Particular attention will be given to the less tangible aspects of the matter – the pupil's beliefs about the nature of success and his beliefs about luck and chance.

Armed with this information, the head of year would then interview the pupil. It is here that counselling skills are essential. Clumsy questioning will reinforce existing defensiveness. For many pupils the interview situation is contaminated with associations of trouble. Many pupils have learned that the steady proffering of the response, 'Don't know, Sir', renders the teacher impotent. Confrontations will merely lead to more polarized attitudes. We use the methods of behavioural counselling, building on the pupil's strengths, and extending our efforts very gradually. Diagrams and visual methods are used to interest the pupil and help him work out the steps he could take. Graduation of demands is crucial: we get the pupil to arrange the steps in order of difficulty, and begin with the easiest. Perhaps we too easily ignore the possibility that the underfunctioning pupil feels overwhelmed, and predicts failure, or that he sees the whole field of achievement as so confused that he does not know how to clarify it and change the situation. Our strategy is to build up an individual plan of which the pupil is fully aware and to involve other teachers in support measures. This means that colleagues are aware of the phased plan, offering reinforcements of praise, interrupting the previous pattern of blame and pejorative remarks.

Underfunctioning can be general or specific. Specific underfunctioning is related to a subject and here the pastoral worker has to recognize his limits. Faulty learning or missed steps, together with difficulties arising from a specific disability, fall within the province of the subject specialist. Family pressures also enter into underfunctioning and these are a matter for the pastoral worker. It is not the presence or absence of parental interest which is significant, so much as the way in which that interest is expressed. If the cumulative impact is negative, then parental concern will be counterproductive. Parents and child will need help. It is particularly difficult when a pupil is compared with a brighter young brother or sister. Often parental comparisons are paralleled by teacher ones. The child then reacts by that form of passive resistance to infringement of identity which we call underfunctioning.

This diagnostic approach which is the heart of pastoral work can be taken further through the monitoring of pupil's progress. This is merely an extension of the form tutor's responsibility for periodic

11

reviews of pupils' work as described by Blackburn (1975) and Marland (1974). The basic development is:

1. Form tutors review individual progress.
2. Form tutors' contributions used by heads of year to detect trends and needs of, e.g. (a) the less able and gifted; (b) boys versus girls especially in relation to mathematics and the sciences; (c) different age groups.
3. Further examination and exploration through working parties of problems. This could include: (a) surveys of attainment in reading, etc.; (b) investigation of study skills.

Monitoring the trends in attitudes which develop as pupils pass through the school is vital. Pupils' views of the relevance of subjects to careers and life and their perception of the difficulty of certain subjects need to be known. Those interested in developing this perspective will find the following model of interest.

A BASIC MODEL FOR MONITORING THE LEARNING PROCESS

Realistic thought about accountability is crucial. Disregard of variations in basic inputs and within school processes would lead to arbitrary and inaccurate judgements.

The aim of the model is to concentrate not on the relative achievement of different pupils but on the relative success of the school in achieving important agreed objectives:

1. INPUT
   Pupil characteristics:
     (i) General ability
    (ii) Neighbourhood attitudes and values
   (iii) Attitudes of family towards school, general tendencies
   Staff resources:
     (i) Experience and training
    (ii) Educational philosophy
   Organizational variables:
     (i) Educational methods and general educational organization
    (ii) Size
   (iii) Buildings – split site – purpose built

12

2. LEARNING AND INTERACTIONAL PROCESSES

Value climate of school: Including rewards and punishment/integration of pupils

Ideal pupil model: Boys/Girls Academic/Non-academic

Decision-Making and other processes which ensure success in school and affiliation with its aims.

3. OUTPUT

(i) The picture of himself built up in the individual

(ii) Level of aspiration and desire to attain a standard of excellence

(iii) Social skills

(iv) Academic attainment

Philosophical and long-term issues:

(i) Is school solely a place where pupils acquire the beliefs and behaviours which allow them to take their place in society without disrupting it?

(ii) Is it solely the place where pupils acquire the experiences and credentials which define their subsequent position in society?

(iii) Does it function to aid the full development of the individual?

Pastoral care is concerned with the 'health' and functioning of the organization as well as with individual pupils. It moves diagnosis and evaluation from the pupil to the success of the school in achieving outcomes which are generally agreed to be important. I hasten to add that this does not mean consensus – for those who wait for complete consensus in a school will still be waiting at doomsday. The key question is how the school adapts to its intake. If we are to relate pastoral care to performance then the mode of adaptation has to be one which neither reinforces nor confirms the existing state of affairs when the intake is disadvantaged or holds attitudes which are antipathetic to school. The three basic adaptations are:

1. *Passive*: Merely accepting the limits of the environment and intake and lowering teacher expectations;

2. *Substitutive*: Stressing effort rather than success. (Note how negative the predictions are in this strategy);

3. *Active*: Assessing strengths of the intake and also identifying the learning skills which will have to be provided to give the intake success.

Pastoral care is therefore concerned with guidance for success. Raising the level of performance means devising methods of:

(i) Looking at the way negative attitudes to work and learning develop
   (a) as pupils move up the school,
   (b) in certain sections of the school population.
(ii) Evaluation of general approaches to teaching, examining
   (a) the existence of too low expectations for those who are seen as less able,
   (b) the rewards and targets offered, ensuring they are meaningful.
(iii) Then asking questions such as
   (a) Does our general classroom approach stress the desirability of the passive pupil?
   (b) What strategies have the pupils developed for evading demands and insulating themselves against teacher influence?

IN-SERVICE TRAINING

We have seen that pastoral care has been bedevilled by unclear objectives and a paucity of skills in the head of year. The 'get to know them' approach was defective on two counts. Rarely were the ways in which we should know pupils spelt out. Even odder was the assumption that 'getting to know' the pupil would produce a change in the pupil rather than the teacher. Accompanying this was a curious overemphasis on getting the pupil to tell us about his difficulties as if this automatically ensured change. A trouble shared is not necessarily halved. Expressing difficulties is only the start of pastoral help.

It is currently fashionable to stress the tensions between form tutor and head of year as if they were unique in the school. Academic departments are divided by similar forces. Resistance may mean that pastoral care has not been related clearly to basic educational objectives. Sometimes the duties allocated to tutors are trivial, and therefore scarcely likely to commend themselves to those with a sense of professional status. Lack of clarity can arouse the fear that if the tutor responds to the head of year, they could be opening themselves to a spate of demands which would erode their competence as teachers.

14

In-service training misconceptions can be corrected by negotiation. Tutors can be helped to observe pupils more accurately, gaining deeper knowledge of pupils' reactions to frustration, their preferred roles in group situations and the incentives to which they respond. Group sessions can help dispel undue reliance on global attributions such as 'unreliable' or 'immature'. Observational training and presentation of methods of modifying behaviour should fall within the sphere of the head of year.

Detection of pupils who are at risk depends upon the observational skill of form tutors. Phillips (1978) in his research into achievement and anxiety found a surprisingly large number of his sample wished that the teacher would slow down so that they could understand what he was saying; many were unduly anxious about answering questions; whilst expectations, both of teachers and parents, were a source of stress. Guidance programmes can include cartoons and simple transparencies which open up such topics in a constructive way, but we also have to train tutors to help anxious pupils without making them feel deviant. Alertness to changes in behaviour or appearance is important. Signals of fatigue or irritability can be ignored or even dealt with punitively. Changes in appearance may indicate that something is wrong at home – yet the response of some tutors is merely to admonish the pupil, effectively creating a barrier to the expression of difficulties.

The head of year must take responsibility for selecting and introducing materials and activities which are necessary to the achievement of intermediate objectives. In-service training of this type prevents the misuse of activities and materials, but also brings a sense of purpose and direction to the pastoral effort.

Pastoral care will be directed to the development of study skills and to the fostering of positive attitudes towards achievement. It is not merely a matter of skills, but of a deeper approach in which the processes of learning become the centre of an activity-based dialogue between teacher and pupil. We are not providing recipes, but helping pupils build up an individual style of learning – even in study skills there is no 'right' way or single path to success.

A group of tutors can develop a set of study skill tapes which are available to pupils to take home or use at lunchtime. Alternatively, they can be used in tutorial periods. Such tapes will look at the problems associated with homework, answering questions, reading to generate new meanings and efficient revision. Pupils should be taught about the attitudes that lead to success or failure: the sense of being a passive reactor to forces beyond his control or being responsible for his own fate have a pervasive influence on achievement and perseverance. At the extremes are two fundamental patterns of achievement behaviour:

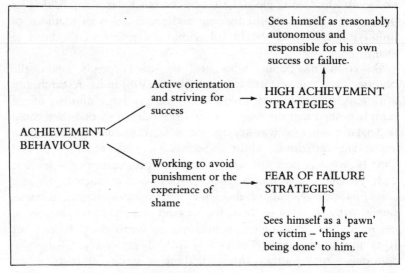

Fear of failure can be described as the situation in which pupils work mainly to avoid blame or punishment rather than because they actively desire success. Such pupils tend to believe that the causes of success or failure largely lie outside themselves. They use excuses such as 'It's the teachers – they're no good', or 'This course is useless'. Frustration or failure produce such reactions, but whatever form they take, the essence is that pupils deny their own responsibility. Simple materials can open up these vital areas for discussion, for example a tape in which a pupil is heard talking to a friend about failures or poor performance in an examination, perhaps blaming her friends for asking her to go out. The friend questions the validity of these statements, showing that she has an equally rich social life, but plans the use of her time.

In pastoral care we have an opportunity to help pupils become aware of the subjective nature of achievement. Group activities help pupils to examine:

EXPECTATIONS of success or failure and the way they influence learning behaviours.

COMPARISONS of self with others; negative and positive ways of using this basic tendency.
BELIEFS about the source of control and the nature of success.

The low achiever tends to stress the properties of the environment and the high achiever those of the person. Basically, guidance should help pupils to see that effort and skill are more important than luck – it is surprising how much our society is chance and luck oriented. The pupil who sees the source of control as primarily lying outside himself probably:

1. Fails to appreciate the links between his behaviour and what befalls him.
2. Has not developed the skills of planning and of working economically.
3. Is unduly susceptible to the negative influences of others.
4. Tends to attribute negative intent and purpose to others, especially those in authority.

These factors lead to passive learning and the inertia which seems to be a major problem in many schools. Cartoons, tapes and case histories can be used in guidance sessions, but the head of year and form tutors must decide how they will build up the following skills, which are associated with achievement.

Basic learning skills for guidance programmes

1. GOAL SETTING

This is a vital skill. It is important for all pupils, but it is vital for pupils from disadvantaged backgrounds and for those who have not internalized the desire to achieve and attain a standard of excellence.
This activity must be carefully planned, the emphasis being on:

(a) CONCRETE BEHAVIOURS – not the vague 'work harder', but improve by, for example, 'checking all my spelling in English essays this week as soon as I finish them';
(b) Targets which are SPECIFIC – the pupil can assess his success;
(c) Goals in which the pupil has a REASONABLE CHANCE of success.

2. CO-OPERATION

Co-operation is a skill which can be learned. Friends can be taught to work together and help each other achieve goals. Pupils can be set 'helping exercises' where they make suggestions and then proceed to help their partner during the ensuing week.

3. USING MISTAKES CONSTRUCTIVELY

Pupils often ignore the teacher's comments or fail to see a mistake as an opportunity for learning. One early study of achievement behaviour showed that the mothers of pupils with high achievement motivation set high demands but had encouraged them to use mistakes and failures constructively as an occasion for reassessing the viability of behaviour. They also emphasized the likelihood of eventual success. Careful discussion of the ways in which positive learning can emerge from mistakes will yield dividends.

4. ORIENTATION TO THE TASK

Another key feature is training pupils to orientate themselves to the task successfully. Unnecessary failure or waste of time occurs because pupils have not been taught to stop and think about:

- the nature of the task;
- the best way of tackling it;
- the most effective way of presenting the results.

5. PLANNING SKILLS

Pupils should be helped to produce plans suited to them for homework and unsupervised study. These plans will include:

- breaking up the working periods into sections devoted to various activities;
- the balance between reading and other activities such as note-taking;
- the amount of time devoted to testing what they have learned and the way they will do this in different subjects;
- organization of retrieval systems;
- taking notes which emphasize the structure of the subjects.

18

6. OVERCOMING DIFFICULTIES

This introduces the key element of perseverance, but avoids suggesting it is sufficient by itself. The methods used could involve:

- decision-making exercises where groups of three to four pupils work together;
- tape recordings where two solutions are presented and pupils have to assess them;
- written character sketches in which a portrait is given of a pupil who is trying to resolve some learning difficulty – small groups then discuss the strategy illustrated in the sketch.

7. SUPPORTS

These include simple graphs, record forms or, in the case of sixth-form pupils, diaries which act as self-diagnostic tools. Many younger pupils need these tangible signs of progress.

8. PLANNING AHEAD

This can be discussed, although diagrams which break the goals down into termly steps are important. The younger the pupil, the less developed is his time concept and therefore the less useful are remote goals. Sharpening career plans and emphasizing the usefulness of certain subjects to those plans increase the investment of energy in school work.

Methods

These methods will be used in structured programmes of guidance:

- decision-making exercises;
- role-play;
- simulation and games;
- tape recorded scripts;
- case histories;
- self-evaluation devices – diaries, record forms, etc.

A caution

Not only must the methods be adapted to the age of the pupil, but

19

there must be consistency in applying the approach. A single teacher can achieve something. For real results, however, a co-ordinated attack on underfunctioning is essential. Consistency does not, of course, mean similarity of method in each age group. It does mean realistic development and challenge based on what has gone before.

MANAGEMENT SKILLS

Schools are not only for pupils: they are for teachers who have a right to satisfaction in an arduous task. Pastoral care helps to produce this satisfaction by creating a framework of order based on effective procedures for early detection of problems. Good pastoral management assesses the impact of demands upon teachers, relating the pastoral tasks to what is done elsewhere. Schools still exist which require tutors to write reports when they are exhausted at the end of the autumn term and coping with plays, pantomimes and carol services. It also seems strange to issue reports at the end of a term when pupils and parents have a fortnight in which to forget them. Phasing of tasks should ensure minimal conflict of interests and reduce undue stress on the tutor. For each year there should be a chart which shows what has to be done, when it will be done and how difficulties are to be anticipated.

Sound management means that the role specification of the head of year will indicate which pupils he will deal with directly. Like the head of department, he deals with the majority indirectly. Underfunctioning pupils, the withdrawn or aggressive who require additional social skills might well be his province. This does not mean he has to rely solely on individual counselling. An equivalent of the withdrawal system operating in remedial education can be employed, allowing the head of year to run small guidance groups.

Building and maintaining links with the external agencies is part of the head of year's task. Informed co-operation based on real knowledge of the task and standpoints of the agency must be accompanied by interpretation of the viewpoint of the school. Little understanding of the constraints on teachers in the secondary school seems to be the norm in many cases. The danger is that sometimes the help and interaction seem to be one way. This seems to be especially true of the social services, who seek information and help from the school and yet, claiming the need to preserve confidentiality, deny it to those who have to work daily with pupils. Close co-operation and better communication may improve this situation. We also have to learn to use the educational psychologist and others more fully as resources in pastoral care.

Division of labour lies behind the need for heads of year in the secondary school. But there should also be a planned division of labour *within* the group of year heads. One year head might develop special links with the youth service; another a greater understanding of the problems of bereavement or the single-parent family; another a greater understanding of drug-taking, alcoholism or sexual problems. In this way, members of the pastoral system act as points of reference for their colleagues when certain problems occur.

2

Adolescents and Activities

Chris Watkins
(Lecturer in Education, University of London Institute of Education)

ADOLESCENTS AND INTERACTION

This perspective on adolescence reminds us of the considerable social learning which is taking place during the second decade of life. The process of developing identity involves trying out a view of oneself in the social world via interaction with others, and being sensitive to the response which those others make. Adolescents are continuously involved in experimenting with their self-presentation and judging the reactions thereto. This is an active process on their part, sometimes knowingly so. McPhail (1967), for example, showed in his interviews with adolescents about the role they played in critical incidents with adults, that up to 40 per cent gave their motive as 'I just wanted to see what would happen', 'I had to find out', and similar. It would be wrong, however, to suggest that all adolescents are aware of this experimental learning and could report it as such (for example, many of the class who are having their first lessons with a new teacher will not see their 'testing' behaviour this way). Those we can help in pastoral care are those who initially lack the reflective capacity to manage their own behaviour: these may be the young people who are *not* learning by action.

Secondly, this approach to adolescence makes a different sense of the importance of the peer group than does the usual stereotype of slavish conformity. It can be seen that the peer group is an important arena for trying out a social identity. As Salmon (1979) points out in her excellent review of peer group studies, 'the absence of a stable audience with whom to test out a developing view of oneself in relation to others had resulted (for adolescents making numerous changes of school) in a greatly impaired ability to understand oneself and one's peers'. Salmon notes 'three main functions that have been put forward for the peer group: intimacy, consensual validation, and the provision of a frame of reference'. Here we may begin to understand the function of talk with age-mates. In one of the very few studies of what adolescents really do with their time, Csikszentmihalyi (1977) showed that 14.7 per cent of time was taken up in talk with peers as the primary activity, and a further 18.1 per cent as a secondary activity. Talk with adults made up 4.1 per cent of the time as a primary activity, and 4.0 per cent as secondary. Those who know playground and corridor conversations may infer that much of this talk is about social events and self-presentation. The function of these discussions may be to create and receive feedback on one's own and others' activities.

THE ROLE OF PASTORAL CARE

If the pastoral care team can use active methods which include the model of experimental action plus subsequent discussion, they may replicate the naturally-occurring process and bring about significant learning. Further, and of equal importance, to adopt openly a developmental approach to pastoral care would be a constructive move away from some of the more common distortions of pastoral work, for example the inadequate social welfare or the ineffective discipline via external controls. In day-to-day terms, form tutors who are able to use more creative techniques in their tutor periods are less likely to fall into the traps of making registration last thirty minutes or of 'getting to know' pupils for no obvious purpose. Pupils too may develop a different notion of pastoral care, one which helds rewards for them by giving them skills which contribute to their own personal success.

The activities to be considered in this chapter (role-play, simulation and games) are initiated by teachers and depend on their teaching skills. It may be useful here to consider the history of the use of such active techniques in the formal curriculum. Such approaches were originally put forward with great claims for their results by some proponents: Boocock and Schild (1968) identify an 'acceptance on faith' stage in the American experience when enthusiasm for a new approach greatly outweighed evidence on the effects. When evidence began to gather on the effects of active techniques in formal learning as compared with other techniques, it seemed that active methods were no worse and possibly better in some respects than other methods (Gibbs, 1974). The results are equivocal and it seems wise to conclude that there is no panacea as far as formal learning is concerned.

In the more informal sphere of social learning it is more difficult to make comparisons between active and other methods, since it has so far proved difficult to suggest a set of definable learnings which may act as criteria. We should still make every effort to set objectives and thence evaluate our methods. But there are difficulties in constructing a 'social curriculum' and its associated measures of achievement that do not fall into the trap of being extremely value-laden or specific to a particular group. It may be more profitable at present to view these approaches as tools for exploration in certain areas rather than tools for teaching 'known facts'. The product, therefore, is not so much a set of factual learnings, but more an extended understanding of *processes*. Processes of judging others, of understanding others, of communicating with others, and of interacting with others are included here, as are processes of making decisions, solving problems and coping with difficulties which may arise in any of these areas. The general aim is a greater understanding of the principles involved together with an increased self-knowledge regarding one's part in them and an extended language for expressing and reflecting on them.

An associated point arises from the proposal to re-create in the school context a learning process mainly observable in the peer group. Negotiations in the peer group are not confounded by considerations of differences in formal power: in that sense the statuses are equal, and this important distinction marks off many peer relations from many adolescent–adult relations where the statuses are not equal. It is important, then, that teachers take care over utilizing their formal status and power lest the exploration becomes limited and the problems are answered but not really solved by the participants. Glandon (1978) has directed our attention to the 'hidden curriculum' in simulations: we would not be doing our pupils a service if the implicit learning they extracted from an experience was, for example, that adults know all the answers. But having made the point that exploration is better than easy answers, this is *not* to suggest that the techniques require a

24

teacher to be *laissez-faire*: they are properly constructed techniques where the teacher has responsibility for controlling the structure.

ACTIVE METHODS OUTLINED

Three main types are to be described here. The borderlines between them are not always as distinct as the descriptions may suggest. Many variants and hybrids are possible.

1. Simulation

This method attempts to replicate certain features of reality (for example a job interview, a group tackling a new problem) which have not yet been encountered, so that the main elements can be experienced but without the real-life consequences that would be attached to behaviour. The situation is almost taken as a cultural 'given', and experimentation is on how best to handle the situation.

2. Role-play

This is similar to simulation, but generally covers more limited social interactions, often just two people, with less constraint imposed by the situation. The added aim is for one person to learn how the other sees her/his behaviour. This is achieved by the technique of role-reversal where having first played his or her own role in the interaction each person then has to play the role of the other. Examples could include a pupil role-playing a conflict or a misunderstanding with a teacher, a tutor-in-training role-playing an interview with a member of the tutor group, and so on.

3. Games

There are many possible games. Almost any set of transactions between a group of players may be termed a game, but in pastoral care the focus is often on social situations that are neither highly structured nor predictable in outcome. Games in these areas look more like variants of 'Desert Islands' or a 'balloon debate' than

Monopoly or Snakes and Ladders. Players are presented with a number of strategies which they must evaluate, select from and proceed to implement. The aim is to develop particular skills of thinking, decision-making and problem-solving.

A crucial element in all these methods is the 'post-play' discussion. This is where analysis takes place and the transfer of learning to other contexts can be discussed and evaluated. An atmosphere of joint exploration is aimed at: negative criticism is discouraged whereas positive criticism, especially suggestion on how the strategies could be improved is welcomed. Again therefore it should be stressed that the teacher is active in this phase. The activity centres on:

1. drawing out the various perspectives which different members have had on the experience, and the different strategies they adopted;
2. identifying the salient events which occurred and their possible effects, both on the later course of events and on the feelings of the participants;
3. evaluating the advantages and disadvantages of the various strategies which were adopted and of any others which can be envisaged;
4. considering whether valid generalizations may be made, in the form of general principles of human interaction;
5. discussing which other situations may have features in common with the one enacted, and which of the learnings may be transferred to those situations.

Much of this activity may be structured by the use of simple questions which focus pupils' attention on each of the elements above:

What were you trying to do?
What did you achieve?
How did it feel?
Why did the different people see things differently?
What did you feel was the most important thing that happened? Why?
What was the effect?
How did you feel when . . . ?

What did he think when you . . . ?
Whose approach seemed to work? Why?
What else could have been done?
Do most people behave in this way?
What other situations are like this one?

Obviously not all these questions would be used, interrogation-like, they are merely suggestions from which the teacher may select. The teacher's role here is to help pupils to structure the experience and elaborate on what they have learned. In this role the teacher may sometimes be neutral, especially when he/she considers that expressing his/her point of view may inhibit pupils expressing theirs, but the teacher is not passive. It certainly seems possible that an *unstructured* discussion of some social issues may serve to reinforce prejudice and stereotype if pupils merely find group support for some of their attitudes. This is contrary to educational aims. Active intervention to question and sometimes confront prejudice is required, together with a follow-up on the personal and social functions of stereotyping. Thus the post-play discussion should never be neglected. Discussion is not the only approach: written methods or further active methods may be utilized in the reflection and analysis which can centre on questions like those suggested above.

In the post-play phase pupils are helped to elaborate their ways of expressing what has happened and what were the perceived effects. This is an important aspect, based not on the simple theory that 'expressing feelings is a good thing', but on the idea that adequate language skills are necessary in order to reflect on one's own behaviour. Many adolescents are fluent in the language of action: they have ways of behaving which are almost automatic in response to some event or situation. These active methods try to encourage reflection on behaviour, using the medium of language to extend the meaning of situations and events, and thence encourage more satisfying strategies. During adolescence both the breadth of vocabulary and complexity of language for expressing personal and interpersonal issues are developing continuously. We can help in this development and thereby give young people greater facility to ascribe meaning to their feelings, difficulties and experience. For many who have seldom reflected on their behaviour this will be new and possibly at first the benefits will not be clear. Thus it is important to spell out the purpose and pay-off of these activities.

The introduction of a simulation, role-play or game to a group of pupils is important in a number of respects. As we shall see in the detailed discussion of each technique, thoughtful selection of the situation to be explored will help to make the rewards clear. An initial briefing, however, can clarify the objectives and this will give students some idea of what to expect and how to proceed.

The model of learning which is built into these methods may be summarized as:

1. Act
2. Understand the particular situation
3. Generalize
4. Act in new circumstances

and this approximates to adolescents' experimental learning. The contrast with the 'information-processing' approach to learning which underlies much of the curriculum can be seen by comparing the above with this:

1. Reception of information
2. Understand general principle
3. Particularize
4. Act

This latter model might also underline inactive teaching of social principles, where pupils are informed but their action may remain unaffected.

WHAT CAN BE LEARNED?

Without wishing to give the impression of claiming another panacea, it seems useful to list the potential outcomes of active methods. The concepts underlying this list may also be profitably borne in mind when constructing new simulations, games and role-plays.

1. The ability to 'put oneself in others' shoes' and see things from their perspective is a fundamental ability in co-operative social interaction. These 'role-taking' skills can be fostered by the role-reversal techniques. These are different skills to those of

role-enactment, which are more the concern when the drama teacher uses role-play methods. Our concern here is not with dramatic skills but with cognitive skills of imaginatively constructing another perspective, and anticipating the situation from that point of view. Some information is obviously required in order to construct the other perspective in a realistic way, as also is personal flexibility. One end result of teaching role-taking effectively is that the pupil has an awareness of himself as one member of various dynamic interacting systems of other people.

2. An understanding of the feelings evoked in self and in others by a variety of situations, together with the language for dealing with those feelings, may be extended. The latter element is not always given the importance it deserves: a more elaborated language for denoting feelings is an aid to reflecting on them and a tool for organizing self-knowledge.

3. New roles and social skills can be tried out in a safe situation, in which the real-life consequences are temporarily suspended. The other side of this coin is that old faulty strategies may be identified without having to contend with the full force of the real-life consequences. This category would also include the skills of interpersonal communication, of putting one's viewpoint across to others, and of presenting oneself in positive ways. Trying out new lines of behaviour may help their growth as well as their maintenance, because the person will have experienced what it feels like to behave that way, and the feeling will no longer be new. Finally, to experiment with new ways of behaving may be better than only talking of new ways of behaving, running the risk of never actually achieving a change in practice.

4. Learning to assess the costs of an action and the consequences expected may improve anticipation of these elements in other situations. This skill is very much associated with the skills of decision-making, which can be taught in school. It is important to recognize alternative solutions and to evaluate each of the alternatives.

Having listed four general areas of possible learning, it is obvious that there is some overlap between these areas and certainly much interaction between them in day-to-day situations. However, separating them in this way may help to identify which *sort* of ability is lacking for a particular person in a particular situation. Each of the three active techniques is more relevant to some of these areas than to others. For example, role-play may be most appropriate for area 1 (role-taking), whereas for area 4 (decision-making), a well-constructed game which makes those skills specific may be most effective.

HOW ARE THESE ACTIVITIES USED?

In this section some points will be made concerning the construction and use of simulation, role-play and games, together with a consideration of some of the difficulties and self-defeating strategies which may arise. Each will be covered in turn although many comments may apply to other or all methods. One example and suggestions for further reading will be given.

1. Simulation

A major contribution to the success of a simulation is in the choice of issue or situation to be portrayed. A realistic and important issue will obviously have greatest potential. The situation will probably be well known to pupils even if they have not yet experienced it directly; it will be concrete rather than being a somewhat rarified 'moral dilemma'. A moral issue may well be represented, but the reason for choosing the situation is that it represents an issue which young people want to cope with in a more satisfying way. So, for example, rather than constructing a simulation to explore 'parent–peer conflict' as a moral dilemma, it may be more profitable to identify a concrete issue such as 'being out late', or 'how I use my money', where pupils may be experiencing a real difficulty.

It follows then that with a well-chosen situation the rewards for involvement in the simulation should be meaningful and the justification should be clear to the pupils. Ensure this is the case by making them explicit in the introduction. In the last example we could suggest that the simulation would help students examine alternative ways of behaving, anticipate the reactions of other actors in the situation, calculate the costs and consequences of their action, and find a suitable strategy.

Sensitivity is required in introducing a simulation. In the contexts where these techniques are likely to be used (careers, social education, pastoral care), the method can probably be introduced out of a theme already under discussion. Instead of 'today we're going to do a simulation', a suggestion of 'why don't we see what happens?' will be better received and motivate the pupils to explore.

Some preparation of the group is required. Fears of embarrassment and of 'drying up' are anticipated by the teacher, who can suggest how to cope. For example: 'you may imagine you'll dry up. Before you start, think of a few phrases you might use in your role, and if you do find it difficult, carry on as best you can'; or 'you'll probably be a bit nervous and giggly to start with, but this will wear off as the situation develops'. With older pupils, fruitful discussions can be held on these processes and methods of coping with them. Warn participants against overacting or portraying a stereotype: there is no point in oversimplifying the reality to be portrayed and pupils who do this via stereotyping should be discouraged.

Actors may be chosen in various ways. Volunteering may be the least threatening approach with which to start. If some of the group are not taking up roles, suggest things to look out for in the interaction, so making their role as audience an active one. You may find it useful to notify them of some of the post-play questions suggested earlier. When you allocate individuals to particular roles, make sure that the role does not violate a salient personality trait or personal difficulty, such as asking a withdrawn student to portray an effusive adult or asking a recently bereaved young person to portray someone similar to the one lost.

In simulations the description of the situation and the characters should be detailed enough to 'set the interaction going', but not so much that the role-holders have little responsibility for the enactment. Scripts are inappropriate, except occasionally to give someone a starting line. Hamblin (1974) suggests the following scheme for planning a simulation:

(a) a description of the basic event
(b) the role-holders in the situation
(c) the relations between these characters, and the nature of their interaction
(d) the rewards and punishments involved
(e) the barriers to attaining the outcome
(f) the nature of the intended outcome.

These ingredients should all be present at some point (not necessarily in this order) in the description. Enough information is given to allow actors to construct the role to be portrayed: this information often includes a little of the character's background experience, the perception of this particular event, and some alternative lines of action from which to select.

How long should the enactment take? There is no real answer – a full simulation of an interview could take half an hour, some group problem-solving tasks could take more than one session, but most interaction scenes only need five minutes to generate a good discussion. Probably the best strategy is to start with brief situations.

The post-play discussion invariably takes longer than the simulation. Here the teacher can stimulate discussion by asking for pupils' opinions of the actions taken, the motives attributed, the feelings evoked, the overall process of interaction and so on. This then leads to an evaluation of the experience: were the roles played realistically, how better might they have been played, were there other alternatives? During the discussion the teacher will have in mind the objectives she/he has set and the possible learnings which may be developed. Where the aim has been to practise new skills in handling the situation, the simulation can now be re-run. Finally a discussion evaluating the method is valuable: what other similar situations are there, how could this simulation be improved? In this way the technique can be developed, since student suggestions can be incorporated into the description the next time it is enacted.

An example of a simulation where the situation is an interpersonal one which may contain conflicts of interest:

THE CHARACTERS

1. Joanne, 15, has a Saturday morning job where she earns £4 a week. She's just decided to start saving for a new pair of jeans (in at least three weeks' time) and her mother, who thinks Joanne has had too easy an attitude to money, has said that Joanne must buy the jeans with no help from her.
2. Diane, also 15, is Joanne's best friend and has been for about two years. They spend a lot of time together and nearly always go out together, taking considerable care over their appearance.
3. Michael, 23, is Diane's older brother. He has just become a partner in a firm supplying boutiques and often sells clothes

cheaply to his friends. He's a bit suspicious of Joanne because he thinks she goes out with another group of friends without telling Diane, whom he thinks might feel hurt.

THE SITUATION

It's Saturday afternoon and Joanne has arrived at Diane's house to make arrangements for that evening. Diane has just bought a new sweater from Michael and very much wants Joanne to have a similar one when they go to the ice-rink tonight. Michael forgot to go to the bank yesterday and needs some cash in his pocket for Saturday night. But Joanne only has her £4.

*　　*　　*

Before acting out the scene, each character should consider the costs and consequences of behaving according to the following alternatives, but not discuss with the others until the scene has been acted.

JOANNE

a. Refusing the offer of the sweater and keeping to the decision to buy jeans.
b. Accepting the offer and promising to get the rest of the money from mum before tonight.
c. Trying to get Michael to accept £4, with the rest to be paid next week.

DIANE

a. Giving up the idea of similar sweaters and saying you'll wear something you've worn before.
b. Not bothering to persuade Joanne and wearing your own new sweater all the same.
c. Making every attempt to persuade Joanne to get the sweater somehow.

MICHAEL

a. Telling Joanne it's the last sweater you've got and persuade her to find the money.
b. Taking £4 now and the rest next week.

c. Not selling the sweater to Joanne and taking the risk of finding another buyer this afternoon.

For further examples and discussion of simulation see: Hamblin (1974) pp. 172–9; Hamblin (1978) p. 158; Davison and Gordon (1978); Taylor and Walford (1972).

2. Role-play

This technique is often used to explore two-person interactions. Consequently it is more likely to focus on a relationship or type of relationship, rather than a general social situation as in simulation. Even more often, then, the selection of the issue will arise out of discussion of a particular difficulty that one person is experiencing with another. Role-play might be used, for example, in the context of a tutor's discussion with one member of the tutor group. Some of the difficulties coped with in this way may have themes which are generalizable to a whole group (see pp. 42–44), but there is one major theme which is generally amenable to role-play techniques in groups – that is the theme of interpersonal communication. Here we can build up component skills such as: (i) those of good listening; (ii) of putting one's viewpoint across to others; (iii) of being aware of the impression one creates; (iv) and of being able to adopt non-conforming styles in communication and bargaining.

Again, the technique is not introduced 'cold', but in the context of discussing themes. The rewards and justifications for this mode of learning thus make themselves clear. Difficulties pupils may encounter must be anticipated, and advice given on how to cope with initial embarrassment, drying up and overacting. Choice of actors is less problematic, especially in the context of a discussion with one pupil, but in the group situation where pupils may be asked to role-play in pairs it is sometimes necessary to allow pupils to opt out if they find the prospect disturbing.

Role-play should be kept brief. Three minutes is sufficient in the first instances: it is better to repeat an episode rather than prolong it. A short enactment is enough to generate a number of discussion points: an overlong period may make the role-reversal scene more difficult, may increase the chance of a stereotype being acted out or of participants drying up. The role-reversal element requires that each person sees and acts the scene from the standpoint of the

34

partner, thus simulating the partner's experience of the issue. If this is the chosen purpose, then the actors can change roles, carry on the enactment, and then discuss how the issue feels from the other's position.

Role-reversal can also develop *reflexive* role-taking skills, that is the ability to put oneself in others' shoes but in order to view oneself from that standpoint. This is central to effective self-presentation, and can help many adolescents who unwittingly and unintentionally create an impression (often non-verbally) which clouds their intended message in the eyes of the receiver. In this case the role-reversal scene should try to approximate the scene first played: the partner tries to give each person a glimpse of him/herself in the way she/he enacted the role originally. If you use this technique with a pupil by playing his/her role yourself, it is useful to start discussion by asking: 'How realistically do you think I played your role?' Very simple examples can be handled very effectively here: for example, someone's style on entering a room can be quickly examined by saying: 'Now you sit here and I'll come in the way you did: see what impression is created.'

The post-play discussion is of major importance: here the teacher centres the discussion on the processes which have emerged in the case of an individual improvised role-play, or on the aims that have been set in the case of a planned role-play. In either case the discussion may profitably move to an evaluation of the method and its advantage for finding new ways of behaving.

An example (of a planned role-play for possible use with groups):

'CHANGING MY MIND'

CHARACTERS AND SITUATION

Alan, 14, has just agreed to go with his dad to Bristol next weekend when dad picks up the older brother David from college at the end of term. But Alan has just remembered that he made a vague promise to go fishing with his best friend next weekend, so is just about to tell dad he's changed his mind.

Father is very keen for Alan to get a glimpse of college life: he hopes Alan will eventually go to college like David, but feels that he presently spends time on activities which aren't helping his school work.

1. The group divides into pairs and each pair decides who is to be labelled A and who is B.
2. For the first role-play A plays Alan and B his father: each spends a couple of minutes thinking about the role, the situation and how they might behave.
3. Three minutes role-play.
4. Discuss for five minutes. Consider the following:
    (a) how did each person feel?
    (b) did Alan succeed or did things get worse?
    (c) what arguments did father use?
    (d) did they negotiate some other answer?
    (e) could they see each other's point of view?
5. Now B plays Alan and A his father: spend some time thinking how you will behave.
6. Three minutes role-play.
7. Final discussion in pairs and evaluation in group.

For further examples and discussion of role-play see Hamblin (1974) pp. 158–67; Hamblin (1978) p. 155; Shaftel and Shaftel (1967); Chesler and Fox (1966).

3. Games

As the name suggests, games are not so strongly concerned with replicating a real situation. Rather they are a set of transactions which focus on one element of a real situation, but approach it in an unusual way. Games are not all sheer flights of fantasy. What is required, then, is to analyse from a particular situation the skills or competences you feel pupils are lacking, and then to construct a game activity to teach, exercise and develop this particular skill.

For example, in learning to cope with the demands of homework and the increasing importance of self-directed work, one of the component skills in this situation may be that of ordering the various alternatives which compete for time. A game could be constructed which teaches and exercises this skill, with the basic idea of getting pupils to put in priority order various demands for time in a variety of hypothetical contexts. Another example would be in careers education, where one ingredient of vocational choice is seen to be knowledge of the life-style associated with various jobs.

Having identified the sub-skill towards which attention is to be directed, we can now take the first steps in constructing a game. It is important to note how tightly structured the game is to be. A highly structured game may have predictable outcomes for the pupil and this is appropriate when information is to be taught or a particular limited skill developed. A less structured game may involve more elements of exploration for the players and therefore less predictable outcomes (an example here might be a loosely-structured group problem-solving game where players might learn about the problem, or the process of solving problems, or the group's composition, or the style adopted by the various members). When first using games, it is probably best to start with a fairly high degree of structure until pupils are acquainted with the technique.

But what *sort* of structure is provided? Great care must be taken to anticipate any implicit messages which may be generated by the game's structure. It is possible to build in implicit messages which are contrary to our overall aim, so that the game becomes self-defeating. We may need to forget the usual examples of board games such as Monopoly, as many of their features do not serve our purpose. The idea of 'moves' taken in turn by each player may be inappropriate: it is certainly difficult to identify an example of turn-taking in 'real-life' interactions, and the implicit effect of 'moves' may be to disallow the more complicated real negotiation. Similarly, to have progress through the game determined by chance (dice, spinner and so on) is to give a distorted message to the players. This may be all the more counterproductive for those players with a tendency to view the world in a 'fateful' way, where luck and chance are felt to be of major importance. There are some situations, nevertheless, where an element of chance or an unforeseen contingency are valuable: for example, during the course of a group problem-solving game such as 'Survival on a Desert Island' (where the group's personal resources and limited environmental resources need to be marshalled for survival), an extra 'crisis' can be introduced to test the group's flexibility: while planning a scheme for a freshwater reservoir, castaways suddenly have to deal with the effects of a hurricane. These unpredicted demands are possibly best introduced by the teacher.

A third feature of games which we need to examine is that of scoring. The games which are most useful do not necessarily decide a winner at the end; indeed many games aim at co-operation rather than competition. 'Co-operative Draughts' is a case in point: here the two players aim to exchange all the black and white draughts so that they end at opposite sides of the board. The game differs from the usual rules in that there is no jumping or moving backwards and no draughts are removed. The game is won if each player's last draught is moved to the last open position on the opposite side of the board at the same time. This example shows how exciting well-known games can be creatively modified to suit other educative purposes. If the games you develop do include scoring, check that you are not building in the message that life is a zero-sum game: that is, that what one person wins can only be at the expense of another's losses. Try instead to build in the idea of joint maximizing of rewards. There is a larger point here: each game probably carries an implicit model of man and his supposed way of behaving. Does your game see man as basically competitive? Does it encourage strategies which utilize short-term aims rather than a more reflective strategy? Does it reward manipulative approaches to the other players? Does it view people as only responding to rewards?

Turning now to those features necessary in the design of a game, the following list may help your planning:

1. The objectives of the game: what knowledge or skill do you intend to convey?
2. The roles of the participants: are pupils to be themselves or imagine themselves in another situation? If the latter is your choice, give role descriptions.
3. Players' goals: what are the pupils to aim at in the game? This needs to be spelt out clearly.
4. Players' resources: what can each pupil use to influence the outcome in his/her favour? These may be concrete, physical or abstract, personal.
5. Interaction between players: how can they affect each other and each other's outcomes? Are they partners and collaborators? Or negotiators? Or opponents?
6. How does play progress: what is the sequence of interaction, what choice points are included, how does the game end?
7. External constraints you may wish to place on the players' choices.
8. Materials required.

Remember that games turn out to be more effective if you have developed them in partnership with the people who are going to use them. A schema such as that above can help construct the first draft of a game: the next stage is to go to a group of pupils and ask them to play the draft version of it. Their comments and discussion will lead to much valuable modification of your planned activity. This point, of course, is also valid for simulations and planned role-plays, and it is surprising how much pupils gain from the developed version. Indeed most games can be fruitfully played on a number of occasions, either with increasingly complex rules or situations presented, or to develop a skill which has been taught earlier.

The particular elements you will need to modify will be specific to your game, but some general comments can be made (with thanks to Megarry, 1976, for some).

1. Try to make sure that no player spends much time 'idle'.
2. Try to exclude confusing materials in your game, or cues in the materials which are irrelevant to the task (unless of course you have designed a game to develop pupils' skills in coping with confusing or irrelevant information. This would certainly be a worthwhile enterprise in the study skills area).
3. Avoid, if you can, complex calculations which the players must perform at any stage.
4. Avoid writing in any unnecessary or unclear rules.
5. Do not reward speed in completing the game or learning the rules of the game rather than the skills or knowledge you have intended to reward.

Having constructed and developed a game, many of the earlier comments on how to introduce an activity to a group of pupils also apply here. There is one further point about the introduction: rather than spending time trying to explain the rules before play starts, it will be more effective to let the players learn the rules as they play the first round.

When it comes to the post-play discussion one further point is added: where the game incorporates elements loosely representing features of a real situation, it is useful for pupils to identify these elements and discuss their interpretation. So in the example of 'Survival on a Desert Island' where the teacher introduces a chance hurricane, post-play discussion would include students'

39

interpretations of this element, what it might represent, and what similar occurrences they know in real life.

EXAMPLES:

1. A SIMPLE COMMUNICATION GAME

Objectives
(a) to encourage taking the other's perspective in communication.
(b) to develop a recognition of the need to encode one's language for the listener.

Roles
This game is played in pairs, where one pupil is the instructor and the other is to follow instructions.

Players' goals
The instructor's aim is to direct the other player in a simple day-to-day task: putting on a jacket. The other player is not committed to this aim: he/she just follows instructions.

Players' resources
The instructor can only use spoken words to convey his directions: no demonstrating or other non-verbal communication. The other merely does what he/she is told, does not ask questions or communicate with the instructor.

Interaction between players
Since the person without the jacket does not share the aim of putting on the jacket, she/he is not basically co-operative towards the instructor and takes *every instruction literally*.

Sequence of events
At the start the jacket is lying on a table.

The game can have hilarious results while being played and can serve as a light-hearted introduction to many issues in communication. Similar situations where the effects are more serious will be brought out in the follow-up activities.

2. A SIMILAR COMMUNICATION GAME

As above but the task is different: here, the instructor has to describe to the partner a diagram which only he (the instructor) can

40

see. The joint aim is for the partner to reproduce accurately the original diagram. Simple diagrams are sufficient to begin with: a series of progressively more difficult diagrams could be developed if your aim is to develop this particular skill.

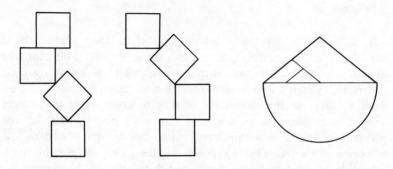

3. A GROUP PROBLEM-SOLVING GAME

Objectives
(a) to analyse group co-operation in solving a problem.
(b) to show some of the behaviours which may help or hinder group problem solving.

Roles
In groups of five, each person is to contribute towards the task given to the group. Each member is given an envelope containing a random selection of pieces cut from squares as below:

Players' goals
The aim is for each player to end up with a complete square in front of him. Only when all five players have a completed square is the task finished.

Players' resources
Players cannot ask others for the pieces required to complete their square: no member may speak. The only way to get a piece from another is for that person to offer it.

Interaction between players
Non-verbal communication is not allowed. The task therefore is

41

carried out in silent co-operation. Members may pass any of their pieces to any other group member at any time.

Sequence of events
Each player is given an envelope, the rules are explained and the task is begun.

This game is especially interesting when *some* players have completed their squares but others cannot do so. Thus for the group to complete the task some individuals must break up their completed squares and search for an alternative solution. If you wish to increase the likelihood of this outcome, you may select 'rigged' combinations for some of the envelopes, so that for one player a solution is within easy reach, but it is not one of the solutions as shown. Other versions of this game are possible with sentences cut up into single words and distributed to the players.

For further examples and discussion of games, see Hamblin (1974) pp. 180–2; Davison and Gordon (1978); Stadsklev (1974); Stanford (1977); Krupar (1973).

SUGGESTIONS FOR FURTHER USE

It is sometimes difficult to imagine how to extend the use of a new technique. This section suggests other areas in which simulations, role-play and games may be effective. *These suggestions* are not exhaustive, nor are they exclusive. Neither are these suggestions a rigorous typology or classification: they are a somewhat incoherent collection.

Simulations

The basic theme is learning about unknown social situations. There may be unknown people, an unknown context, an unknown way of behaving, or any combination of these. The basic aim is greater knowledge of the situation, how to 'handle' the event, present oneself positively and communicate effectively.

Suggested areas:

Working in groups
Roles in groups
Co-operation and competition

42

Maintaining one's own identity within a group
Meeting someone new (same/different sex, same/different age)
Initiating conversation
Going to an interview
Going to a family wedding, funeral, party
Approaching others
Returning goods to a shop
Dealing with the public as part of a job
Dealing with competing demands in a job
Life-styles of various jobs

Role-play

Here the basic theme is learning about relationships with known others. These may include difficulties, conflicts, frustrations, feelings of unfair treatment, issues of power and authority. The basic aim is greater understanding of the relationship, the other's perceptions and one's own part, communicating effectively and coping with any difficulty. Suggested areas:

(a) *with peers*
Coping with confrontation and escalation
An invitation to truant
Others getting me into trouble
Embarrassment, feeling silly
Being teased
Conflicts of loyalties, changing my mind, saying 'No'

(b) *with parents*
Being compared with others
Taking responsibility at home
Spending my money, going out
My effect on my brothers and sisters, their effect on me

(c) *with teachers*
Changing my reputation
Asking for something, a change of decision
Taking responsibility for my work
Asking questions in class

(d) *with other adults*
Talking to relatives
Being stopped by an official

43

(e) *with workmates*
Coping with 'initiations', being the novice
Making new friendships
Making mistakes

(f) *with the boss at work*
Taking instructions, not understanding them
Being paid wrongly
Unfair workload

Games

Here the basic theme is a particular set of facts and/or skills which
have been identified as necessary elsewhere. These may be skills of
thinking, decision-making, evaluating and planning. The basic aim
is to improve these skills in a variety of areas, at home, in school
and elsewhere.

Suggested areas:

> Solving a mystery (each person has one clue)
> Using information
> Identifying differences and similarities
> Inference games
> Decisions at school (options, stay or leave, careers)
> Decisions every day
> Level of risk in a decision
> 'Brainstorming' alternatives in a decision
> Forced choice games
> Organizing homework
> Saving money
> Creating a revision timetable
> Planning a trip, visit, holiday
> Co-operation games
> Communication games

SOME CONCLUDING COMMENTS

I have tried to describe active methods so that they are amenable to
the particular aims and constraints of pastoral care. When
considering the use of these activities in tutor time it is clear that

timing is important. If you have, say, thirty minutes with your tutor group and can complete the register in five, you may have five minutes to introduce the activity, five or ten to play it through and ten or fifteen for the follow-up activities. With a shorter period of tutor time it may be necessary to devise follow-up activities which allow pupils to record a few main points and their reactions, so that the main discussion may be held at the next meeting.

This point again brings us to consider the structure which is created by the post-play activity. The questions in this chapter have been suggested in the hope that the post-play activity will be well structured and will extract significant learnings. Discussion is not the only activity possible, and when we have to carry over the discussion to the next meeting, written responses may be convenient. For this purpose we may select some of the questions on which discussion is to centre, but we may also include other types of tasks. For example, simple self-assessment items which focus on the theme being explored can be very helpful: putting in order of importance the various alternatives open to a player, sorting other similar situations into liked and disliked, comparing outcomes from various lines of action, and so on. Processes like 'How I judge others' or 'People I model myself on' may also be incorporated, but for these self-assessments as for active methods generally it is important that the learnings are not seen as static.

Finally, I have tried to suggest one way in which pastoral care could become more creative. A positive involvement with social development and the development of other personal skills, all of which have a spin-off for academic development, may create a more forward-looking approach than some schools have at present. Encouraging students to take responsibility for their own learning and giving them the skills to take charge of their lives in this way, rather than watching them sink or swim, may have positive spin-off for many aspects of the school's life. But this is not to claim a panacea: active methods will not revolutionize education overnight, nor will they end conflict in our schools. They may nevertheless equip more students with the ability to succeed in school, and as a form of feedback may help school to become a truly adaptive learning environment.

3

Development of an Activity for use in Pastoral Care and Tutorial Periods

Maggie Bradbury
(Social Worker, West Glamorgan)

STOP! WAIT...GO! is a game in that those involved are presented with a logical sequence of tasks which must be worked through to achieve a particular result, and the tasks are introduced in a particularly stylized way. The game has no 'winner' or 'loser' as such. Each individual has responsibility for making a decision, which must be justified to a group in discussion. A group may then aim to present an overall decision reached by consensus through discussion of individuals' justifications. Alternatively, a group spokesman may describe the range of opinion within a group, if the members have reached a variety of decisions on those courses of action to be taken in meeting the problem posed by the given situation.

Thus, a group may actively negotiate to present what they consider to be the most appropriate course of action, or they may choose to describe their collective appreciation of varying viewpoints.

THE OVERALL OBJECTIVES OF THE ACTIVITY

1. *The creative and educative use of pastoral care time*

Creative – in that the game comes from and leads into other

46

activities, and can be presented in a manner which emphasizes this dynamic process.

Educative – in that it requires the same principles and methods of good teaching that should underlie the work on the rest of the timetable.

'Good teaching' involves:

(i) the careful preparation and review of materials and activities.

(ii) the selection and variation of tasks and their pacing, appropriate to the group involved.

(iii) effective activity management at the beginning and end, as well as during the session.

(iv) a flexibility of approach, so that the plan for the session may be adapted to those circumstances which occur within it.

(v) evaluation and constructive use of feedback.

(vi) a consistent and constructive awareness of pupils' and pupil/teacher interaction.

2. Linking pastoral care and the curriculum

Separating the aims of pastoral care from those of the curriculum is unrealistic. The pupil, as learner, may be working upon material which differs from that presented in subject lessons, but the skills developed in the learning process are applicable to everything he does in school and outside it.

3. The acquisition of skills

The provision and practice of certain skills, notably in decision-making and communication, in a safe setting, may be *transferred* to actual situations encountered.

4. Part of a programme of structured guidance

As pastoral care cannot be thought of as a random, unstructured practice, the game should not be a 'one-off' time-filling exercise, *but one of a series of events planned for the groups who use it.*

The two main areas of skill to be worked upon are those of decision-making and communication, embodied in the actual task of the game and the means by which the task is effectively operated.

The game can be an extended, conscious enactment of the decision-making process. The components of this process are:

1. Awareness of the need to make a decision.
2. Obtaining and selecting information to assist choice of action.
3. Evaluation of this information.
4. Reaching a tentative decision based on selection and evaluation.
5. Justifying the decision to self and others, assessing its finality or permanence, coming to terms with dissonant elements in presentation of the decision as a performance.

In discussion, individual styles of decision-making may be discovered and explored – preferred levels of risk – and there may be recognition of the sources of influences which shape decisions, and of tendencies to make decisions on the basis of impulse or expediency.

It is important to develop decision-making skills because the ability to make a decision is crucial to personal development; in building self-control; in taking responsibility for one's behaviour; in achieving a sense of competence by meeting the challenge presented by those situations in which decisions have to be made; and in using personal judgement to select from a variety of courses of action.

In developing skills of communication, the game requires appropriate means of communication at certain times, between teacher and pupils, and between pupils themselves. The teacher's practice of speech in the forms of instruction, direction and discussion may be repeated amongst pupils working in their groups. The game incorporates a useful model of the constructive use of classroom talk. The limited time available should help rather than hinder discussion. Both teacher and pupils may be encouraged to make their 'messages' concise. They may experience the ways in which effective communication is delayed or prevented. Too much teacher or pupil talk, the inappropriate noise levels of 'shouters' or 'mumblers' may prevent a well-judged decision being made or reviewed.

Finding out about communication patterns and processes in the classroom, and about the ease or difficulty with which discussions are held can be a most valuable follow-up in the game.

Questions of this sort might be introduced:

1. How did you get your opinion across to the others in your group?
2. Exactly how did you tell them what you had decided to do?
3. Were some people easier to listen to, and to understand? Why?
4. Were you persuaded to agree or disagree with anyone by the way in which they actually spoke to you?

Time is a main part of the game's framework, but there must be no suggestion that the group which reaches a decision in the quickest time 'wins'. Better to plan an extension of the activity than to limit discussion and encourage rushing.

The discussion phase of the game involves skills of listening and speaking, in that decisions are presented and justified between group members. An awareness of others' standpoints may develop through practice of these skills, and this may lead to increased understanding and toleration of others.

The game, therefore, both enacts and reflects a decision-making process, and operates through effective communication skills.

Objectives are important because they spell out a desired goal, and give structure and purpose to the activity. Structure is vital. This ties up with the individual's organization of himself and his ideas, his picture of himself in relationship to others and in various situational contexts.

The activity must be relevant to the participants, and credible. Questions will be asked.

1. Why do we have to do this?
2. Is it worth it?
3. This isn't a lesson, is it?

There is more to presenting a game than issuing the physical materials and directing the basic activity. The tone of initial questions and comments will provide some idea as to how to present the game as a credible activity. If pupils and teachers can be shown that it is concerned with relevant and realistic experience and is part of an educative process, confidence, interest and effort may be generated. Perhaps a foremost objective is to present the game as being useful to the pupils – that is, directly concerning their lives and life-skills.

Planning the game gives form to the possibilities suggested by clear objectives, and is a further creative enterprise, drawing up the contents of a framework, always being prepared for development and adaptation.

Clear objectives and sound planning are the foundation of the game. It is important to consider, before using it, these *basic* considerations.

1. The number of pupils.
2. Their age, sex and imputed ability.
3. The time available with the group. 20–25 minutes required for the game.
4. Other tasks to be carried out in the time.
   e.g. registration. These tasks can be used as a convenient excuse to avoid introducing activities. There is no reason to avoid planning a well-organized session where necessary and important tasks *and* activities can run together.
5. Possible interruptions during the time.
   e.g. latecomers. Anticipation and contingency planning apply as in subject lessons.
6. The activities preceding and following the time available.
   i.e. is the session to be first of the morning, last in the afternoon, or sandwiched between two subject lessons?

THE ORIGIN OF THE GAME

STOP! WAIT . . . GO! originated from work with two girls who seldom seemed to think or act independently, who were very unsure about their school work fearing demotion to a lower class, and who were having difficulty with peer relationships. Their ideas or opinions were usually introduced by the apparently more dominant member of the pair with 'We think . . .'

The phases of the game stem from their particular situation. It was important that the girls be provided with an activity in which they would have the opportunity to express individual viewpoints without each other's verbal influence, but to work at the task in the same place and at the same time so that they could explore in immediate discussion their agreement or disagreement on decisions made separately.

In fact the 'quieter' girl was determined and articulate in presenting her own viewpoint. The two agreed on courses of action in two out of the six situations presented to them.

It was evident, from piloting this activity with two pupils, that it was possible to adapt it for use with larger groups and within the tutorial setting.

THE GAME

The game is for thirty pupils, in six sub-groups of five members.

The name

The familiar traffic light command signals and colours catch attention and label the tasks of the action phase in logical sequence.

The cards

SAMPLE TOPIC: TRUANCY

STOP! presents a situation in which a decision has to be made so that a certain course of action may be followed.

One member of the group may be elected spokesman and read out the situation to the rest.

OR

Each member may have a separate STOP! card.

OR

The STOP! card may be passed around the group.

Use of an overhead projector transparency or large poster card for display to the whole class is also possible.

The members of the group have a minute to think about the situation, *without any discussion*.

51

Front   Back

WAIT . . . gives a choice of possible courses of action. These could have been drawn from points made by pupils in a preparatory discussion of the topic, or may be alternatives drawn up by the teacher(s)/pupils planning the game.

It is very important that there is a clearly expressed invitation to draw up an original, personal course of action, apart from the selection on the card.

It is preferable that each member of the group has a separate card to study while making a choice. This avoids others waiting, or a group spokesman reading alternatives in a 'leading' tone. It may be quite possible to pass or read out a card with groups who are familiar with games' activities.

Again, an overhead projector transparency or large poster card may be used to display the WAIT . . . alternatives.

Think!
Do you . . .?
1. HOPE THE FUSS WILL DIE DOWN AND YOU WILL NOT BE FOUND OUT.
or
2. INVENT A REASON FOR YOUR ABSENCE.
or
3. GO AND OWN UP.
or
4. YOUR OWN CHOICE.

Front   Back

Studying the STOP! and WAIT . . . cards could take up to five minutes, without discussion.

GO! signals the opportunity for each individual pupil to record his

52

chosen decision privately, in writing. Individual answer slips can be drawn from a flap stapled to the main card.

One GO! card containing 5 answer slips is needed for each sub-group.

OR

GO! instructions can be written on a transparency or poster card, and answer slips distributed to all pupils.

Up to a further 5 minutes for recording decisions and reasons for choice could be allowed. This must be done without discussion.

Depending on the individual, written decisions may be in brief note form or more elaborate, extended explanations, but these are triggers in the discussion phase.

The written activity has a three-fold purpose: (i) individual effort – no collaboration; (ii) commitment to the decision; (iii) trigger for discussion.

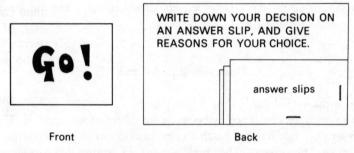

Front   Back

The individual action phase may take up to 10 minutes. This will vary with the groups involved. At least fifteen minutes should be available for discussion and summary.

THE PHASES OF THE ACTIVITY

1. Introduction

Preparing the group.
Presenting the materials.

The amount of teacher-explanation and direction will depend on the characteristics and experience of the group.

The introductory phase is *essential method teaching*. The teacher may use an entire 20–25 minute session as the introductory phase, demonstrating the use of the game with a small group before the rest of the class, or working with the entire class on a sample situation. In doing this enthusiasm and a model for play may be effectively transmitted.

2. Individual action

The game.

Each of the stages is carried out *silently*, and it is best that they should be timed by the director of the activity, teacher or pupil.

In later discussion the effect of time on decision-making can be brought out, particularly in relation to impulsive decisions and their possible consequences.

In the first or early sessions each sub-group could work on the same situation from a particular topic area. In later sessions several sub-groups could work on a variety of situations – see the sample at the end of the chapter.

3. Discussion (figs 3.1 and 3.2)

This is the verbal part of the activity.

The primary discussion is between members of sub-groups. They may or may not have to reach a consensus decision on the course of action to be taken. The presentation of some evaluation and synthesis of their discussion by a representative spokesman is important because it extends skills of communication.

A sub-group spokesman reports back to the entire class the range of choice within his group, or if part of the task is to reach a consensus, what this is and how it was reached.

It is obviously more complicated and initially more time-consuming if six *different* situations are in play although these are concerned with the same topic.

If there is to be an entire class summary session, each sub-group spokesman will introduce the STOP! situation, and the WAIT . . . range of alternatives for discussion, as well as the results and content of the discussion: depending on whether, particularly in the early use of this game, the teacher wants the entire class to join

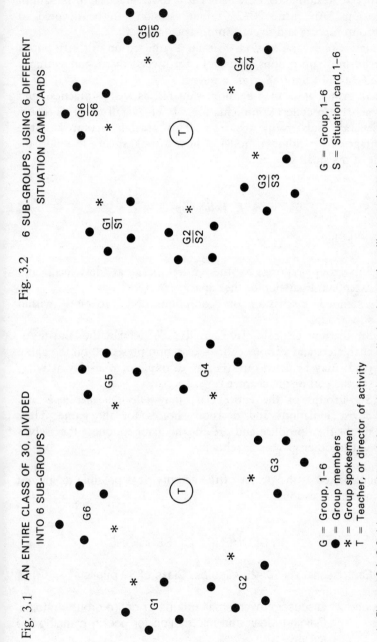

Fig. 3.1 AN ENTIRE CLASS OF 30, DIVIDED
INTO 6 SUB-GROUPS

Fig. 3.2 6 SUB-GROUPS, USING 6 DIFFERENT
SITUATION GAME CARDS

G = Group, 1–6
● = Group members
* = Group spokesmen
T = Teacher, or director of activity

G = Group, 1–6
S = Situation card, 1–6

In Figures 3.1, 3.2, I have positioned the teacher centrally, but he or she will move about the groups.

Spokesmen for the groups may report to the entire class from that central position, or from their own groups.

55

together at session ends, or whether it is more practical to remain in sub-groups. An entire 20–25 minute session can be devoted to sub-group reports and overall summary.

It may take several sessions to train a large group of thirty pupils to break into sub-groups and rejoin for a class discussion within a limited, but not limiting, time sequence.

Small group work may be more valuable, as well as practical, and the teacher can collect comments for a brief overall progress report on separate sub-group activities. This teacher action has the advantage of providing a model of how a spokesman can report on behalf of his small group.

4. Follow-up

This could be:

1. Sub-group reports to the entire class, as described, and extended discussion of the topic.
2. Extended discussion on communication processes within sub-groups.
3. Simulation or role-play activity, in which the situations, characters and various courses of action presented on the game cards may be acted out. (For an example of role-play activity, see the end of the chapter.)
4. Sub-groups or the entire class may select *another topic* and devise situations and decision choices for the game. They might then produce and present the game amongst themselves and to other groups in school.

Having looked at the phases of the activity, it is possible to suggest a sequence of sessions.

A SEQUENCE OF SESSIONS

Each session – 20–25 minutes. Class of 30 pupils.

Session I   Discussion with small groups or entire group on topic. Gaining ideas and information for use in planning the activity.

56

Session II	*Introductory phase*
	The teacher demonstrates the use of the game. Method transmission to pupils.

Session III	*Individual action phase*
	The game, played in 6 sub-groups. One or more starter situations may be used.
	Discussion phase
	Primary discussion between members of sub-groups. Groups' spokesmen prepare summaries.

Session IV	*Discussion phase*
	The sub-group spokesmen report to the teacher and entire class on each group's decision-making activity. A 2-minute report could be presented by each spokesman. The teacher then summarizes, to close the discussion phase, pointing out areas of consensus, the range of opinion, varying standpoints amongst the 30 pupils involved.

Session V	*Follow-up phase*
	Example: as in the fourth suggestion for follow-up work (p. 56). The teacher conducts a 'brainstorm' of ideas from the entire class for a new topic. This is similar to the initial exploratory discussion of Session I. Ideas can be written up on a blackboard, with pauses to discuss their relevance and potential for the STOP! WAIT . . . GO! format.

Session VI	Each sub-group may devise a STOP! situation and WAIT . . . alternatives based on the new topic, and produce game cards for another sub-group to try out.

Another cycle of sessions may then begin, using pupil's own material.

The discussion is structured in that it is focused upon a particular topic, based on set STOP! situations and certain WAIT . . . alternatives provided by the game planners.

It must be emphasized that to structure is not to restrict. To return to the idea of framework, such structuring provides guidelines within which ideas may be ordered. If the time is to be used purposefully, the structuring of discussion is vital, otherwise diversions, however valuable in themselves, may be introduced, and the immediate topic and task lost.

Timing is important. Allowing for other events in a tutorial period – registration, giving notices, various administrative tasks and possible interruptions – it is perhaps most realistic to plan for a 20–25 minute activity session, which ideally might occur 2–3 times a week to retain impetus and meaningful sequence.

Some schools have timetabled pastoral or tutorial periods as they have subject lessons, in which case 30–45 minutes may be available, with fewer extraneous tasks to hold up the activity.

Apart from the amount and use of time available *within* a session, other aspects of timing must be examined.

1. When should an activity of this type – a game – be introduced to the group?
2. ... at what stage of the group's relationship with the teacher as tutor?
3. ... with how many members of the group? All at once, or a small pilot group?
4. ... at what time of the week, or stage of the term?

These are further *basic* considerations.

The game should not be introduced for the sake of doing *something* without careful consideration of how it is to be introduced and followed up – that is having the *overall objectives* firmly in mind.

Control of the activity is built into the game. The purpose of silent and verbal phases must be explained and demonstrated by the teacher in the introduction. As the tasks are varied, so may be the groupings. It is important to build up experiences of individual and shared tasks, of self-reliance and of co-operation with others.

Both material and verbal presentation are important for the successful use of the game. Indifferent preparation and presentation are perhaps to be thought of as part of a chain of negative expectations. Verbal presentation will be adapted to varying groups more than the written instructions and information which are suitable for a wide range of age and ability levels.

It is important to be economical with resources in preparing the activity, with materials and teacher time, not only because of the present economic climate, but in seeing an activity of this type as part of a dynamic process in which much else needs to be done and which claims personal and general resources.

PRODUCING THE GAME

The game's materials can be mass produced on duplicated sheets from master copies, and its separate parts cut from these.

Example

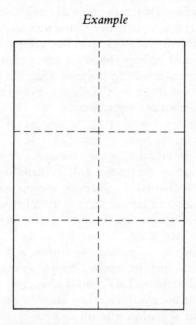

Six STOP! situations could be written on an A4 master copy. Different coloured stencils or carbons could be used for attractive presentation. Copies could be made on very thin card, or on duplicating paper. WAIT... and GO! cards could also be produced in this way.

If coloured stencils or carbon are not available, felt pens, crayons or paint can be used to outline and fill in outstanding titles and directions on the fronts and backs of cards. The colours should emphasize the traffic light theme.

Game cards may be produced *individually*, using felt pens on a stack of pre-cut thin cardboard. Cards could then be covered in transparent adhesive film, so that although this method may prove more expensive, initially, in time and costs, the cards will last longer and keep their attractive appearance.

The preparation of large poster cards and of overhead projector transparencies may be considered appropriate. This avoids duplication and a bulk of individual cards.

Whatever materials are used, careful printing or type, and use of colour are strongly recommended. Think back to the credibility of the activity, and the effort put into commercial productions.

A game can be prepared more swiftly by a team working on its various parts, and a team may draw upon a wider range of planning and production skills. This team may be assembled in in-service training sessions, or in teacher/teacher–pupil workshops. It has already been suggested that pupils producing their own game is an extension of the initial activity. Ideas for other games may emerge. A sequence of activity involving game-making can be as important to the acquisition and practice of skills as playing the end product, or directing its use with other groups.

This chapter will end with a set of six STOP! situations and WAIT alternatives on the topic of truancy.

These are based on preparatory discussion with pupils.

First, a word about the topic and its handling. Working on truancy leads to the discussion of varying standpoints on that topic. Within some schools and homes there is a tradition of truancy and collusion with those who truant. Various stereotypes of truants may be held. Those pupils who do truant may be labelled as idlers, troublemakers, evaders, or perhaps as heroes and system-fighters. Those who never do may be labelled creeps, swots, cowards, or as the responsible and reliable. Labels must always be questioned, and accurate evidence of the tendencies they point to must be sought.

The policy of the school in relation to truancy must be clear – it may have to be very clearly expressed: not easy if the policy is inconsistent. The possible position of parents must be anticipated. Loose condemnation or approval of apparently fixed parental or school attitudes and policy are not constructive.

It is important to look at long- and short-term consequences of truancy for the individual, and to consider the effects of and influences towards truancy amongst groups of individuals inside and outside the school and the home. It is a topic in which personal responsibility for action can be emphasized, reflecting its importance in decision-making.

Criticism of the STOP! situations and WAIT . . . alternatives for choice may arise – do these provide ideas and ready-made 'excuses' for confirmed or would-be truants? Do they reinforce avoidance strategies? This type of criticism does not appreciate the objectives of the activity, nor the aims of pastoral care as an educative process. It is likely to support a view that in the discussion of such topics, pupils and/or teachers are practising skills of manipulation and persuasion.

It must be said, very firmly, that opening up topics and exploring them through structured activities, encourages pupil and teacher appreciation and analysis of problems which can be met and shared in a programme of pastoral care.

Stop! Situations		*Wait . . . Alternatives*
		Do you . . .
1. Your dog is ill, and no one is at home during the day to look after it. Your parents say the dog will be all right.		1. Stay at home with the dog, without telling your parents? OR
	DOG	2. Get your register marks and then go home, twice, during the day? OR
		3. Seek some advice on what to do? OR
		4. YOUR OWN CHOICE.
		Do you . . .
2. Mum has asked you to look after your baby sister for the afternoon. She has an appointment to keep. Next day you go to school without a note.		1. Explain the situation to a teacher.
		2. Say you were ill, and promise to bring a note.
	BABY SITTER	3. If Mum is too busy to write a note, and you know you must have one, forge a note. OR
		4. YOUR OWN CHOICE.

3. You have left school at 1.30 pm after getting your register mark for the afternoon. Calling in at the Post Office on the way home, you meet the Headmaster who asks your name.

CLOSE ENCOUNTER

Do you . . .
1. Rush out of the Post Office without replying.
OR
2. Give your name and wait for the next move.
OR
3. Say that you're a bit late for school this afternoon, because you were asked to call at the Post Office.
OR
4. YOUR OWN CHOICE.

---

4. Your friend meets you as usual on the way to school. It is his birthday, and he has been given some money. He suggests you both go into town, now, to spend it.

CELEBRATION

Do you . . .
1. Refuse outright, telling him not to be stupid.
OR
2. Immediately agree to take this chance to have what sounds like a good time.
OR
3. Say you're not sure that it is such a good idea, and try to explain why.
OR
4. YOUR OWN CHOICE.

---

5. You are with 3 close friends at break. They are planning to miss afternoon lessons, and say that if you don't join them,

Do you . . .
1. Say you'll go with them, because you don't want to break up the friendship?
OR

they'll not forget you let them down.

COMPANY

2. Say you'll join them, but plan to make an excuse after dinner, so that at the last minute you can't go?
OR
3. Say you'd rather not take the risk, and tell them they can do what they like?
OR
4. YOUR OWN CHOICE.

---

6. You are dreading a particular lesson because you haven't done any homework and you don't really understand the work.

PANIC

Do you . . .
1. Miss the lesson, and lie low around school?
OR
2. Go to the lesson and talk to the teacher about the work?
OR
3. Go to the sick room and ask to be sent home because you are feeling ill?
OR
4. YOUR OWN CHOICE.

Role-play as a follow-up activity

This is based on the situations and characters of the game cards. Taking STOP! SITUATION (1), from the sample set.

Your dog is ill, and no-one is at home during the day to look after it. Your parents say the dog will be all right.

63

The following scenes, set at home and at school, are two possibilities for role-play activity and arise immediately from the given situation.

SCENE 1

One of your parents, arriving home unexpectedly from work, has found you at home with the dog, and wants to know why you are not at school.

Character 1   the girl or boy who owns the dog.
Character 2   the mother or father.

For a few minutes, the two players think about the implications of the scene in relation to the original situation, and how they are going to behave in it. For a further few minutes, they role-play the scene. Then, for up to five minutes they discuss what happened in the scene, their interpretation of the situation, and how they felt about the characters they played.

Was the parent angry, disappointed, worried, sympathetic?
Was the girl or boy alarmed, defiant, calm, sorry?
Did either character make any suggestions about what might happen at home or at school after this situation?
Did the characters have an argument about the dog?
How much did each character understand the other's point of view?

This sort of question emerges in post-play discussion.

SCENE 2

You have been missed in morning lessons, although you collected your register mark. You have been visiting the dog. At afternoon registration your tutor asks where you have been.

Character 1   the girl or boy who owns the dog.
Character 2   the tutor.

These questions might come up in discussion.

Did the pupil decide to share his problem with the tutor? How
did he answer the tutor?
Did the tutor think that the pupil was worried about something?
Did they, together, find some way of improving the situation for
the pupil, while not making things more difficult at home or
at school?

Sub-groups of up to 6 members, who have been playing STOP!
WAIT . . . GO!, could divide into pairs for this activity, or into trios,
where the third member is an observer of the role-play, and
contributes to the discussion.

SUGGESTED TIMING

For each scene, involving pairs and/or trios:

2 minutes – thinking about the scene and characters.
3 minutes – active role-play.
5 minutes discussion.

The teacher may wish to bring the entire class together for the end
of session,

OR

sub-groups of six could join up again to discuss the activities of the
three pairs or two trios within them,

OR

pairs and trios could work on a second scene from the starter
situation. Again, 20–25 minutes is required in all.

65

4

Management of innovation in pastoral care

Dewi Williams

(Head of Guidance, Olchfa Comprehensive School, Swansea)

A defect in our pastoral system is the tendency to abrogate responsibility for pastoral care to members of staff such as heads of year. Pastoral care is seen as predominantly their responsibility: something for which they are paid. Thus a split develops between pastoral and curricular activities. Pastoral care then becomes a responsibility outside and supplementary to the classroom; so a referral process develops, but usually of disruptive pupils only. Pastoral care can then become warped into a disciplinary system, unless staff are alert to the danger. A disproportionate amount of time is invested in dealing with referrals and investigating incidents.

A further process can be detected, which is not confined to schools – that of trivialization. Posts are established so that significant responsibilities will be discharged, but the holders find that under the pressure of immediate demands, more and more time is spent on routine, trivial matters. Pastoral care is not exempt from this process, which seems to be related to the size of the school and the number of posts of special responsibility within both the school and the administration of the LEA.

If we value the contribution of pastoral care, we must examine the effects of these processes, taking into consideration the time and effort that is misplaced. An analysis based on the following questions could be undertaken.

1. How many referrals are made to the pastoral staff?
2. By whom? To whom?
3. Is there a disproportionate number from and to certain teachers?
4. Are the same pupils referred time and time again?
5. Are they frequently from certain sections of the school?
6. For what reasons are pupils referred?
7. Are anxious, apathetic, underachieving pupils included?
8. Is there an assumption that achieving and/or well-behaved children do not require pastoral care?
9. How much time is spent on the investigation of incidents?
10. Do pastoral activities portray a pattern of incident with predictable response?
11. Do pastoral staff feel that nothing does or will improve the present state?
12. What proportion of time do pastoral staff spend on administration? How much of this could be eliminated without loss?
13. Do trivial, repetitive matters lead to the neglect of important duties?

If it appears from our analysis that we need to improve the system, then what must be remedied? There is a tendency to blame heads of year for the inadequacies of pastoral care systems, or for their interpretation of their role as punitive agents. But it seems to me that they become trapped in this role by the expectations of teachers, which are revealed by the selectivity of referrals, and find it difficult to escape: they are, maybe, more the victims than the perpetrators of the role. The remedy must lie in shifting more of the onus of responsibility to the classroom; but to cope with this responsibility, the class teacher will need greater pastoral skills and sensitivity, and in some cases a change of attitude and role interpretation.

What are the skills required?

1. Greater understanding of the social, educational and developmental needs of pupils.
2. The ability to detect when pupils are not coping with demands.
3. A range of strategies to remedy deficits.
4. Sensitivity to the signals of evaluation and devaluation emitted to pupils.

From this analysis of skills, it is apparent that two tasks must be tackled; the first, developing the teacher's sensitivity, range of expertise and techniques; the second, making the teacher aware of the skills required by the pupil to cope adequately with the demands made on him. Clearly, these two aspects are interdependent and mutually promotive; and on them will depend the quality of our pastoral care. Here lies the need for innovation.

But where do we begin to innovate? As a guide it is necessary to evolve a simple model. Within a school many variables interact to affect attitudes and behaviour. For our model we focus on two that are crucial: self-image, and closely related to it, perception of causality; that is, does the pupil feel that success and failure are dependent upon his own efforts, or upon factors outside his control such as luck. The feeling that control resides with him implies choice: whether or not to undertake the necessary activities that will bring success. If he feels that success and failure do not depend on him, then he has little choice: for then there is no point in making an effort. These two variables largely determine the pupil's potential for achievement. Therefore they must be central to pastoral care. Our concern must be the attitudes that promote or militate against this potential, and the habitual ways in which the pupil responds to his perception of it.

But we must also remember that both the pupil's achievement potential and response are being continually affected by the signals of evaluation and devaluation emitted by the school, through the remarks and attitudes of staff and school organization.

The pupil's responses can be grouped into two: productive and unproductive; that is, those conducive to success in school, and those that undermine his capacity to achieve. The latter can be either active – devaluation, defensiveness, suspicion, arrogance, belligerence, truancy and vandalism; or passive – disorganization, helplessness, withdrawal, apathy, anxiety, underachievement, and low motivation. Innovation must be planned to move the efforts of pastoral work from dealing with unproductive behaviour to promoting the pupil's perception of himself as someone capable of achievement; therefore the focus must be on developing a high level of motivation, persistence, resilience, responsible behaviour and the ability to defer gratification.

At what stages of the pupil's career is it best to concentrate our attempts?

For assistance here, we can utilize the analysis of critical points elaborated by Hamblin (1978). These are times of decision and change, when feelings of uncertainty and loss of confidence are apt to appear. Failure at these stages can damage the pupil's potential for success. Therefore, innovation should be designed to help pupils cope with these demands.

When do these critical points occur?

1. Transition to secondary school.
   (For analysis of pupil's needs and skills see p. 71.)

2. Third-year subject choices.
   Needs.

   a. Greater self-knowledge.
   b. Job information.
   c. Ability to relate them realistically.
   d. Enhanced decision-making skills.

3. Fifth year.
   Needs.

   a. Study skills.
   b. Coping with examination anxiety.
   c. Entry into, and preparation for, employment/unemployment.
   d. Preparation for sixth form.

4. Entry into sixth form.
   (For analysis of needs and skills see p. 81.)

Marland (1974) comments that pastoral care cannot be conducted in a vacuum. This is just as true of innovation. As the analysis of critical points indicates, we need to structure our innovations carefully by producing programmes which aim to accomplish definite tasks in order to satisfy defined needs.

We shall probably begin innovation with the form period. But one must reckon with the casual perception of form periods which has developed among staff and pupils. 'A time when you're not expected to do anything' was a typical comment from a sixth-former. There is a further difficulty: a misconception has arisen among members of staff who are reluctant to allow the time to be wasted. They see form periods as a time for preparation, marking, doing homework, extra practice and communication. In many schools the form period has developed into an essential

69

feature of the communication system; it is the most convenient and least disruptive time for relaying messages on sports, parents' evenings, clubs and extracurricular activities. These perceptions must be modified by an in-service training programme.

To structure our innovation we will need to produce programmes to satisfy the following requirements:

1. Providing activities to help pupils to acquire specified skills and coping strategies.
2. Familiarizing teachers with these particular skills and needs.
3. Promoting the professional development and general expertise of the teacher.

Therefore we must write three sets of materials. The first is designed for the teacher and is concerned with a particular area of innovation. It sets out:

1. The aims.
2. The objectives.
3. The needs being met.
4. The tasks to be accomplished.
5. The rationale behind the activities.
6. Suggestions about methodology.
7. Lastly, it should contain any other information that will make the programme as self-contained as possible and easy to implement. It is planned so that minimal demands are placed on teaching staff, thus making it more acceptable.

The second set of materials will also be for teachers, but will deal with broader issues, such as the psychological and sociological processes at work in the school and classroom. It will consider such topics as the school as a system signalling valuation and devaluation, labelling processes, classroom relationships and teacher expectations and assumptions.

Materials for pupils should also be as self-explanatory as possible, because there is a risk that they may be distributed to pupils without explanation or preparation, or may not be used as intended. But they should also give the teacher an opportunity to develop his own materials and exercise his creativity and specialist skills.

The materials below have been used in first-year programmes: they include teachers' notes for induction, social education and study skills programmes, and some samples of activities for pupils.

FIRST-YEAR INDUCTION PROGRAMME

Teachers' notes

This induction programme is intended to help pupils feel accepted and secure in school. It is necessary, therefore, to:

1. Provide them with the skills they will need.
2. Detect pupils who are having difficulty in making the transition.

Pupils' needs and skills

1. Information
   (a) On staff.
   (b) Layout of buildings.
   (c) Procedures for absence, sickness or injury. Knowledge of school procedures and personnel will help to allay anxieties.
2. Coping with the differing demands and teaching styles of many teachers. Failure will undermine his confidence; he will be more secure if he is able to predict the attitudes and reactions of others.
3. Organizing his work (see notes on study skills, p. 72).
4. Looking after his property.
   Continually losing property may arise from a sense of disorientation in a large school.
5. Understanding:
   (a) school rules and their rationale;
   (b) the unwritten rules of the school.
6. Making full use of the academic, social and leisure opportunities of the school.
7. Dealing with bullying.
8. Understanding the pastoral system. Pupils often acquire the impression that the pastoral system serves to meet the teachers' need for control.
9. Allaying anxieties engendered by fear of PE apparatus and of taking communal showers.

SOCIAL EDUCATION

Notes for teachers

HANDLING SITUATIONS

These situations can be presented to the class for discussion. Arrange pupils in groups of three or four, and present the situations below for discussion. Group decisions can then be presented to the class for further discussion, and for reconsideration by the groups. Pupils should come to realize that there are several ways of handling these situations. Emphasize the assessment of probable outcomes. The aim is not to provide pupils with recipes, but to develop their capacity to consider the advantages and disadvantages of proposed solutions.

Both problems and solutions can be role-played.

SITUATIONS

1. Your best friend tries to persuade you to miss a lesson which you find boring or dislike.
2. Pupils behind you keep kicking you under the desk.
3. You lose your pen and next day you see another pupil with one like it.
4. You are wrongly accused of damaging or defacing school property.
5. An older pupil demands money/sweets from you.
6. You discover that your exercise book has been defaced in your absence.
7. You have forgotten to prepare for a test; the teacher is strict.
8. You have forgotten or mislaid your textbook; you see one nearby.
9. An important school fixture clashes with a special club night or TV show.
10. You suffer a lot of teasing or name-calling.
11. A friend insists on copying from your book.
12. You are late for school; your friends suggest you truant. You don't wish to, but they accuse you of being afraid.

FIRST-YEAR PROGRAMME OF STUDY SKILLS

Teachers' notes

Aim: to raise the pupil's level of satisfaction from, and achievement in, his study.

72

Objectives:

1. To encourage pupils to analyse their methods of working.
2. To inculcate good working habits.

Pupils should consider the following:
1. Time of starting.
   The most common difficulty is inability to start and maintain regular concentrated work.
   (a) Pupils should analyse their domestic routines and select a starting time, to which, ideally, they can adhere *strictly*. Their habits will assist them in getting down to work each evening.
   (b) The later they start, the more tired they are likely to be and will work less effectively; if their work takes longer than anticipated, the less time they will have to complete it.
2. Posture.
   Its effects on alertness and, therefore, effectiveness.. Attention should be drawn to the importance of:
   (a) sitting fairly erect on a firm chair;
   (b) table of suitable height;
   (c) position of light.
3. Environment.
   (a) Eliminating distractions.
       (i) If possible, a separate room.
       (ii) No distraction from radios, television or pets.
   (b) Avoiding a stuffy, hot atmosphere.
4. Organization.
   (a) Timetables: need for two durable copies.
   (b) Books and papers should be kept tidy so that pupils can begin work at once.
   (c) Each evening books and equipment should be packed for the following day.
   (d) Locating information quickly.
       (i) In note books.
       (ii) Keeping a record card system using key words.
       (iii) Use of dictionaries.
5. Use of reference books.
   Please note the following in the library.
   (a) *Children's Britannica.*
   (b) *Oxford Junior Encyclopaedia.*
   (c) *Hutchinson's New 20th Century Encyclopaedia.*

    (d) *Whitaker's Almanack.*
    (e) *Everyman's Classical Dictionary.*
    (f) *Dictionary of Fictional Characters.*
6. Resolving difficulties.
    (a) Spelling: noting down difficult words and mistakes.
    (b) Learning groups of words from a spelling book.
    (c) Keeping a pocket dictionary handy.
    (d) Isolating difficulties with precision; eg pupils should not be allowed to dismiss themselves as careless, but identify the situations in which they are careless.
    (e) Consulting teachers – at a convenient time.
    (f) Absences.
    Catching up by:
    (a) Copying up notes.
    (b) Checking on work covered or set.
7. Doing homework.
    (a) Keeping a homework notebook and jotting down requirements, comments and instructions, plus date of completion.
    (b) Taking breaks (about 5 minutes at the end of each half-hour).
    (c) Tackling hard or easy subject first.
8. Memorization.
    'Within 24 hours of a 1 hour learning period, at least 80% of detailed information is lost' (Buzan, 1974) unless pupils actively retest themselves.

Both long-term retention and understanding will be better if they spread out their learning rather than trying to cram it into a single session.

    (a) Learning a small number at a time.
    (b) Familiarization: attending to meanings and looking for associations.
    (c) Recalling periodically by:
        (i) Testing by parent, etc.
        (ii) Writing out (eyes closed – assists with visualization).
        (iii) Using cassette recorder, allowing gaps for response.
        (iv) Rearranging material in different ways: eg notes, diagrams, charts.
    (d) Working intensively.

9. Examinations.
   (a) Working out a revision timetable 3 weeks before examination, allocating time for weak subjects.
   (b) Revising dissimilar material on same evening.
   (c) Examining diagrams, charts, tables, etc.
   (d) Noting down key words during revision.
   (e) Building up a set of summary cards.
   (f) Periodic testing.
   (g) Reading examination questions carefully, noting each word.
   (h) Allocating time for each question, including planning and checking answers.

ACTIVITIES FOR FIRST-YEAR PUPILS

These activities were designed for pupils in a large comprehensive school with a predominantly middle-class intake. Thus they might impress as being too sophisticated for use in some schools. However, this impression underlines the importance of designing and adapting materials to suit individual schools.

(The cartoons were drawn by two pupils from the first-year sixth form.)

Welcome to your new school

We hope you do not feel too much like the boys in the cartoons. However, you may be a little confused, but as soon as you learn to find your way around the school, you will feel less anxious. The following activities will help you to get to know the school.
1. Make a copy of the map.
Note a. Where is your form room?
     b. Where are assemblies held?
     c. Where is your house tutor's room?
     d. Where are the toilets?
     e. Where can you obtain meal tickets?
     f. Where are school lunches served?
     g. Where is the nurse's room?
     h. Can you find the school library, the gymnasium and the swimming pool?

75

2. Make 2 copies of your school timetable (just in case you lose one). It is better to use a piece of card 2″ × 3″ which can be kept in a transparent plastic folder.

Homework

In your primary school you may not have been given homework. However, you will now be expected to do some work at home. You should, therefore, give some thought to how you will organize your homework.

A.
1. Discuss the following:
(a) What time will you begin each evening?
(b) Is it better to start early or late; before going out
to youth club, etc. or on your return?
(c) Is it better to begin with an easy or a difficult subject?
(d) Will you give extra time to 'weak' subjects?
2. Now draw out a homework timetable. Don't forget to include
the starting time each evening.

B.
1. The appearance of your work is very important. What kind of
   impression does your work give?
(a) Hurried? Thoughtful?
(b) Is it neat? Writing legible?
(c) Do you underline headings and leave margins?
2. Write out an example of how you will present your work.

Looking after property

We hope you will not be as careless as the pupil in the cartoon.
1. How could he have avoided this situation?
   Make a list of the measures he should have taken.
2. What equipment is likely to be mislaid?
3. What should you do if you do lose something?

Using the library

You may be puzzled at first by the arrangement of books in the
library, but it is easy to use when you understand the system. The

78

librarian will explain the classification to you, but to help you further we have drawn out the following activities.

Books are divided into two main groups.

Fiction
Story books or novels.
Books arranged:
Alphabetical order – author's surname.

Non-fiction
(a) Sport, inventions, animals, famous people, travel, school subjects.
(b) Reference: Encyclopaedias, dictionaries, atlases, gazetteers.

Books arranged:
In topics: note topic numbers.

1. Find the fiction, non-fiction and reference section of the library.
2. Write down the titles of six reference books. Do any of these specialize on one topic?
3. Find both the classified and author catalogues (consist of cards arranged in drawers).
4. What does each card show?
5. What use can these cards be to you?
6. What is the purpose of the number in the top right-hand corner?
7. Look up 'football'. What is the topic number?
8. Find the section on chemistry. Use the wall chart near the librarian's desk.
9. What subject do you find under 591.4?

Getting to know the library

The following exercises are meant to help you to get to know the library's reference books: that is, books, such as encyclopaedias, dictionaries, gazetteers, which we consult for information. Look up the reference books given, and see how quickly you can find the answers to the following questions.

Children's Britannica
1. Where was the dahlia first discovered?

79

2. Who was Chardin Jean Baptiste?
3. What was the Locarno Pact?

The Oxford Dictionary

The meanings of miscible, plexor and quiddity. How is occu $\frac{(r)\ (rr)}{}$ ed spelt? 1 'r' or 2?

Junior Pears Encyclopaedia
  1. Who is the holder of the European record for freestyle swimming for 100 metres?
  2. Who was Mithridates?
  3. What is the time at Lagos, Nigeria, when it is 12 o'clock midday at Greenwich (winter time)?

The Junior Encyclopaedia
  1. Who was Villon Francois?
  2. Find out as much information as you can on Medals and Decorations.
  3. What is a cassowary?

Oxford Junior Encyclopaedia
  1. Who built the Taj Mahal?
  2. How many different kinds of fish are there?
  3. Who first used anaesthetic?

The following programmes are presented later in the term. 'Exams' is issued to first-year pupils about three weeks before their first examination, and is intended to help them plan their revision. 'Danger! man at work' is for November, after pupils have had experience of doing homework. It is more searching than the initial activity on homework.

Examinations

Panic! Will this be me?

To ensure that you will not be like the boy in the cartoon, you should prepare now for the examination.
  1. Decide what time you will begin work each evening and *keep to it* (the earlier, the better).
  2. How long will you work without a break?
  3. List all your subjects and enter them on your timetable.
  4. Will you allocate the same amount of time to each subject? Or will you give more time to weak subjects?

5. Avoid spending long periods on the same subject.
   It is better to vary the subjects you revise.
6. It is worth jotting down brief notes as you revise.

Draw up a revision timetable using this format.

	Starting time	Subjects to be revised
Sun		
Mon		
Tues		

Write notes in answer to the following:

1. Do you start work at the same time each evening? What are the advantages of doing so?
2. Do you think that your sitting position affects your alertness?

Danger! man at work!

3. Does the temperature of the room affect your ability to concentrate?
4. Is your table/desk at a comfortable height, and well positioned in regard to lighting?
5. List the distractions that occur when you do your homework.
6. How can you save time by having books, notes and other equipment immediately available?
7. Decide on three ways which will improve your study methods.

SIXTH-FORM INDUCTION COURSE

The following materials are part of a sixth-form induction course. Obviously, the skills required cannot be learnt during an induction course; but we can make pupils aware of these skills, which will then have to be developed systematically; some could be introduced in such courses as General Studies. Here is an example where the pastoral and curricular sides become inseparable.

Skills

These are the skills pupils will need to develop if they are to cope with the demands of sixth-form work.

1. Using free time constructively: working without supervision.
2. Coping with heavier workloads; requires ability to plan work and set objectives with realistic time limits to ensure systematic coverage.
3. Coping with less clearly defined demands.
4. Setting own standards of excellence.
5. Appraising books and arguments: detecting main parts of concept or argument.
6. Appreciating the difference between inductive and deductive thought.
7. Enhanced study skills.
   (a) Reading: skimming, scanning, intensive, selective.
   (b) Note-taking: linear, block, pattern.
   (c) Use of library: tracking down information quickly.
   (d) Essay writing. (i) Structure.
   　　　　　　　　 (ii) Interpreting not cataloguing facts.
   (e) Checking progress. Progress may not be monitored until examination; without the frequent testing as in 'O' level, pupil may fall behind without realizing it.
   (f) Taking action when in difficulties: isolating with precision source of confusion/error.
   (g) Revision and examination techniques.
8. Coping with anxieties.

Exploring attitudes

Teachers' notes

Pupils may enter the sixth with attitudes that will prove obstacles to their success. We must through discussion make these attitudes explicit, so that pupils are aware of them and their implications for their work, or lack of it.

These attitudes seem to centre around three issues:

(a) *Plenty of time*

1. The lower sixth is a laugh.
2. The upper sixth sit in the lounge, and they have an examination this year. We need not be too bothered.
3. There's plenty of time – two years.
4. The results of 'O' level came out only three weeks ago. There is no way I shall start work at once.

5. What is the sixth-form lounge for anyway – if not to lounge in?

It is often assumed, wrongly, that sixth formers will somehow learn to use study periods effectively.

(b) *Comparisons with 'O' level*

1. I only worked in the last year for 'O' levels and I did quite well.
2. It can't be worse than 'O' levels.
3. Notes are published on these topics: there's no need to make your own.
4. Marks are lower than at 'O' level.

Pupils need help to realize the intellectual requirements and characteristic methods of subjects.

(c) *Lack of close supervision*

1. Teachers don't chase you for work as they used to; they don't demand work from you.
2. Teachers don't know whether you've done the recommended reading anyway.
3. An important part of education is discussion with your friends.

Note-taking exercise

Teachers' notes

Objective: to teach pupils the importance of structuring notes.

The importance of note-taking in advanced studies cannot be overstressed. Pupils often take notes by copying out sections of the original without regard to logical structure or the relative importance of facts. The following exercise is intended to draw their attention to these deficiencies.

METHOD

1. Students to make notes from selected unfamiliar material, but without being given any explanation of the purpose of the exercise.

2. Collect material and notes.
3. After two weeks return notes only.
4. Students to reconstruct main theme of material from notes.
5. Discuss usefulness and weaknesses of their notes.
6. Distribute model notes and original material for comparison.

The following points should be discussed:

1. Notes should be meaningful after lapse of time.
2. Main points should be clearly distinguished from sub-points in format.
3. Need for economical expression.
4. Note-taking not simply a record, but a tool to assist understanding.

Reading skills

Teachers' notes

Aim: to help pupils consider and enlarge their range of reading techniques and apply them to the demands of their subjects.
Method: discussion should focus initially on the various techniques of reading, depending on the nature of the book and the reader's purpose. It would be particularly useful if pupils could apply these techniques by setting them exercises or providing examples based on their textbooks.

Pupils' notes

You may feel taken aback by the vast amount of reading that confronts you, lengthy lists of vast tomes. It will be impossible to read it all. You will need to consider how you read books, how you will select what to read, and how much you will read.

When you learn to read, it is usual to start at the beginning of a story and proceed page by page, sentence by sentence to the end. If you are to read profitably in the sixth, this technique will have to be discarded. 'Start at the beginning' may be bad advice when reading some of your books.

How and what you read will depend on the nature of the book and your purpose.

Novels, textbooks, reference books and set books will demand different techniques.

Your purpose in reading can vary. If it is:

1. A search for information. You should pay close attention to contents indexes, summaries, key sentences.
2. To understand a difficult passage. Concentrate initially on main points before proceeding to greater detail. Note especially key sentences.
3. To follow a writer's argument. Skim through, isolating and simplifying main steps.

Using study periods

Pupils' notes

When you receive your timetable, you will quickly note that unlike your fifth-form timetable you have several free periods. What use will you make of them? Each year some students idle their way through them — will you be one?

Over the year these periods will build up into a substantial amount of time; obviously, using them productively can make a considerable impact on your standard of achievement. If you waste them, you will undoubtedly increase your anxieties and dissatisfaction. Therefore, it is important that you give some thought to how you will use them. But this will not be enough, you must carry out your plan — the sooner, the better. Resisting the temptation to put off work until later will be your biggest problem.

Consider the following:

1. How many free periods do you have per week?
2. How much time will this add up to over a year?
   (Assume there are 35 effective weeks per school year.)
3. How many periods will you use for study?
4. Which ones?
5. Draw out a study timetable. It may be necessary to modify it during the year in response to the changing demands of your subjects. But it will help you to acquire the habit of systematic study.

The following points must be considered:

1. Notes from previous lessons will need to be written up. It is better to do this as soon as possible while the material is fresh in your mind.
2. For some topics further notes will be needed.
3. You will need to prepare beforehand for some lessons, eg tests.
4. On which days will regular assignments be set?
5. Extra time may be needed in laboratories, etc.
6. You will need time for reading in the library.
7. The study period timetable must be related to your homework timetable.

Having worked out your timetable, albeit a provisional one, you come to perhaps the most important question.

How much time will you allow to elapse before you actually start work in your study periods? 3, 5, 10, 15 minutes.

N.B. Intending to work is not enough!

Appraisal

Pupils' notes

A key skill in advanced study is appraisal; that is, estimating the value of an argument, hypothesis or opinion. To develop this skill we must know what to look for. It is by no means a simple matter. Below are some of the questions you must ask when appraising material; you can discuss these points during General Studies periods.

What is the author's purpose?

(a) Telling a tale.
(b) Explaining a topic.
(c) Analysing conflicting points of view.
(d) Attacking or trying to persuade.

If the author is presenting an argument, try to extract the main point at issue, and then the steps in his reasoning. Then ask:

(a) What evidence does he put forward?

(b) Does he separate clearly facts, hypotheses and opinions?
(c) Is the conclusion warranted?

The following is a list of the main weaknesses found in arguments.

1. *Lack of precision*:
   (a) Vague and undefined terms.
   (b) Sweeping statements.
   (c) Oversimplifying complex issues.
2. *Inadequate evidence*:
   (a) Essential facts overlooked.
   (b) Unfair selection of instances.
3. *Irrelevancies*:
   (a) Incidental points attacked; main points ignored.
   (b) Attacking, not the argument, but the arguer's character, past, etc.
   (c) Appealing to sentiment – use of emotive terms.
4. *Unfair arguments*:
   (a) Distorting main argument to embrace more extreme positions.
   (b) Taking the conclusion for granted during the course of the argument.
   (c) Stating the same point in different words.
   (d) Unsuitable comparisons.

In planning materials certain tasks await us: choosing the areas for innovation, selecting content, arranging and writing the materials and considering teaching techniques.

Pupils can assist in the preparation of materials. At the end of the first year, they can help in contributing ideas to an induction course: this has the advantage that the experiences are fresh in their minds. Three first-year pupils who had a strong interest in drama were delighted to have the opportunity to participate. Given an outline of what was required and a cassette recorder they produced original and perceptive materials on the problems encountered during their first year. Similarly, pupils from the art department have produced drawings and cartoons for programmes.

To guide our writing, statements of intent are necessary; they will be needed later for evaluation. Such statements are often couched in global terms; for example, to enhance the self-awareness of pupils. Aims expressed in this way have a satisfying ring, but, unfortunately, it is almost impossible to know if or when we have achieved them. However, if we specify objectives, using practical and precise terms, it becomes possible to judge whether we have achieved them. But this is not without its dangers: our objectives may be so narrow as to eliminate unexpected but valuable results and broader aims; they may also fail to take into account the complexities of the classroom and these can vary from class to class.

To forestall this, it has been advocated that objectives should be written as the programme develops, but this can lead to badly planned programmes. Possibly the best solution is to produce tentative objectives, which can guide the design, but can be modified in the light of on-going appraisal, become increasingly defined or broadened, or changed if found to be inadequate.

During much of the chapter I have equated innovation in pastoral care with the production of materials to meet specific critical points in a pupil's career and promote a positive self-image and a feeling of having control and choice in achievement. But are there no other areas that demand the attention of the innovator? Our model indicates that in all our activities we emit signals of evaluation and devaluation; some emanate from us as individuals, others from the social system or organization of the school. Labelling processes are active, forcing an unwanted identity on a pupil. Our expectations can produce the behaviours we predict. We can respond to problems in mechanical, stereotyped ways. How does the innovator deal with these?

These aspects should form the basis of in-service training, which must be at two levels. The first, familiarization and acquiring the knowledge and techniques to implement the specific programmes. Without this our materials can be easily misunderstood, indiscriminately applied or subtly distorted. The second must deal with the development of more constructive, professional attitudes, which involves self-development. Teachers must examine their interaction with pupils, their expectations and the assumptions they habitually make.

It may be argued that in-service training is the responsibility of the LEA or some other body. But these courses need to be supplemented and implemented within the school. It is not unusual for a teacher to return from such a course fired with enthusiasm, only to face apparent intransigence and indifference. Sometimes he has no opportunity to present his information and experience to the staff. We need to build mechanisms for in-service training into the structure of the school, to serve the needs of school-based innovation, and to help disseminate information and techniques from externally organized courses. Part of the innovator's task is to build up a supportive atmosphere in which open discussion of problems and proposed solutions becomes possible. The innovator cannot overlook staff relationships.

In organizing in-service training for staff at the second level, as discussed above, I have found the following programme of topics useful.

Teachers' in-service training programme

INTRODUCTION

In this programme our aims are to develop further our professional expertise and teaching skills and to increase our awareness of social processes operating within the classroom. An essential element must be an honest and critical appraisal of our interaction with our pupils, since this interaction lies at the heart of the educative process.

The following activities are designed to alert us to important sociological and psychological processes. Their apparent familiarity may obscure the wide implications they have for the quality of our teaching and the social climate of the school.

In answering the questions, would you make your responses as specific and concrete as possible; global statements will be far less useful.

Encouraging desired behaviours

Becker (1969), after studying teachers' classroom interaction, concluded that we give unwitting encouragement to deviant as much as desired behaviours. This may be discouraging; but we have impressive evidence that teachers can be trained to change specific aspects of their behaviour toward pupils, and that apparently small changes can have dramatic effects.

We need to consider which behaviours we strengthen. In doing so, we should bear in mind that actions which are immediately followed by rewards are *repeated and learned*, whereas actions or behaviours which are not followed by rewards are dropped. Rewards may be of many kinds: verbal and non-verbal expressions of approval and praise, smiles, head nods, or physical and verbal demonstrations of acceptance.

We should consider:

1. Which classroom behaviours should be encouraged?
2. Are desired behaviours ignored or unrewarded?
3. Which behaviours do we unwittingly promote in the classroom? How do we actually promote them?
4. What rewards can we offer?
5. Do pupils place the same value on a reward?

SELF-RESPECT

The way pupils regard themselves is crucial for responsible behaviour and achievement. If they have little self-respect, they will find difficulty in interacting with others, may be oversensitive to real or imagined criticism; and may believe that others dislike them. Some build up a facade of compulsive masculinity, and are then constantly afraid of exposure.

One of our tasks must be to build up the pupil's picture of himself as responsible and capable of achievement. This is an essential element in all teaching. Hence we need to consider:

1. In what ways can we build up pupils' self-respect?
2. Do we rely for control on such techniques as: 'bawling out', sarcasm, abuse or putting them in their places?
3. What is our concept of a good pupil? Is it acceptable to them without loss of integrity?

TEACHER EXPECTATIONS

Our expectations of what individual pupils can achieve may lead us to expect little from them. Differentiating between pupils can increase differences in attainment and behaviour. In this way we promote the fulfilment of our own expectations: we expect little and get less. Hence we should consider:

1. How can our expectations actually produce behaviours?

91

2. What assumptions do we make about the ability and character of different sections of the school?
3. Do we regard some groups of pupils as abnormal or inferior? Do we convey this to them by (a) our comments, (b) school organization, (c) choice of subjects, (d) timetables?

PREJUDGING

The perceived environment determines our behaviour. Our preconceptions filter our perceptions, and so will crucially affect our assessment of a situation, what we consider to be important about it and its implications. How far are our perceptions of the school and hence our behaviours dominated by the following prejudgements? How far do they limit our response to situations?

1. It's as simple as that.
2. You have to be down to earth.
3. The thin edge of the wedge.
4. Put them in their places.
5. It's a matter of common sense.
6. Get them, otherwise they'll get you.
7. Quell the first offender.
8. It's either them or me; it's not going to be me.
9. The fear of losing control of the class.
10. Not to punish is soft.
11. If a pupil returns unpunished by the head of year, nothing has been done.
12. If a pupil has little ability or difficult family circumstances, there's not much you can do.
13. The pupil who frequently breaks school rules will become delinquent.

SOCIAL MODELLING (the kind of example we set)

Finally we must consider what impressions of ourselves we give to pupils. They are exposed for long periods to our influence, and readily observe what we say, do and how we express our feelings. They may, on occasion, be puzzled by discrepancies between our conduct and precepts.

1. How do we fail to present ourselves as competent models worthy of imitation?
2. What are the disparities between our words and actions? eg

92

demanding homework on time but being dilatory in marking it; complaining if pupils come to school without equipment, but being disorganized ourselves; complaining about punctuality but being late for lessons.
3. How do we start the day: actively, or giving the impression of waiting for the valued activity to start?
4. What happens after the register has been marked and during form period? Does it convey to the pupils an impression of work avoidance?

Organizing in-service training

How do we organize in-service training programmes? Here we must distinguish two possibilities: training for the whole staff, or for a section involved in a specific programme.

The first problem will be allocating time to in-service training. We have used three strategies:

1. A whole day involving all the staff; the school closed.
2. A whole day's training for a section of the staff, eg those concerned in first-year induction courses. This was done during the course of a normal school day. The staff concerned were released from their teaching commitments by bringing in ancillary teachers. To minimize disruption, classwork was preset.

These strategies require the support of the LEA.

3. Lunch breaks or immediately after school, of staff concerned in particular programmes. This strategy is not as effective as 1 and 2: lunch breaks tend to be hurried and the impact of several short periods is weaker; but it is useful in maintaining the impetus of a programme, for providing support and obtaining feedback.

The second will be the production and distribution of materials. The following schema may prove useful:

1. Discuss with head, senior management and advisory service the possibilities of in-service training, outlining aims, objectives and materials.

93

2. Prepare materials: further discussion with above.
3. Duplicate materials (extra copies needed).
4. Distribute to staff about ten days beforehand to allow time for preliminary discussion – any earlier and material could be put on one side and forgotten.
5. Preliminary meeting with chairpersons of groups.

The third problem will be to ensure adequate coverage of the materials. To achieve this, the following strategies are suggested.

1. Allocate staff to small groups of four or five. Three tends to be too small and leads to the formation of too many groups. More than five, group tends to function as a committee. Aim: informal, frank discussion with maximum participation by all.
2. Composition of groups.
   Groups need to be carefully selected so that: (a) staff from different disciplines, with differing experiences and attitudes, come together; (b) dissident members are separated.
3. Choice of chairperson.
   It will be necessary to designate a chairman for each group; (a) to ensure groups keep to task; (b) share group's observations at the plenary session.

Chairperson must be capable of dealing with disgruntled members and ensuring fruitful discussion.

4. Briefing of chairpersons. It is essential to discuss the materials thoroughly with them beforehand.
5. Allocation of topics to groups. In order to cover the material thoroughly, it will be necessary to allot topics to groups to explore in depth. Their observations are reported to the plenary session. Thus a wide range of topics can be explored.

In implementing programmes, the selection of staff is crucial. It is important to remember that good programmes have been ruined by faulty implementation. In innovating we need teachers who will show enthusiasm and commitment and a readiness to appraise new ideas and techniques. It may be that there will be no opportunity to choose staff, which makes the task of the innovator more difficult. Entrenched attitudes are a major obstacle. In my own experience of innovating in the first year, we had to resist expectations from 'strong' disciplinarians that it was essential to lick pupils into shape. Pastoral work demands skills other than bulldozing.

Another danger is that programmes will be given to ineffectual teachers in the vague hope that somehow they will improve or, at least, do no damage. Underlying these attitudes we can often detect the assumption that our innovations are marginal, not part of the serious business of teaching and not worth the time of the more valued members of staff. In-service training can usefully deal with these assumptions. Innovation requires teachers with enhanced skills and sensitivity, and it would be unrealistic to expect teachers who have not acquired the basic skills of classroom management to implement it successfully. If in their attempts to do so, classes become thoroughly disorganized, this would discredit the whole programme.

How do we select staff for particular programmes of innovation? The following procedure might help.

1. Discuss programme with headmaster, senior management.
2. Inform staff (at staff meeting), request volunteers. Many may volunteer for reasons other than a desire to participate in innovation; eg to escape from difficult classes.
3. Meet volunteers to explain nature of programme more fully, stressing the need for commitment. Some will then withdraw.
4. Meet head and senior management to make selection: crucial factor – the relationship the volunteers have with their classes.
5. Contact volunteers who were not selected, to explain that they can participate in other areas of innovation.

As soon as we ask for volunteers and our proposed innovation becomes known, there will be repercussions throughout the school. The reaction is akin to throwing a pebble into a rock pool: ripples reach even the most secluded crannies; crabs, shrimps and small fry scurry to their hideaways; and limpets cling with grim determination to their niches. This clinging to entrenched attitudes and behaviours, perhaps the commonest reaction, is revealed in comments like these.

When are we going to do all this?
What's wrong with the present system?
We need time to settle after all these changes.
What's the point of it?

It won't make any difference.
The pupils are getting on all right without it.
Our job is to teach.
We managed pretty well before.
Leave well alone.

Innovation can be seen as a threat; often as something that will undermine school discipline. Difficulties are magnified into insurmountable obstacles. Paradoxically, greater resistance seems to come from staff with pastoral responsibilities: a reflection on the holding-system into which pastoral care can develop. Yet these are the staff who should be most interested in the kind of innovation we wish to produce.

However, we must remember that in innovating we are initially making extra demands on staff, who already have considerable teaching commitments and other duties. We are involving them in interacting with pupils in possibly unaccustomed ways. This raises anxieties about loss of control which is the innovator's biggest bogey. Possibly as a hangover from our first experiences of classroom management, when we might have experienced considerable disorder, we seem unable to rid ourselves of the fear of losing control of our pupils. This anxiety will undoubtedly be expressed during in-service training.

5

Study Skills as an Element in the Output of the Secondary School

Sue Russell
(School Counsellor, Gwent)

The idea of secondary-school *outcome* is easier to appreciate when we look at Hamblin's (1974) Basic Process Model, which gives it perspective. Socialization is seen as the process by which an individual acquires standards, values and behaviours of a certain kind. Hamblin explains this socialization by saying that the model should look at: (a) the process by which a pupil affiliates or disassociates himself from the school; (b) the objectives of the school and the actual outcomes; (c) the outcomes which should be analysed with the following in mind: (i) intended versus unintended; (ii) the costs of these outcomes to pupils and staff; (iii) the strategies which have to be used to shape behaviours in the desired ways; (iv) the detection of critical events which determine whether or not the outcomes occur.

Using Hamblin's analysis of the output of a secondary school, we can detect the processes which impinge upon it, either distorting or facilitating. The most valuable, and probably the most permanent element in the output, is the self-image of the pupil.

Next, we would ask about the level of aspiration of the pupils: this part of the output is salient to the curriculum. From Hamblin's

97

analysis of the output come vital questions. Is the school developing in pupils a desire to work for some standard of excellence? Has the conception been built up that controls are internal? Or do they see themselves as victims of luck or fate? We need to show the pupils that attainment comes from planning, skill and perseverance.

We would find Wall's (1948) idea of adolescence to be relevant here. Adolescence was seen as the period of construction of the philosophical, social, sexual and vocational selves. Hamblin (1975) sees this as important but would extend it by careful examination of the way in which the school, through classroom transactions and rituals, builds up the perception of the self as a learner. A negative perception of the self as a learner can produce predictions and behaviours leading to psychological truancy. Boocock (1972) talks of the nature of 'perceived irrelevance' of the task and finds that pupils who do not see meaningful connections between what they do in schools and what they would like to do or expect to do in their own future, are not likely to perform well academically. Boocock is also critical about the 'reward system' and its unfortunate consequences.

The programme at the point of the critical incident of entry aims at giving pupils a good start in their secondary school career. The major factor in the entry to school is adjustment to teachers. Pupils encounter different teaching styles and different demands about the presentation of work, with, of course, variations in discipline: an induction programme at this critical incident of entry would deal with all these points using different activities. It may be extended to cover homework, how to take notes and present work attractively. Many able pupils from poorer backgrounds have had no experience of homework and are unlikely to get any help at home. The programme presents an ideal opportunity for study skills to be introduced for the first time. Below are two extracts from an induction programme I prepared for a comprehensive school in South Wales. Both are designed to be used as discussion vehicles for the form tutor.

Presenting your work

You have now been in school for two weeks and are beginning to do quite a lot of written work in your exercise books.

Sometimes, when a teacher is marking your work, he will write on it, 'Presentation poor' – so today we are going to look at this word *presentation*.

By presentation we really mean how your written work looks. So *neatness* will be important. But let's look at some other tips:

1. Use a ruler to _____ underline the heading
   _____ underline the date
   _____ underline the side heading
   _____ underline the answer

You could also use a ruler to draw a line between two separate pieces of work.

2. What to write with – fountain pen or biro? Whatever you write with, there are important things to remember.

Do not press too hard with your biro – it will go through to the next few pages.

Your fountain pen may blot – so do not shake it near your book! and – keep some blotting paper in your exercise books.

3. Your work will always look better if you use the same colour ink: this means, always use a blue biro or always use a black biro.

4. Felt pens. If you use felt pens to colour in a map or diagram, it will look much nicer but be careful not to press too hard.

Remember: ask your teacher how to present your work if you are not sure. These are suggestions: talk about them with your friends. Then discuss your ideas with your form tutor.

GETTING ON:

Soon we will be having our half-term holiday. Already you have been here half a term and are looking forward to your first tests.

You probably know that you do not have any examinations as such: instead, in the first year, you will have four tests. They are called Quarterly Tests, but your homework also counts toward your final mark.

Your tests are coming along very soon so let's begin to think about how we should revise our work.

In Maths there is a special tip: check that you know your work by going over new questions from your textbook.

Another special tip for Geography: check you know about the country by drawing the map and then labelling towns, rivers and other important things. This tip can also work in Science – draw your diagram and then label it.

The general tip about revising would be to:

Read carefully
Make notes (on separate paper) *as you go*

Then you can read over these notes again as a way of checking that you know your work.

Always test yourself after you have been revising
Revise at the same time each evening
Revise in a quiet room

Now
Think about these tips and see if you could suggest any other tips to your form tutor.

WHAT ARE STUDY SKILLS?

There is an obvious link between study skills and underfunctioning, but this is not fully appreciated by many teachers who write on reports: 'Jimmy is capable of better'; 'Jane is not working to the best of her ability'. Do teachers ask themselves why? They could conclude that pupils' study skills are weak; but, in order to do so, they need to differentiate between the report, 'can do better', and 'makes no effort'.

If teachers do fail to link underfunctioning with study skills, then there must be many pupils who are unaware of studying as a skill. Studying means swotting and swotting is a panic activity done twice a year before examinations. 'No one loves a swot' and as Patterson (1962) suggests, pupils may deliberately 'underachieve' in order to gain social acceptance. Girls are particularly vulnerable here, since many of them feel that academic success is somehow unfeminine and will make them less attractive to the opposite sex. To counteract such feelings, any study skills programme would have to stress the organizational element of study skills. Organization will create a regular pattern, freeing pupils to do other things. Clearly, there is more to study skills than is immediately appreciated and the following fifth-year programme demonstrates the amount of detailed explanation given to pupils.

The programme is designed to be used by form tutors with their forms; indeed, there is a very heavy emphasis on teacher involvement. The form tutor is the adult who is continually and consistently making the effort. The programme stresses the importance of the teacher–pupil relationship by caring for the pupil and how he performs but the reverse occurs when the pupil feels he can talk to the teacher when he *himself* feels that his performance is going 'off'.

Stressing a high degree of teacher involvement with the pupils' study skills should not be seen as 'wet-nursing'. The teacher must appreciate that as the pupil moves towards higher education, he is moving toward independent study in the sense of working without immediate surveillance.

STUDY SKILLS IN THE FIFTH YEAR

The focus of study skills in the fifth year is a business-like examination of the conditions of success and failure for 'O' level and CSE. The emphasis is on organization and efficient use of study time but the main task is to show pupils that studying is a skill and skills can be learned. Table 5.1 highlights the areas that have to be stressed in a guidance programme.

Table 5.1   The main causes of ineffective study and of poor results

1. Inability to cope with anxiety.
2. Rigidity of thought and study habits.
3. Inadequate reading skills.
4. Unplanned and sporadic attempts at study.
5. Low rate of productivity, resulting in inability to complete work in the set time.
6. The inability to develop an argument in a reasoned and coherent way.
7. A lack of structure in written work and thinking, including a logical structure.
8. Failure to use the teacher's comments.
9. Poor note-taking.
10. Inadequate retrieval plans.
11. Inadequate strategies for tackling examination papers.
12. No methodical plans for revision.

This particular guidance programme stresses a high degree of teacher involvement and so the teachers taking part in such a programme will need to have a working knowledge of the above-mentioned causes. This working knowledge could come from a briefing by the school counsellor or the head of fifth year but basically the notes for any briefing would include the following details. Anxiety is a danger signal and the form tutor must be able to help the pupil locate the *real* source of threat and then deal with it in a realistic way. We need to appreciate that anxiety is not necessarily a bad thing but how we react to any anxiety will be important. Anxiety can produce amazing quantities of energy but can also produce feelings of inadequacy and helpfulness. The form tutor can reassure pupils that they are not alone in experiencing anxiety but then detect in each pupil their reaction to anxiety-provoking situations. The programme will aim to give pupils effective study skills as a coping strategy for anxiety and also show that there are different ways of studying. The emphasis is on efficient use of study time: time spent studying is not equated with success in examinations. Some pupils will need to be shown that often the more time you spend studying can mean the less you are learning.

The timetable may well appear to be vague but it is not designed to be done at whistle-stop speed; indeed each form tutor should proceed at the best speed for the pupils in his form. The programme should begin within two weeks of the start of the autumn term: the timing of the programme will depend on the amount of time allocated by the school for pastoral or guidance periods for each form. Each unit can be discussed and used by the

Table 5.2 Programme timetable

Unit	Topic
1.	What do I think of studying?
2.	Organizing your studying.
3.	Effective revision.
4.	Reading and note-taking.
5.	Note-taking and writing answers.
6.	Weekly diary.
7.	Examination techniques.

pupils in a thirty-minute session, and it is fair to attempt a unit each week. It should be noted that after the first units of general explanation there is a sharpening of focus on the elements of study skills: reading, note-taking and writing answers.

Once the general units have been covered, the form tutor may slow the pace down to cover the more detailed units of study skills. Alternatively the form tutor could decide to go through the complete programme and return to consolidate the units on reading and note-taking. The form tutor is better equipped to decide the pace of the programme as he is the person who knows the pupils best.

STUDY SKILLS PROGRAMME

What do I think of studying?

The following diagrams highlight the factors which determine your success or failure in a course of study. Attitudes are evaluations concerned with like or dislike of the object of the attitude – here the focus of attitudes is on study – and with the tendency to approach or avoid it.

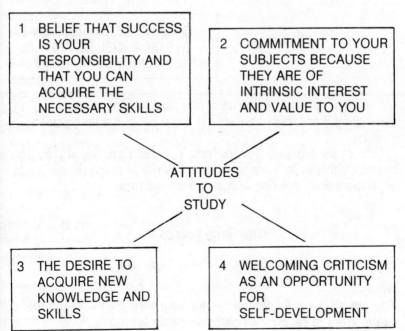

A little thought will suggest that these attitudes point to *your being in charge.*

Things are not happening to you
Come on!
Take responsibility for yourself

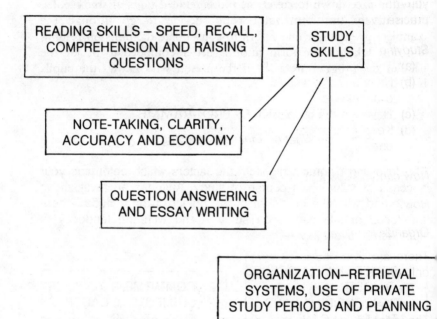

The four areas given here are crucial for success – by developing these skills you will get more out of the time you invest in study.

Lots of people say, 'I work hard, but don't get anywhere'. The sensible thing is to learn to study efficiently – then you can enjoy your spare time, relaxing with a clear conscience.

Organizing your study

THE BASICS: WHY, WHEN AND HOW?

Why?
You are studying for yourself – for your own pleasure and future career – not to satisfy your parents or your teachers.

104

You can make an impact on a malleable world if you have zest, determination and a belief in yourself.

When?
Most of your studying will be done at home in the evenings but if, you do have an unexpected free period then have something precise to do – *don't just waste it.*

Studying at home
   (a) Try to create a work area in your bedroom.
   (b) Neatness and tidiness will save you many panics before your examination.
   (c) Have a place for paper, rulers and other necessities.
   (d) Keep carefully all notebooks and build up an index for each one.

Now can you see that this sense of order is a basic requirement?

How?

Organization is the key to effective study

There are three basic postures that can be adopted for study – only one is really productive.
   The recumbent style: this is taken lying flat. This way you are more likely to daydream or even sleep, than study.
   The relaxed style: usually done with a graceful sprawl in the armchair. A difficult position to make notes in and usually means Mum yells because you are breaking the springs!
   The competent style: here the student works at a well-organized desk or table. A clear separation of work and leisure means that you can completely relax once you have completed your self-allocated study tasks.

Your basic structure comes from your timetable:

   1. Give yourself frequent breaks: these are essential if you are to maintain efficiency. They should not be too long – about ten minutes is enough.
   2. End each study period by assessing what you have learned. You can test yourself in any way that suits you.
   3. Try to end each period of study with an activity or subject which gives you both pleasure and a sense of success.

Before you finish, check what you are going to study the next day. This will allow you to get started immediately.

Do it!

Don't put things off!

This helps you to do things and not avoid them.

Effective revision

Revision can never start too early – try to revise the work as you proceed through the course.

You will find it becomes part of you.

Have a system for recording and storing your notes.

It is important to space your revision – this means that you allow time between revising different subjects. This allows you to deal with each subject properly. You are able to put your notes from the one subject away and get ready for the next subject.

Things are in order.

You are in control.

Now read through the following sheet – there are many tips for you to use.

Are any more helpful than others for you?

Now think about three situations in your work where you wish to improve: rate them in order of difficulty.

Discuss the easiest situation with a friend – your friend is to try and be helpful and make concrete suggestions about what you could do.

Then it will be your turn to help your friend.

Use this diagram:

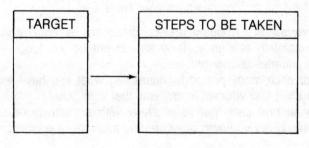

Bring it along next week and report on your progress. If you feel ready, then go on to the next situation. Consult your form tutor if you feel you want to. Remember – go at the speed you want to. You're in charge.

GENERAL POINTS

1. Work to a carefully planned timetable.
   (a) Write down what time you will start revising.
   (b) Do not work beyond 10.30 p.m. – it is unlikely that you will be fresh enough to revise at this hour.
   (c) It can be helpful to work in units of an hour e.g. from 6.00 p.m. – 7.00 p.m. 'French Vocabulary'; 7.00 p.m. – 8 p.m. 'Maths Theorems'.
2. (a) Give yourself a break of a few minutes between each subject.
   (b) About half-way through your revision session give yourself a break of 20 minutes–30 minutes: make it a complete break by leaving your desk, make a cup of coffee, etc.
3. Keep your notes (essays, exercise books) in a clear index system: this would mean keeping all the work for one subject separately.
4. Break down your notes into sections with clear headings: these headings can also be written on summary cards and used in the final revision.
5. Read through a chapter first to get the whole idea of what you are going to revise: then go back and make the section headings, picking out the main points.
6. You should be aware that some subjects have a summary given at the end of the chapter: this would include main points.
7. In certain subjects it is helpful to begin by drawing a diagram and then labelling it with the relevant facts, e.g. Geography – labelling a map of a country with location of industries, etc., Maths – a geometry rider.
8. If you find during your revision that you are not sure about a topic, then ask your subject teacher to explain it.
9. It will be helpful to anticipate exam conditions by answering questions set in them with the same strict time limit.
10. (a) Try to explain your feelings of stress to your parents

107

calmly. They will then be able to help by giving you the peace and quiet necessary for revision.

(b) Even when you are depressed or upset, try to have the will power and determination to carry on revising.

Study skills for reading

SOME HINTS:

If you are feeling worried about your work then plan the use of your time more carefully.

Have definite times for studying at home and stick to these times.

Begin working as soon as you get to your bedroom or the place where you study.

When you are in difficulties with your work, set out to discover why or try to do it in a different way.

READING AND NOTE-TAKING

1. It is often helpful to scan a chapter or passage very quickly to get the main ideas; and then to begin to read carefully.
2. Difficult sections should be noted and gone back to once the general meaning of the passage has been appreciated.
3. Check meanings of unfamiliar words in a dictionary.
4. Look at the chapter and section headings before you begin to read: these will probably become the key words of your notes.
5. As you read make a list of key words or phrases as an aid to your memory.
6. Underline or mark the key points in your notes so that they stand out: it is the key points you will recall first during the exam, and these key points are the ones you will expand to provide the full answer to an examination question.
7. As part of your note-taking, construct diagrams to contain essential information.
8. Look out for words like 'first' or 'second' which indicate the main points.
9. Always arrange your notes to give a brief, logical summary.
10. Always recall main points when you have finished reading: test yourself by jotting down the points you can remember and then check them against your notes.

11. Re-writing the main points in your own words is a valuable test of recall: then check this back against your notes to see how successful your recall has been.
12. To help yourself with the understanding of a passage, make a list of questions about it.

The most important function of good note-taking is that of highlighting the salient points rather than what is peripheral. This means you are writing down what is absolutely necessary to the subject of your notes – this is the salient. The next most important function is to reformulate the ideas in your own words.

You can use coloured pens, capitals or diagrams to make the *important* points stand out.

Be adventurous in your note-taking where possible. Use a diagram to contain essential information.

Perhaps you could try something like this:

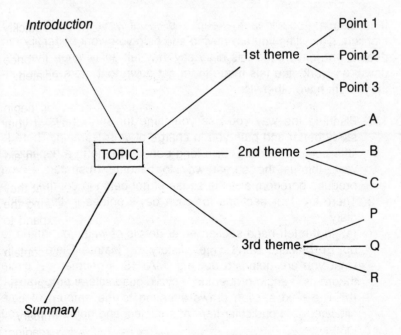

When you have made notes from your reading, try and write them again in your own words.

109

It is a good idea to show your notes to your friend – you can check again whether you have got the key points – the salient.

When you are writing an answer to a question, always try to read the question carefully to make sure you know exactly what you are being asked.

Make quick notes – this can be the framework for your answer.

It is a good idea to help your study by writing an outline answer to a question you have devised.

Always make a plan – you could write down what you were going to put in each paragraph.

Try to make sure all your ideas are relevant to the main theme of the question.

Try to make sure that each paragraph leads on to the next one.

Discuss these thoughts with your friend. Then ask how your friends write their notes. Maybe you have a good tip to pass on.

Weekly diary and organization of study time

It is also a good idea to keep a *diary* of your work. This will highlight difficulties you are having and help you work better. Some people who have used this diary say they felt guilty when they put down 'no work' and this made them get down to it more often than they might have otherwise.

1. Planning the way you use your time for study helps you to study better and puts you in charge of your learning. There is little point in working for a long period of time in a haphazard way: this is the surest way to become frustrated – you produce boredom and the sense of not being in control.
2. There are four sections for each day's entries in the weekly diary.
   (a) In the left-hand section enter details of what you intend to do. *Be precise.* Don't write 'History' or 'Maths'. State *exactly* what you are going to do, e.g. MATHS – geometry – circle theorems – angle properties – cyclic quadrilateral properties.
   (b) The next section draws attention to the amount of time allocated to a particular item of a subject and helps to put you in charge.
   (c) The third section draws your attention to the amount of time you are devoting to testing yourself. Here you are raising

110

questions and *ACTIVELY ORGANIZING* what you have learned. This is fundamental – the nearer you are to an exam the more time you should spend on this. You could be – rewriting your notes in your own words – making up a question and then answering it – constructing a diagram and then labelling it.

(d) In the right-hand column you become your own best critic of your study methods. It is your future and the responsibility belongs to you.

Make comments immediately. They should be practical.

eg 'Must give more time to test myself',

'Wasted time – must read question more carefully.'

3. As an active learner you must decide how long you study and what time of the day you study best.

Each one of us is different and so you have to make these decisions yourself. You should not, however, study for long periods without short breaks.

The length of each period is a matter for you.

Examination techniques

MAKING THE MOST OF YOURSELF

1. Cheer up! You know more than you think you do.
2. Get these examinations into perspective. They are the culmination of something much more important – five years of study.
3. Make sure the night before that you have all the items of equipment you'll need next day.
4. Avoid an overdose of last minute revision – reading through summary cards would be helpful.
5. On the night before the exam try to have a couple of hours complete relaxation.
6. Go to bed at your usual time and try to get a good night's sleep.
7. When the paper is put in front of you – RELAX! You've waited a long time for this. So enjoy it!
8. Read the paper through very carefully – note any compulsory questions. Read through the paper again carefully – there is nothing worse than answering a question you *think* the examiner has set rather than the one he *has* set.

111

9. Try to plan your answers carefully.
10. Keep an eye on the time and divide up the paper equally. Don't undervalue the last question but realize that this question is to be answered last because you felt you knew more about the others.
11. After the exam – forget it. No post mortems.

The writer feels that the next step in such a programme would be to detail study skills which are relevant to particular subjects. Subject teachers could pass on new study skills for the benefit of all pupils.

As mentioned earlier, the programme takes the form of discussion sessions with the form tutor taking the lead. The form tutor becomes involved and cares about the progress made by the pupils in acquiring the study skills. The form tutor is the person who checks on the use of the weekly diary and maybe, even 'nags' if it is not being used properly.

Examination anxieties and a lack of study skills reduce the rewards that pupils get for their hard work and a programme at this point can reinforce the pupil's self-picture positively. The aim of the programme is for the pupil to feel 'in charge': these feelings come from the organizational element and the sense of order it produces. When things go wrong pupils use the form tutor as a consultant who helps them develop a style of study that is productive.

6

Staff Development and the Problems of Teachers

Ann Silcox
(Head of Lower School, Tavistock)

THE PROBLEMS

Communication

Hamblin (1978) states that poor communication impinges on teachers in a school more strongly than it does on pupils. As King (1973) indicates, formal and standardized communication is the chief method used by many schools. Certainly the practice in many secondary schools of relying on daily or weekly written sheets to convey its messages can serve to antagonize the staff. It can lead to misinterpretation particularly if it is the main method used.

Written sheets do, however, provide a quick and relatively efficient way of reaching all staff. Factual messages may be conveyed accurately. They may contain two kinds of information – for the whole school and for staff only. Some schools achieve this by dividing one sheet in two, the two parts separated by a dotted line. Others produce two different sheets, either with different headings or on different coloured paper to avoid confusion.

Traditionally, information was communicated by means of staff meetings. In many schools staff meetings serve two main functions: to impart factual information and to provide a means of staff participation in planning and solving problems. For both functions to be served adequately, different kinds of meetings are essential, and the number of staff present seems to be crucial.

One school calls a staff meeting every Monday morning. The weekly sheet is discussed by the headmaster and any additional items mentioned. As there are more than 100 staff members, and time is very limited, no discussion is possible. Rarely are all full-time members of staff present, and the purpose of informing every teacher thus fails. Because of the very nature of the meeting some teachers feel they are receiving weekly orders. It seems to serve to increase the feeling of 'us and them', and some of the co-operation which previously existed is broken down. Disgruntled staff may stop attending.

Schools often have excellent systems of ensuring that all staff are able to take part in the decision-making process. These usually follow the same basic pattern. In one school heads of department meet regularly once a fortnight. The agenda always includes the item 'matters for discussion at the next meeting'. Heads of department are then expected to hold a meeting of all their teachers, during that fortnight, to discuss these matters with them. At the next heads of department meeting these teachers are then asked to describe the feelings expressed by their staff. Discussion and negotiation then follow. All teachers should thus be able to express their views, ideas and plans and feel that these are considered in the departmental meetings. The numbers of staff present are small enough to ensure that all teachers can take part in the discussion.

Too often these systems – so good on paper – fail to work in practice. Teachers still feel they have no way of expressing their views and the system designed to break down barriers to co-operation serves to create them. Teachers feel that decisions affecting them are made without true consultation.

The reasons for this breakdown are sometimes easy to detect. Heads of department may fail for some reason to hold their own departmental meeting. The views they subsequently express are thus their own and not those of their department. When discussion has taken place, staff may still feel that a personal opinion has been voiced by their head of department rather than the collective one. In a bigger department there may be many different opinions and staff may see it as impossible to express all these with the same conviction. Perhaps the most important factor, however, is feedback to the staff. If the heads of department explain why decisions are made, and why particular ideas were accepted, then teachers are likely to feel more involved and committed to their implementation. Often, however, the feedback becomes a simple

114

communication of the decision made – the rationale behind it ignored.

Much of the information which needs to be communicated in a school is about individual pupils. Form tutors, in particular, are often aware of the circumstances of the children in their care which the other staff should know. Some teachers, instead of communicating this to their colleagues, see it as a form of power, and withhold the information which would help their pupils. They have knowledge which their colleagues do not have. Sometimes the pastoral team too keep much vital information secret. Teachers therefore need to seek advice when pupils become disturbed, or suddenly behave very strangely, and come to the pastoral head. This increases the pastoral head's sense of importance and power, but can hardly do the pupils good. House or year heads sometimes see dangers inherent in passing information on to other staff, and consequently feel that they must be in charge of personal information. A more constructive attitude is that teachers should be trained to use this information in a professional way. Seeing the teachers concerned, individually, and talking about it, gives the opportunity to discuss these dangers: e.g. the consequences of labelling children as a result of one incident.

Attitudes

Hargreaves (1972) sees attitudes as an integral part of relationships and a central concern in education. Teachers are part of the membership group of the staffroom. Within this membership group, however, many smaller groups exist.

These groups may be seen working within a staffroom particularly when a decision affecting the whole staff is being made. If, for example, a major change, like altering the internal examination system, is being considered, individual teachers who feel strongly about this begin to gather support. They seek agreement from members of their reference group and use this as a basis of comparison with the other groups.

Each group usually has an opinion leader, who may be difficult or easy to detect. Hamblin (1978) describes how, working with the opinion leaders first, in difficult classes, he used them as targets for positive help. Similarly, within the staffroom, if the opinion leaders are consulted and worked with, then decisions are more likely to receive general support and be more successful.

Katz (1967) suggests that attitudes are favourable towards particular objects which satisfy the individual's particular needs and unfavourable towards objects which thwart or punish him. Some teachers' attitudes are ego-defensive, protecting them from seeing their own unpleasant qualities.

Sense of isolation

Many large schools today contain scattered buildings, sometimes on the same campus and sometimes on sites physically far apart. Often several staffrooms are provided throughout the school, as it may be impossible to get to a central staffroom in time for breaktimes, etc. This fragmentation can bring about a very real sense of isolation, particularly in young teachers. Schools have tried various ways of overcoming this problem: for example, centralizing the communication centre, placing pigeon-holes in one room so that they are obliged to go there at least once a day; placing all members of a department together in one area of the school – block or floor – so that young staff are near their head of department. This becomes impossible, however, when the main consideration is, for example, to keep the lower two years of a school in one area. The head of department may then be based a long way from his youngest teacher. The year head then has to provide the support needed.

Sometimes staff who have been in a school for some years gradually isolate themselves, perhaps for personal reasons or because they no longer feel able to cope with a change of emphasis brought about by a new head. Their commitment to the school and old colleagues disappears. As time passes it becomes increasingly difficult for them to overcome their self-inflicted isolation, much as they may wish to.

A science teacher with several years experience gradually stopped coming to the staffroom after breaking off an engagement. Her colleagues did not realize this for a few weeks; and when their attempts to draw her into their lunchtime activities were rejected, the group gave up. She stopped helping with out-of-school activities, and mixing out of school with her colleagues.

Her friends became very concerned but got nowhere on their

own. Eventually, with the year head, several teachers made a planned attempt to draw her back into the life of the group and school, asking her advice and inviting her to various functions in an attempt to bolster her self-confidence. Despite initial rejection she gradually responded and became a member of the group again, although not as close as before.

Ideological viewpoints

Cosin (1972) provides a fourfold classification of educational ideologies. Elitism advocates the maintenance of the established standards of cultural excellence through the traditional methods of selection. University and grammar school teachers may be seen to support this ideology. The technocratic-rationalizing ideology is concerned with the vocational relevance of education and paper qualifications. Romanticism is concerned with the development of all of an individual's innate abilities – children should have the right to give free rein to all their innate potentialities. Egalitarianism gives central importance to the principle that all people have the right to be educated and raises questions about the distribution of power.

Not all these ideologies are compatible, although all may be represented in one staffroom. Most individuals, while adhering to one rather than another, usually express them moderately, and see defects in them all. Teachers who prescribe to one rigidly and express its viewpoint strongly can cause problems.

In the comprehensive school, for example, exponents of the elitist ideology may work against the principle of equality of care and concern for each individual pupil, being striven for by the pastoral team. One teacher saw his role as getting as many pupils through their external examinations as possible. When faced with a mixed-ability group in the first year, he taught the brighter children only.

As a form tutor, he saw his job as that of marking the register but not forming a relationship with his pupils. His previous experience in a streamed grammar school provided him with only limited skills for working with the comprehensive range of ability. He was, however, a keen rugby coach and was encouraged to use his expertise with the first-year team. While most of his teaching time was timetabled with examination classes, departmental meetings took the form of discussing various techniques, using audiovisual equipment with younger classes. Conflict did occur in pastoral meetings but gradually he began to extend his role, as the head of year worked with him on materials for his tutor periods.

The extreme romantic can also cause problems where the senior staff are working towards a consensus of realistic disciplinary measures in their school. Often their beliefs are deeply felt and debate has little or no effect. They continue to ignore measures agreed upon by their colleagues.

Inexperience

Probationary teachers coming into a school at the beginning of the year face a very real problem in assimilating a mass of information and procedures in a short space of time: the practical details of marking a register; understanding the timetable well enough to pass details on to their tutor group; finding their way around a large school; and remembering the faces and names of key members of staff – for example, their head of department, head of year, etc. Many schools partly overcome this by arranging a staff meeting on the day before term starts, but often the inexperienced teacher is confronted with a mass of faces and instructions which serve further to confuse the situation. Perhaps a meeting a few days before, with just the key members of staff, would be more effective in helping with the details of organization – the day-before-school meeting could then serve as a social occasion to welcome the newcomers.

These new teachers, although inexperienced, often have enthusiasm and creativity. Unfortunately, their inexperience is a source of frustration when they are learning to differentiate between gaining control and their wish to achieve a good and honest relationship with their pupils. They do not always recognize how to avoid trouble.

Hamblin (1978) sees a link between teaching methods and the underlying attitudes which lead to disaffiliation and sometimes disruptive behaviour in the classroom. Inexperienced teachers therefore need to be provided with skills to produce a stimulating environment for their pupils, one that will extend their experience and not limit it. As Bernstein's (1971) work shows, pupils with a poor verbal culture need the experience of using language to extend

118

their understanding. Passive teaching methods inhibit this and the pupils see the classroom environment as irrelevant.

Probationary teachers

Young, inexperienced probationary teachers often seem to experience feelings of isolation and desperation. They need help in feeling that they can be both in charge of their situation and change things. As it is, they often deal with problems in a way that disrupts their relationship with all pupils: for example, punishing the whole class for one pupil's misbehaviour. Teachers and pupils alike feel themselves being dragged into a spiral of interaction in which neither feels happy but neither can change.

Heads of department in their attempts to help are often hindered by the distance between their room and the classroom of the young teacher. Moving certain pupils to the classroom of a more experienced colleague often makes the situation worse, as this may be just what the students are hoping for. As Hamblin (1978) points out, some punishments may carry the more valuable rewards of toughness and an identity as someone prepared to challenge the system. They get the reward of approval of their peers. The move may, however, bring with it a feeling of resentment when the pupil is returned to his normal venue. It rarely serves to improve the confidence and classroom skills of the teacher.

Many schools provide sessions for probationary teachers during out-of-school hours. They are asking for practical and constructive ways of coping with their situation. Their enthusiasm can easily wane, not just with the pressure of the everyday tasks of marking, etc., but because of disruption of a carefully prepared lesson. Their reactions, often abortive in settling the minority, need to be analysed and more positive possibilities substituted.

The senior staff in a school can do much to help. A daily walk around the school by the senior staff at different times can be most helpful to the probationary teacher. If they are encouraged to use these senior staff by inviting them into the classroom to show them pupils' work and to praise them realistically, then the relationship between the class and young teacher can be strengthened.

A young music teacher was helped in this way. Her room was a hut in the playground, and she was having difficulty with a group of second-year pupils of limited academic ability. While a few were singing, the rest were making peculiar noises. The headteacher, making his customary tour of the school, heard this and invited himself into the room, greeting the teacher politely. By praising the singing and suggesting a tape recording, he restored order. The teacher used the idea of taping the best efforts and often invited the head in to hear them. As the singing improved, she was encouraged to invite other senior colleagues into her room, and her feeling of isolation decreased and her self-confidence built up. As the headteacher came to their other classes too, the children didn't see this as anything extraordinary. Many teachers used him as an extra resource.

A PLANNED PROGRAMME OF IN-SERVICE TRAINING FOR PROBATIONARY TEACHERS

Many schools do provide a programme for their probationary teachers, but often these do not begin until well into the autumn term and are haphazard in their approach. The programme needs to use the many resources of the school; for example, heads of department, year and house. They may well take into account the views and experiences of teachers who have just completed their probationary year. The programme needs, therefore, to be planned in the summer term by the senior staff but only after discussion with these people. Much of the material – registers, school map, timetable – is sent by one school in the middle of the summer holidays. The young teacher has time then to assimilate much of the information required before the term begins.

Many schools use about eight hourly sessions after school for their training programme, spread throughout the year. Greater success was achieved in one school when probationary teachers were released from assemblies to attend weekly half-hour periods. These were supplemented by after-school sessions later in the year, when longer periods were desirable: e.g. visits from outside agencies in an 'any questions'-type discussion. Releasing staff during the school day does require planning and co-operation. It does, however, indicate the importance attached to the programme by the senior staff (see Table 6.1).

During the first few days, the programme aims to reduce anxiety and build up the self-confidence of the probationary teachers. It provides them with the information and practical help necessary to

Table 6.1

Objectives of the programme of in-service training

---

1. To alleviate the teachers' feeling of inadequacy and failure by providing the necessary skills and supports to build on their creative abilities.
2. To establish good communication with the pastoral care system and co-operation in the solving of problems.
3. To create a caring environment for the teachers who are then able to offer positive support to their pupils.

---

fulfil the routine tasks of the first day. By anticipating the skills needed throughout the year, and difficulties which need to be faced, the teacher is more likely to achieve success.

Regular sessions with the head of year or house enable both the year or house head and the probationary teacher to exchange views, feelings and ideas – building up good communication between them. Discussion of problems, at this level, ensures greater co-operation; particularly if the house or year head anticipates the areas in which the young teacher is likely to meet failure and gives practical help.

URGENT PRACTICAL DETAILS

1. Register keeping.
2. Programme for the first day of term.
3. Timetable–interpretation.
4. How to give timetable to tutor group.
5. General classroom management.

DUTIES

1. What is expected of the children, of the staff.
2. Supervisory responsibilities.
3. How to avoid trouble.
4. Supports available.

Table 6.2   Programme for probationary teachers

Timing			
1. Middle of summer holidays	1. Covering letter 2. Programme of the 1st day 3. Register marking 4. Timetable 5. Programme of school year 6. Map of school		
2. Day before school starts	Personal introductions to head of year or house head of departments		
3. 1st day	Serving teacher in pastoral team detailed to help with 1. Register 2. Programme for the day 3. Timetable 4. General classroom management		
	General topic	*Areas to cover*	*Materials/notes*
4. 1st and 2nd week	Duties	What is expected? How to avoid trouble Where to go for help	What to do if?
5. 3rd week	Marking	Ways of organizing mark books Phasing of marking Purpose of marking	How to avoid having a lot of marking to do all at once.
6. 4th and 5th weeks	Lesson preparation	1. Keeping records of lessons 2. Relevant teaching methods 3. Resources available	Heads of department involved
7. 6th week	Informal parents' evening	1. Organization 2. Interviewing techniques	
8.	Pastoral periods with tutor groups Informal parents' evening	1. Interviewing techniques 2. Personal development feedback	Games, simulations, role-play

9. 1st–3rd week of spring term	Records	1. Personal records 2. Purpose 3. What records can reveal – nature of disorientation 4. Confidential files: danger of self-fulfilling prophecies	
10. 4th–6th weeks	Disruption in the classroom	1. Positive ways of coping 2. Skills 3. Supports available and constructive use of them 4. Analysis of what is going on	Heads of department involved
11. 1st–last week	Formal parents' evening	Exploration of feelings Interviewing techniques Supports available How to deal with negative feelings	1. Timing dependent on schools programme – i.e. when meetings are held 2. Simulations
12. 1st–3rd weeks	Reports	1. Purpose 2. Format 3. How to write positively and constructively 4. Keeping of records	1. Report slips + forms 2. Report sheet
13. After school 4th week		1. EWO 2. Educational psychologist 3. Health visitor 4. Social worker	'Any questions' discussion
14. 6th week	Planning session for next year	1. Topics covered – relevant – any additions, etc. 2. Timing 3. Development of programme	

Materials which might be included in the programme

Hints

1. Make absent O as large as possible within square so that it is easily visible (see Fig. 6.3).
2. Mark in a pencilled √ inside last absent O when absent note is received so that these are easily checked – lack of notes may be due to truancy or an emergency at home.
3. Make a list of unexplained absences at the end of the week to discuss with senior pastoral staff for checking.
4. Glance through register at the end or beginning of week for absence patterns: e.g. every morning or afternoon session on a particular day – a subject may be worrying an individual pupil.
5. Many odd day absences are often more worrying than a longer period of absence which may be due to an illness.
6. Note lateness by the use of an L. If a pupil is only a little late for a pastoral period use a pencil. A pattern of this kind of lateness may indicate problems with peer-relationships within the tutor group.
7. A pattern of persistent lateness also needs checking – the pupil may be having trouble coming to school: e.g. bullying, which needs investigating.
8. Always keep details in the register up-to-date and the dates for the weeks filled in. This will save time and confusion when filling in forms for the educational welfare officer, etc.
9. Keep all absence notes filed and dated.
10. Talk to head of year about anything which makes you

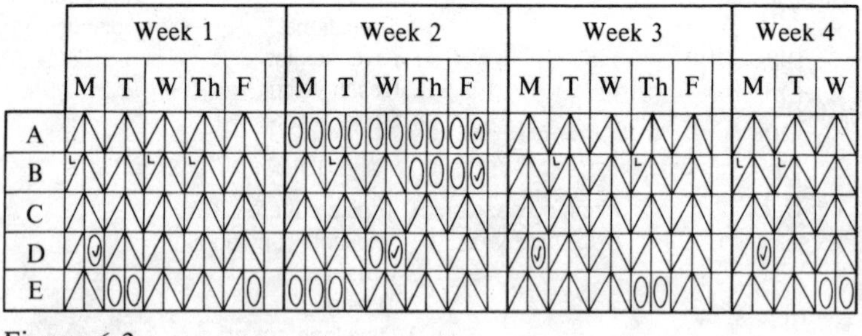

Figure 6.3

uneasy or concerned. They are there to help you and can call on the educational welfare officer if necessary.

Pupil A: Attendance good apart from Week 2 when he had 'flu which was explained by a note.

Pupil B: attendance good apart from two days at the end of Week 2 when he had a cold which was explained by a note. He is very often late in the mornings, which needs to be investigated. If talking to the pupils reveals no cause and the pattern persists, talk to the year head about it – it may be a long-term problem, bullying on the way to school, unhappy relationships within the tutor groups or a more deep-seated problem.

Pupil C: attendance excellent.

Pupil D: an obvious pattern of absence on Monday afternoons which needs investigating. Absence notes are being received regularly so it may be due to circumstances at home. The reason may be a particular lesson which is causing distress. Contact with home may be needed. Talk to the pupil and the year head.

Pupil E: attendance poor – many odd days absence, with no explanatory notes. There may be a real emergency at home: e.g. mother dying of cancer which may be the reason for no notes, or the pupil may be truanting. Talk to the pupil about this, showing him the pattern of attendance which is causing concern. See year and/or the educational welfare officer who may be able to help if this is needed.

TIMETABLE

1. In this school the timetable is based on a four-period day.
2. The cycle is ten days which is divided into two weeks: Week 1 and Week 2.
3. The week number is published every day on the newsheet placed in each staff pigeon-hole.
4. On the period for each day the following information is included: room number; subject; staff initials.
5. See staff names and initials and subject abbreviations on fig 6.4.

DUTIES

'*What to do if*': this material provides a useful starting point for

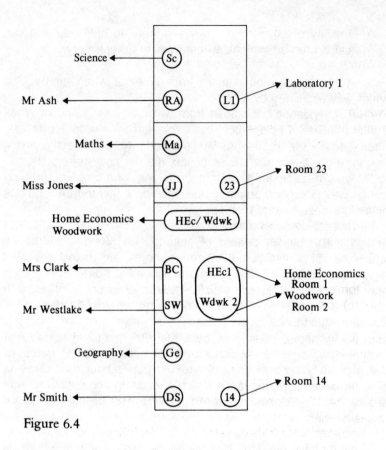

Figure 6.4

discussion in small groups with a more experienced member of staff acting as the group leader.

Situation A: you are on lunch-time patrol duty and several small second-year boys are running around the school. They take no notice of you when you call after them and disappear, only to return after a few minutes.

What would you do?

What is the likely result of your action?

Where would you find help?

Situation B: it is morning break and you are on duty. While you go to the staffroom for a cup of tea a third-year girl comes to you and takes you towards the girls' cloakroom where her friend is crying and bleeding from a large cut in her arm.

What would you do?

What is the likely result of your action?

Where would you find help?

Other situations which may be explored in the same way could include a pupil missing his bus after school, extreme rudeness from a pupil caught smoking, a bullying incident, a broken window.

REPORTS

Hints

1. Keeping well-documented records of pupils' progress and attainment will help when writing reports.
2. Write out record in mark or record book first.

   This: (a) helps to prevent mistakes when writing on actual form;

   (b) provides the basis of your own records on individual pupils;

   (c) helps at parents' evenings as research (Watts, 1979) has indicated parents compare reports with previous records.
4. Try to be positive when describing a pupils' work throughout the year.
5. It may help to compose thirty or so relevant comments before you start as a basis for writing reports which can be easily adapted for individual pupils: e.g. has worked successfully in overcoming his difficulties with vocabulary – well done! Or: Is capable of logical thought – good. He now needs to try to improve the presentation of his work.
6. Try to explain the organization of the class: set 2 means less to parents than middle set.
7. The form tutor comment is important.

   (a) Summarize the report as a whole trying to pick out the good points: e.g. good subjects, effort grades, etc.

   (b) Most parents would like a comment on their child's personal qualities (Watts, 1979): e.g. helpful. *Caution*: They should, however, concern the actual behaviour rather than personal interpretation of it and contain practical suggestions for improvement (Hamblin, 1978).

   (c) Include other apects of school life: e.g. involvement with out-of-school activities.

127

8. See attached copies of the reports used in this school.
   The report form is used for first and second years.
   The slips are used for all other years.
   It is the tutor's responsibility to head report forms with pupils
   names, etc. before they are passed on to subject staff for
   completion.
9. Your year head and head of department will help with
   problems of grading, composing appropriate comments, etc.
   Do talk to them about these aspects.

The programme needs careful adaptations to each individual
school. It develops as the probationary teachers suggest alterations
and additions in the last session, for inclusion in the next year's
programme. Timing is difficult as each school has its own pattern
of parents' evenings, reports, etc. – and obviously the sessions for
these must come before the event.

Teachers working through such a programme have indicated the
need for more time for individual topics, for example disruption in
the classroom and how to cope. They feel that this is needed earlier
in the year and the session needs to be followed up later by further
discussion and skills. A session in classroom management early on
would seem to be a useful addition.

A critical time for such a programme seems to be towards the
middle of the summer term. So many other activities occur at this
time and in particular examination invigilation. This makes it very
difficult to keep the programme running successfully yet the last
sessions devoted to forward planning seem to be extremely
valuable, and evaluating the reactions of the participating teachers is
essential.

TEACHERS WITH UNSOLVED PROBATIONARY
PROBLEMS

Some teachers have a few years of teaching experience, but
seem to have never fully solved their probationary problems. Often
they may be seen to be coping with difficulties, but cannot see their
own contribution to their problems. They thus tend to look for
scapegoats and cast the blame on others. They may not use the
supports available and a pastoral team may either fail to recognize
their need or choose to ignore the signs. Their negative attitudes

128

towards the methods and ideals of the school harden and they join groups in staffroom which strongly support their attitudes. This is where they find the social and emotional rewards they fail to get elsewhere.

These teachers obviously need to obtain some success and rarely hold entirely negative feelings. To involve them actively with probationary teachers is certainly not without its dangers. Their bitterness and the oversimplification of their difficulties can serve to increase the feeling of inadequacy in younger colleagues. Obviously a pastoral team alerted to their difficulties also requires tact and understanding. Certainly when these teachers ask for help – often when the situation has reached crisis point – it should be made available immediately and positively. Again analysis of the specific incident as described by Hamblin (1978), should prove useful.

1. Assessment of the relevant characteristics of those involved.
2. Evaluation of the participant's beliefs about the nature of the situation.
3. Consideration of the relationships between the participants prior to the incident.
4. The issue around which the incident seemed to centre.
5. The audience.
6. Comparison of the intended and actual outcomes.

The implications of the findings should enable the teacher to become more aware of the process involved.

This analysis of a particular crisis should be followed up by analysis of other incidents. The head of department may need to be involved, bearing in mind that teaching methods may also serve to cause disruption in the classroom.

An English teacher of three years' experience seemed to have little difficulty in dealing with her classes. In discussions in the staffroom she seemed confident. However, during a lesson with a third-year class, she came to the senior mistress' room in tears, complaining about the behaviour of a small group of boys, and saying that she could stand no more. A senior teacher took charge of the class, while the young teacher explained how the problem had really begun in the first year and had continued ever since. She was unable to control other groups as well. She seemed to cope with older and brighter classes and enjoyed taking these.

The head of department revealed that he had been concerned by her lack of preparation for many classes – she would indicate that she didn't know what she was going to do just before the lesson started. Books were often not marked and she was late in starting lessons. The head of department pointed out these things to her, and helped her prepare lessons: suggesting new material and explaining how to phase work in the hour-long periods. She was encouraged to include the head of department in praising her pupils' efforts: taking their books to show him, etc. Later she helped plan the induction courses for probationary teachers and run discussion groups.

Gradually her self-confidence grew. The techniques that she had acquired through the head of department made her more successful in the classroom. She no longer needed to be late for classes. As she began to enjoy teaching younger pupils, she invested more energy and time in out-of-school activities: for example, producing a play. The head of department, as a result of this experience, devoted more time in departmental meetings to discussing teaching methods and techniques, and so helped other teachers.

RIGID TEACHERS

These are teachers anxious about their status and dominated by threat. Their rigidity makes it difficult to work with them.

One teacher, who saw everything in his classroom as a battle against wrongdoing, often drew a black picture of his pupils at case conferences. He would reject ideas of rewarding children, seeing this as 'giving in' to them. When he grudgingly agreed to try praise as part of a planned programme his own preconceived idea of failure undermined the exercise. The little success he did achieve he did not recognize as such, either ignoring it or interpreting it as failure. Working with these teachers is difficult and frustrating, and senior staff can only keep trying patiently.

TEACHERS WITH UNFULFILLED ASPIRATIONS

Those teachers who have been at school for some time and see themselves passed over in the promotion stakes cause the pastoral team much worry. They may be in a position of some responsibility but are embittered by the fact that younger colleagues or less experienced people are in authority over them. Sometimes they react by becoming detached and their commitment to the school is restricted. Often they are vocal in expressing their negative feelings to the school and the work of the pastoral team. They obtain their emotional and social rewards by gathering around them a small number of staff who fan these negative feelings. Their resentment spills out in their dealings with the pupils in their care and their relationships with many of the staff. A particular incident can spark off deep resentment. They often gain their satisfactions by halting the pastoral team's programme or by putting it into practice in such a way as to ensure its failure.

These teachers are rarely without their strengths. Hamblin (1978) sees pastoral care beginning with an assessment of an individual's strengths and building on these. Teachers may, for example, be able to relate particularly well to pupils who cause disruption. Members of a pastoral team who plan a way in which they may share their expertise with other members of staff, show these teachers that they are still valued. This may be done by involving them in regular case conferences, asking them to describe in detail how they talk to individual pupils or build up a relationship with them.

MEASURES

Transmitting a caring atmosphere to all teachers

It is important to transmit to all new teachers the caring atmosphere of the school. They all need to feel they are accepted immediately as a member of the team and that they are valuable and important. One school attempts to achieve this by holding an informal social gathering during the early evening, the day before the term begins. They serve sherry and invite the heads of house and heads of department to meet the new staff. If the ethos of the school is experienced as a caring and friendly community then the new teachers feel more secure. They feel accepted and are more likely to transmit this caring concern to the pupils in their care.

This may be followed up later in the term by other social events – skittle evenings or a more formal dinner dance. Variety is important, as expense and the interests of all staff need to be taken into account. An important feature of this must be a clear and personal invitation, as staff often complain that they did not receive

131

an invitation, when in fact they did – but in a written memo which included many day-to-day items of administration.

A sense of belonging and success may be achieved by involving new staff, concerned with first-year pupils, in the organization of a social event for 'new parents'. Held in the early part of the autumn term this provides an opportunity for them to meet parents in an informal atmosphere. If they are given a particular job to do – for example, the organization of the food for the event – they experience success and feel an important part of the team.

The confidence built up by meeting parents for the first time in an informal setting, could with profit be followed up by help with interview techniques in preparation for the more formal parents' evenings. Each probationary teacher should be seen beforehand by the head of department, year or house, to let them know that their feelings of apprehension are normal and help is available. The organization for full parents' evenings in some schools is to put each teacher in a separate room and let parents walk from room to room. This means that each teacher is by himself and this may increase his sense of isolation. In other schools one large room is provided for each department – all the teachers from that department being present. Parents are able to talk to the appropriate teacher. The probationer is thus able to gain support from the physical presence of his head of department, although some individual teachers may prefer to be on their own.

The concern of the school for its staff may be shown at these functions by making sure the new teacher is able to get home and back in time – and that transport later at night is not a problem.

The senior staff should arrange to thank their teachers after these meetings. A personal enquiry about how it went serves not only to increase the teachers' self-esteem and sense of belonging but also provides a valuable opportunity for feedback. A discussion about the individual interviews enables the probationary teacher and head of house or year to gain from an exchange of information and experience.

Provision of a programme of group planning

As Rutter et al. (1979) pointed out, the school values and norms are more effectively transmitted when curriculum and approaches to discipline are agreed and supported by the staff acting as a cohesive whole. Group planning not only facilitates this but also provides opportunities for teachers to support and encourage each other.

Some schools achieve this through regular meetings of each department to plan the outline of the courses they offer. Full staff meetings in very large schools are not always successful, as some teachers feel unable to talk in large gatherings. Most schools, however, are broken up into smaller sections: for example lower/senior schools, years or houses. If staff are encouraged to bring up matters at these smaller meetings, positively, knowing that their views will be listened to, then the decisions made are more likely to be implemented.

SECTION TWO: CURRENT PROBLEMS

7

Integration of Handicapped Pupils into the Comprehensive School

Lynne Chapman
(Student Counsellor, Barking College of Technology)

THE MEANING OF INTEGRATION

If it is unacceptable to segregate children at the age of eleven, according to aptitude or ability, it is surely illogical to select pupils on the basis of their physical ability to get into a school building (Large, 1978). Even so, the egalitarian ideal in itself is not enough to make integration work. Most handicapped children need a degree of positive discrimination in their favour, in proportion to the severity of their disabilities. Therefore, the warnings in the Warnock Report should be heeded: integration will not be a cheap alternative to special schools. Education authorities will need to provide adequate resources, in terms of equipment and personnel, if integration is to have any hope of success.

A notable feature of the Warnock Report is its recommendation that individual categories of handicap be abolished and be replaced by the much wider concept of 'special educational need'. This term includes physical and mental handicap, as well as pupils who are educationally or emotionally handicapped. Such a change, if accepted, would bring within the scope of special educational provision a much larger percentage of the school population than is the case at the present. Indeed, if the findings of the Isle of Wight survey of the incidence of handicap (Rutter, Tizard and Whitmore, 1970) are repeated nationally, it is possible that as many as one in every six children may require special educational provision at some time in his school career. Thus, integration, in any true sense, will include the maladjusted child, the educationally disadvantaged, the mentally-handicapped and the physically-disabled pupil. However, it is proposed to concentrate here specifically upon the integration of mentally and/or physically handicapped pupils, since it is felt that for many schools they present a less familiar challenge.

INTEGRATION AND THE HANDICAPPED PUPIL

It is frequently argued that handicapped children will cope better if allowed to proceed at their own pace in a special school, that they need the equipment that only a special school can provide, and that they are likely to suffer as a result of teasing and bullying at the hands of non-handicapped peers.

Few would dispute that it is vital for all disabled children to receive the very best education that is available, since in later life they will have to compete with the non-handicapped for jobs. They must be able to make the very best of their disabilities. It is suggested that many of them may be more likely to do this within the climate of an ordinary, rather than a special school. First, the disabled child may be stimulated by the presence of normal peers, provided the school has the resources and the good will to allow him adequate access to the curriculum. Next, one must consider the suggestions put forward by Kellmer-Pringle (1970) to account for the lower level of attainment found among many pupils at special schools.

1. A special school is less likely to be situated in the pupil's immediate neighbourhood, involving a long journey to and from school, with resultant fatigue.
2. The school day is shorter, a fact aggravated if frequent absences from school for medical treatment are also necessary.
3. Where there are large numbers of children with different handicaps, some of which are mental or neurological, teachers' expectations may be lowered, so that the most able child is unlikely to be stretched to the full of his ability.

Cope and Anderson (1977) report the comments of pupils transferred from special to ordinary school thus: 'They found the special school "boring" or "too easy" and said that they were enjoying the greater range of subjects available.' The same authors found that pupils in special schools rarely had the opportunity to study sciences or languages and therefore often required special tuition in these subjects when they entered the ordinary school. It must also be considered that within a special school, a class is likely to contain a fairly wide age range, and that therefore a pupil has less opportunity and choice of interaction with peers of his own age than would be the case in an ordinary school.

On the matter of equipment also, the special school argument may be challenged. Large (1978), for example, suggests that many special schools lack the very resources and specially trained staff which, it is often claimed, would be unavailable in ordinary schools. Pedder (1975) cites the case of cerebral-palsied children requiring a great deal of physical stimulation, who are allowed to remain inactive for long periods of the day in special schools. Whilst in no way belittling those special schools which do achieve standards of excellence, it is suggested that a good ordinary school with adequate resources can provide an environment which is more stimulating for many handicapped pupils.

Finally, if one examines the possibilities contained in integration from the viewpoint of social development and adjustment, one may agree with the parents in Anderson's (1973) survey, who put forward 'social benefits' as one of the chief reasons for wishing their child to attend an ordinary school. The pupil who attends a local school is far more likely to retain social contact with other children who live near him, than if he spends his school day at a special school some distance away. Moreover, as Warnock suggests, 'A child must learn how to accommodate himself to other people: he must learn what will be expected of him as an adult'. Since the majority of handicapped people will be expected to function in the normal world, to a greater or lesser degree, upon reaching maturity, it is difficult to see how they are to achieve this effectively if, during the important learning period of their lives, they are actually segregated from their normal peers.

The disabled child needs to learn how to cope with staring, teasing, with bullying and with ill-timed offers to help, since he is certain to experience them at some stage in his life. One could argue, with Wright (1960), that the sooner these coping strategies are acquired, the better for the individual. Certainly, the disabled pupil in the ordinary school is not likely to be sheltered from these intrusions, although research done by both Anderson (1973) and Cope and Anderson (1977) suggests that the problem is not as great as is popularly supposed. It is likely that a handicapped child who has had limited experience of varied physical and social environments needs to acquire specific social skills, such as the ability to establish rapport with others, and to reduce the anxiety and tension often felt by others when interacting with a disabled person. It could be argued that he is more likely to acquire such skills in the context of an ordinary school.

MODELS OF INTEGRATION

Warnock postulates the existence of three models of integration, these being *locational*, *social* or *functional* in type.

Locational integration may well permit a handicapped pupil to attend the same school as his peers and siblings, rather than risk the loss of contact that might occur if he went to a special school. It can also allow a degree of integration for the severely handicapped pupil for whom it might otherwise prove an impossibility. Indeed, in Sweden, where the integration of such pupils has been achieved on a wide scale, it is generally of a locational type (Warnock, 1978). It allows normal and disabled pupils to observe and be aware of each other, but interaction can be limited or non-existent unless it is carefully planned. Cope and Anderson (1977) give the example of special schools and ordinary schools that shared the same campus, but operated different starting hours, lunch breaks and finishing times, thereby severely limiting the respective pupils' opportunities for mixing socially with each other.

Social integration offers much greater opportunities for interaction, but again, may need organization. Handicapped pupils may be unable to stay on after school to participate in social activities unless a transport rota is arranged to get them home. Similarly, when school trips and other activities are planned, the needs of possible handicapped participants should be borne in mind.

Functional integration is felt to be integration in its fullest sense. It includes both the locational and social types, adding classroom integration as well. As Warnock observes, it makes the greatest demands upon a school in terms of forward planning and teaching.

Nevertheless, where it succeeds, it is likely to be of greatest benefit to the child and ultimately, to the school. Both Cope and Anderson (1977) and Garnett (1976) suggest that where functional integration exists, there is a greater acceptance of handicapped pupils by teachers and pupils in the ordinary school. Garnett in particular found that, whilst ESN pupils experienced rejection, teasing and bullying when their special class was merely located in the grounds of a comprehensive school, once some interchange between the two groups began, culminating in shared classes, most of the teasing and bullying disappeared as the 'ESN identity' was gradually lost. It is of interest to note that a prime factor for change was an altering of attitudes among the main school staff. It may be seen that to achieve functional integration, attitudes are even more important than a shared curriculum and social activities. Nevertheless, notwithstanding the demands it imposes upon the school, it is suggested that functional integration is highly desirable and should be attempted wherever possible.

IMPLEMENTING INTEGRATION: PROBLEMS THAT MAY ARISE

To introduce integration is one thing: to implement it successfully is another. To create the maximum opportunity for success it is necessary for three conditions to be fulfilled.

1. There must be adequate resources, to provide the handicapped pupil with what Warnock terms 'special means of access to the curriculum'.
2. There must be a thorough and adequate assessment of the handicapped pupil's needs and abilities.
3. There must exist in the school a social climate within which integration is likely to be achieved (Warnock, 1978).

It is clear that the first two conditions will certainly influence the third, since, when teachers are attempting to teach handicapped pupils in the face of inadequate resources and inadequate information, their attitudes may well be less than positive.

'Adequate resources' must necessarily include school buildings that are accessible to handicapped pupils, and here it is heartening to note that the Department of Education has recently published a

141

booklet including suggestions as to how adaptations may be made (DES, 1979). 'Special means of access to the curriculum' will imply many things. It may mean providing specialist teaching or physiotherapy for a handicapped pupil, or a typewriter for a spastic child who cannot co-ordinate his hand movements well enough to write quickly or clearly. A 'talking' calculator may be helpful to the child with impaired vision (Dahl, 1978), whilst an adjustable chair or desk may be needed for the child who cannot sit in a normal position. It is accepted that the plea for such resources takes place against a background of cuts in the financial provision made available to education, when many schools are faced with a shortage of ordinary textbooks.

Sometimes 'special means of access' is provided by adapting teaching methods. The following alterations were made by teachers of integrated, partially-sighted pupils: (i) reduced use of the blackboard; (ii) more teacher verbalization; (iii) wider use of group discussion; (iv) questioning integrated pupils to ensure that they were following the lesson; (v) allowing the assistance of peers where useful; (vi) co-operating in the tape-recording of lesson material; (vii) keeping a close but unobtrusive watch on the progress of integrated pupils (Jamieson, Parlett and Pocklington, 1977). Therefore, it is suggested that whilst expensive specialist equipment is often vital to the success of integration, flexibility and the ability to innovate on the part of the teacher are inexpensive but equally important factors.

Personnel, in terms of specialist teachers and ancillary staff represent another, much needed resource.

Obviously, it is not likely that 'special means of access to the curriculum' can be adequately provided on an individual basis, unless an accurate assessment has been made of the pupil's needs and abilities before he enters the school. Indeed, Halliwell and Spain (1977) found that a prerequisite for successful integration was for the school to be given full information about the child and the extent of his problems, including a comprehensive explanation of his medical condition. Only on the basis of an all-round understanding of the child, gained from full consultation with his parents, doctors, social worker or psychologist, can the school begin to perceive him as an individual and assess his needs. Moreover, once the assessment has been made, it is important to ensure that the information reaches those who are primarily concerned with meeting those needs, namely, the teachers. Here, one can envisage a vital role for the pastoral care team within the school, acting as a point of liaison and disseminator of information between those who have, and those who need, relevant information about the child.

It is suggested in the Warnock Report that a 'named person' within the school be available as a point of contact for parents and others who need, on a regular basis, to know how the child is progressing. Whilst Warnock appears to see a head teacher in this role, one could see distinct advantages in the 'named person' being a specialist teacher with responsibility for handicapped pupils, who is also a fully-integrated member of the pastoral care team. In some cases a head of year or house, or a permanent school counsellor might well fill such a role. Such a person is more likely to be in touch with the child's day-to-day progress, and can receive immediate feedback from other staff who have contact with the pupil.

Not only may the pastoral care team liaise within the school, and with experts outside it. Where a local education authority appoints an advisory teacher to visit schools accepting handicapped pupils, it seems logical that the pastoral care team should be the focal point for such contacts.

THE SOCIAL CLIMATE OF THE SCHOOL

By acting as a point of liaison, and by disseminating information about the handicapped pupil, the pastoral care team may do much to facilitate the creation of a social climate within the school that is conducive to successful integration. Where information is handled in a sensitive manner, it can do a great deal to promote positive attitudes towards handicap within the school. As has already been suggested, the attitudes held by teachers are of crucial importance, as are those of the disabled pupil's parents, and other children in the school.

Parents

Parental attitudes can encourage or undermine a child's attempts to integrate with ordinary peers. If the parents are overprotective, or doubtful of the child's ability to cope, these views will almost certainly be reflected in the pupil's attitude to ordinary school. Access to a 'named person' within the school may help to alleviate normal parental anxiety. Certainly the importance of a dialogue between the school and the parents cannot be too highly stressed, for there may be a need at some point for the school to provide counselling for the parents, or to provide access to another source of support, and such work cannot be done in a vacuum. Moreover, as Halliwell and Spain (1977) point out, parents need to be able to see and discuss any problems concerning management of the child, from the staff's point of view, as well as the child's. This is more likely to occur where established, friendly relations exist between the school and the home. Perhaps most important of all, the parents of handicapped pupils should receive the same treatment from the school as other parents: the same invitations to social occasions, or to sit on governing bodies. Often, these parents will have felt a sense of stigma on account of their child: the school can do something at least to counteract this by involving them in all the school activities possible.

Other pupils

Where one is considering the attitudes of other children to their handicapped peers, it is worth remembering that some research suggests that children's behaviour reflects underlying staff attitudes. For example, Garnett's work (1976) shows that normal pupils are more likely to reject the handicapped where they and their teachers are seen to be set apart from the main school staff and pupils, and the organization of the school implicitly segregates the handicapped pupils from their peers.

The way a handicapped pupil is introduced into the ordinary school can also affect the degree to which he is accepted. Cope and Anderson (1977) found that pupils who entered the school during, rather than at the beginning of the school year, were less well integrated with their peers. The manner of his introduction is also important, Heron (1978) stressing the need to introduce the pupil as someone 'who is in the class because he is capable of being there'. Furthermore, as Heron points out, the teacher can take active steps to promote interaction between a handicapped pupil and peers. He may take the trouble to ensure that the pupil is incorporated into class working groups, or he may attempt to increase interaction between the disabled pupil and a few 'target' peers in the class. This could be encouraged by regularly placing the pupil in a specific small work group where co-operation between the pupils is necessary for the completion of a group task or projects. Where a handicapped pupil lacks obvious social and behavioural skills, it may be possible to provide a peer model for him to imitate. A child who previously has attended a special school may at first not know how to speak up in a large class, either to ask for help or to answer a question. He may be bemused by the variety of social situations offered by his new, more varied environment. Where a peer is used as a model in such cases, he needs to be carefully chosen. He needs to possess the appropriate social skills; he needs to be willing to help and understand the newcomer; also, as Bandura (1962) has shown, identification with a model is more likely to occur when the model possesses a degree of prestige within a group. Therefore, the peer model may need to be a fairly popular member of the class. Where another handicapped child has previously become well integrated into the class, such a child could provide a particularly useful model for a new pupil: however the dangers of isolating two handicapped pupils thus are obvious, and this course of action would require careful consideration before being implemented.

The use of older pupils as peer teachers and 'elder brothers' to mentally-handicapped pupils in ordinary schools is recorded by Morgan (1977) as a successful means of inducing social mixing and integration. Certainly, the 'pairing' of a handicapped pupil with a sympathetic peer upon entry to the school would protect the pupil to some degree from the initial isolation and confusion he may experience, and provide him with a model for those social behaviours which he has not yet acquired, thus making more likely his eventual acceptance by peers in general.

Where teasing occurs, much of it stems from thoughtlessness and ignorance, rather than from genuine malice. As Cope and Anderson (1977) describe, when the children responsible are found, and it is explained to them what is meant by, for example, 'spastic', then, 'these children are usually very penitent when they realise they have hurt someone's feelings'. One should repeat here that teasing does not appear to be the great problem which many had anticipated.

Teachers

The attitudes towards integration held by teachers must be

considered in more detail, because they can make or break an attempt to implement integration in a school successfully. A study by Halliwell and Spain (1977) of spina bifida pupils attending ordinary schools found that the majority of teachers favoured the principle of integration, but stressed the importance of supports for teaching staff. Significantly, the one teacher whose attitude was unfavourable was having to manage a doubly incontinent child, with virtually no ancillary support. This vividly illustrates one of the fears which may lead to negative attitudes among teachers, and which may be summarized as follows:

1. That educational standards will deteriorate.
2. That teachers will be 'unpaid social workers' rather than teachers.
3. That they will be unable to cope; there may be accidents.
4. That classes will be disrupted.
5. Fears aroused by the teacher's own aversion to handicap.

If one examines these objections carefully, it is clear that the first of them must be viewed as a consequence of one or more of the other fears being realized. There is no logical reason why the presence of a handicapped child in a class should, in itself, cause standards to deteriorate. That is only likely to occur where there is constant class disruption, and an overworked or stressed teacher. The argument is similar to the one used to attack the establishment of comprehensive schools – 'standards will drop' – and is based upon a similarly false premiss. In reality, integration, like the comprehensive system, will prove a failure or a success in direct proportion to the amount of planning and resources which are put into it.

A report published recently by a major teaching union (NAS/UWT, March 1979) attributed what it sees as falling academic standards to the involvement of teachers in pastoral and 'welfare' work, rather than in teaching. The report foresaw a worsening of the situation if handicapped pupils attend ordinary schools in large numbers. This point of view can perhaps be attributed to several factors. As Hamblin argues on pp. 3–20, one of these is a complete failure to acknowledge that there can be any positive links between the existence of a pastoral care system within a school and improved performance on the part of the pupils. Or there may be a pastoral care system within a school, but functioning inadequately, because of insufficient commitment of expertise. Such a system will almost inevitably foster cynicism amongst other staff, and can do little to enhance the name of pastoral care. There is also a third, and very important, factor at work. Teachers who hold negative attitudes towards integration may often be attempting to cope with quite serious problems, without any effective support. Whilst they do not hold to the old tenet that they are there to teach their subject rather than to teach children, they are likely to be under great pressure and receiving little help. In such cases, their fears concerning handicapped children are easy to understand, since they may envisage integration as meaning yet more problems. For answer, it must be stressed that integration cannot be expected to work unless the teacher receives full support from ancillary staff, and from an effective pastoral care team. Many of his fears concerning his own ability to cope with a handicapped pupil arise from ignorance about the handicap. For example, a teacher is more likely to show acceptance and understanding of a hydrocephalic pupil if he has full knowledge of the condition, and has been told what to do if the child receives a knock. Knowing how to cope, and when to summon medical help, will dispel the prejudices that might be aroused by a vague phrase such as 'the child's got a valve in his head' (Halliwell and Spain, 1977). In the same way, the teacher of an epileptic child is better able to approach his pupil in a common-sense way if he knows that epilepsy is *not* insanity; the difference between grand and petit mal; which type of epilepsy the pupil suffers from; and what should be done for him in the event of an attack.

IN-SERVICE TRAINING

Among the many points raised in the Warnock Report was the recommendation that some form of in-service training be made available for teachers of handicapped pupils in ordinary schools. Whilst it is apparent that teachers could benefit greatly from attending special courses provided by the local education authority, valuable in-service training can also be done within the school. Clearly the presence of a specialist teacher in the pastoral care team is relevant here. Someone is needed with experience and knowledge of handicapping conditions, and who is able to teach other staff the skills needed to manage a specific disability, should the need arise.

Moreover, the specialist provides a resource to be drawn upon in other ways, when advice is needed as to the feasibility of particular teaching methods for handicapped pupils. Sometimes the specialist would suggest, and train teachers in the use of, new teaching skills or new equipment. The educational psychologist may participate in such an in-school training programme by training staff in the use of diagnostic skills and by close liaison with the pastoral care team, particularly where the need arises for parental or family counselling involving handicapped pupils. Help may also be given where a visiting physiotherapist is available, to teach staff how to devise exercises and activities for handicapped children who might otherwise be deprived of much needed physical stimulation. In short, the teacher needs particular *skills* which may be summarized thus:

1. Teaching skills: general expertise, skills of class management and skills specific to a particular disability.
2. Management skills: full knowledge of pupil's disabling condition and practical training in coping with it.
3. Diagnostic and assessment skills.
4. Basic counselling skills.

Possessing these skills, the teacher's ability to cope, both as a manager of the disability and as a teacher, will be augmented and his confidence increased. It is therefore suggested that many of the fears held by teachers concerning integration will diminish where there are adequate resources for a handicapped pupil, where a specialist is available to offer supports and skills training, and where a pastoral care team provides adequate supports for individual pupils and their teachers, when problems arise. The head of house or year is often particularly well placed to analyse such problems and to take steps to rectify them, and here one may cite an example of just such an analysis given by Heron (1978). Heron suggests that where problems occur with a handicapped pupil, they can be solved by focusing attention on: (i) the disabled child's behaviour; (ii) the behaviour of the peer group; (iii) the teacher's behaviour. According to the analysis, specific remedial strategies may then be implemented. A representation of this process appears in fig. 7.1 (adapted from Heron, 1978).

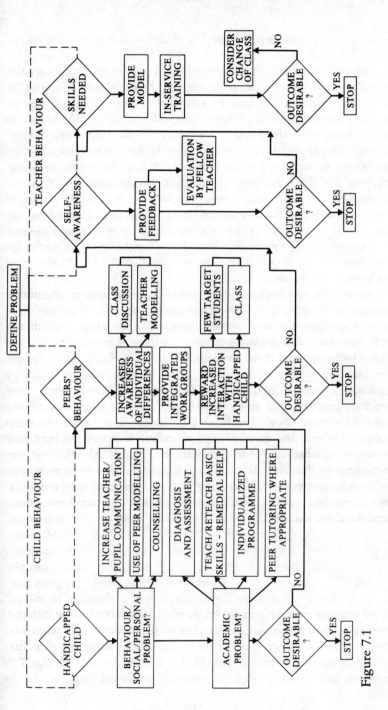

Figure 7.1

Sometimes a teacher may have a negative response to a disabled pupil because the handicap arouses in him feelings of threat or repulsion. Although he may be ashamed of his feelings and attempt to repress them, nevertheless they will be likely to affect his interactions with the pupil. Sometimes, it will be enough for the teacher simply to admit to himself that he has such feelings, before he begins to cope with them positively. It may be helpful if he can explore his feelings with a qualified person such as a school counsellor, or psychologist, who can explain to him the nature of stigma and the irrational sense of threat which the sight of handicap can arouse in 'normal' people. Occasionally, there may be a case for a teacher frankly admitting that he is unable to overcome his aversion, and in these circumstances it may be better for the pupil to be moved to another teacher.

Another aspect of teachers' attitudes to handicap should be mentioned briefly. It is, unfortunately, all too common for those who teach students who are handicapped or disadvantaged in any way to share their stigma to some extent. One thinks here of attitudes sometimes held towards remedial teachers, or of the FE teachers engaged in 'pre-TOPS' course work, who are said by colleagues to run 'noddy' courses (Marshall, 1979). Often these teachers are excluded from important decision-making within the school, because they may have low status in terms of post and salary. There is the greatest need to ensure that any teachers with special responsibility for handicapped pupils should not be perceived in this way. Rather, they should be seen as experts with acknowledged status, functioning within a pastoral care team that has as its concern *all* pupils in the school, not only the handicapped and the disadvantaged.

Counselling

It is felt that every handicapped pupil should have the opportunity for regular meetings with a member of the pastoral care team who has a special understanding of his needs. Whilst accepting the point that no undue attention should be drawn to the child, it is nevertheless believed that the sins of omission here would be greater than the sins of commission. It is not enough that the disabled pupil is coping adequately because he displays no outward signs of distress. Many have become adept at hiding such signs!

Many counselling techniques can be used to enable the nervous or withdrawn pupil to explore his feelings about his handicap. In my own study (Chapman, 1977), I found it helpful to make use of the open-ended sentence technique devised by Hamblin (1974). For example, the pupil is asked to complete a set of sentences, verbally or in writing.

'I think . . . .'
'People in class say I . . . .'

It can sometimes be a useful exercise to ask the child to draw a picture of himself: in my study I found that very few of the handicapped children represented themselves as they actually were, but as they wished to be. The way is then open for a realistic exploration of the pupil's self-image. Self-concept instruments may be of use to some pupils: I have used an adaptation of Hamblin's (1974) 'Actual and Ideal Self Scales' with handicapped pupils, but it is stressed that great care must be taken to ensure that the pupils fully understand how to complete the items on the scales.

Group counselling can provide the pupil with the opportunity for increasing his self-awareness, and the chance to role-play new social skills in a more secure environment. Use may be made of games, simulations, discussions and co-operative tasks within the context of which pupils may learn something of the quality of their interactions with others. For example, the shy child who feels that his contributions are ignored, will learn that it is because he does not speak audibly enough, or with sufficient self-assertion. The group situation then affords him the opportunity to practise more assertive behaviour if he so desires.

The type of counselling which is made available must be determined by the individual needs of the pupil. Whilst one child may benefit from group work centred on the learning of social skills, another may find the group situation too threatening to participate in his own advantage. There should be a flexibility of approach to counselling, allowing for transfer from individual to pair or group counselling where it is felt this would best suit the needs of the pupil.

Teaching staff involved with a handicapped pupil need to be aware of those areas in his personal development where he is likely to be most vulnerable. The handicapped pupil is likely to be at risk in the following areas:

1. Body-image.
2. Peer relationships: opposite sex relationships.
3. Social competence.
4. Vocational aspirations; aspirations towards independence.

Allport (1955) believes that the body-image is the first aspect of the self-concept to be formed in young children. The individual is likely to compare his own image of himself with the type of physique idealized by his culture: this is particularly the case in adolescence. What are the implications here for the physically-disabled pupil? First, any comparison between himself and an ideal must be to his own detriment, and his despair may be compounded by the knowledge that no drastic change in his appearance will be wrought by the altered hairstyle or dress to which his non-handicapped peers may resort. Next, as Wright (1960) suggests, many disabled children cling to the hope that somehow, when they become adults, their handicap will miraculously disappear. With the coming of adolescence, it becomes obvious that this will not happen, and the young person must come to terms with a physique that is with him for life.

Sometimes, where a handicapped child has been sheltered from interaction with normal peers, or has been discouraged, by his parents from the 'mirror-play' – that is, observation and play with his own reflection – normal to young children, the handicap may not be incorporated with the body-image in any realistic way. For example, observing self-portraits by handicapped pupils in a special school, I found that only one pupil had depicted himself as he was, seated in a wheelchair. In these circumstances, realization, when it comes, may be especially painful for the adolescent to deal with, and it may fall to the pastoral care worker to help him through the task of accepting, and learning to live with, a physique that deviates from the rigid norms of adolescent conformity. There is no place here for the offering of false comforts. It may be more useful to help the pupil to explore the most favourable means of self-presentation available to him, and the deeper implications of his physique in terms of relationships with others.

In adolescence, the 'others' – the peers – begin to replace the family as a reference group, as the young person takes his first steps towards independence. The handicapped pupil is likely to encounter much frustration at this stage. First, because for him, the stage of rebellion against parental authority which normally is part of the individuation process, may be only partly accomplished, or may prove impossible. He frequently has little choice over what he wears, where he goes and when. It is not easy to rebel against those upon whom one is, literally, physically dependent. The disabled youngster cannot always slam the door and retreat to his room in time-honoured adolescent fashion. He may cope, either by displaying a great deal of frustrated anger, or by appearing to relinquish the struggle altogether, remaining the 'good', dependent child. Yet another reaction may be to make use of the handicap to get his own way by playing on family sympathies: where this occurs, the stage is set for poor sibling relationships, and at school, behaviour towards others which is unrealistic, and can be manipulative.

Next, identification and association with a peer group is more difficult for him. He may be unable to participate in group activities, such as dancing, which are popular with his age group. In addition, Kershaw (1974) has suggested that boys and girls suffer in different ways. Whilst the disabled boy can be disadvantaged when competing in areas that stress physical prowess, the girl is more likely to suffer in her social life. An ordinary girl may show some interest in a disabled boy, but the reverse is less likely, since teenage boys tend to choose their partners for their physical attractiveness, and a handicapped girlfriend is unlikely to add to a boy's social status. Early experience of rejection may cause a girl to retreat from any social situation which is potentially threatening, so that she becomes withdrawn, or often refuses to go out at all. Again, such experiences may make the girl desperate to prove that she is attractive. In her search for reassurance and affection, such a girl can be exploited by the unscrupulous. In either case, her ability to enter into any normal, meaningful relationships with the opposite sex in later life can be severely damaged. Of course, all young people risk rejection in their relationships with the other sex, but for the handicapped adolescent the risk is much greater. When a boy confides his apprehension that he will never have a steady

153

relationship, he is expressing a very real fear. Underlying his statement is the possibility of a future without marriage and sexual relationships, if he cannot find a partner to whom his handicaps are not overly important.

It is stressed here that any teacher or pastoral care worker who becomes involved with counselling a handicapped adolescent at this very personal level must be quite clear about his own attitudes. There is still a tendency in society to regard the handicapped as eternal children who do not need, and should not expect, normal adult relationships. It is important to realize that the handicapped pupil will share all the fantasies and misconceptions of his peers: he is as fearful and as hopeful as they, and as much in need of sex education and guidance in personal relationships. Those who cannot accept this aspect of the handicapped pupil should not participate in his personal counselling.

Sometimes, rejection is brought about by the young person himself, because of his own attitudes and behaviour. I have already suggested (1977) that the handicapped adolescent is more likely to regard himself in negative terms: the consequent low self-evaluation can affect his responses to other people and new situations. He may be so anxious about social interaction, fearing a rebuff or hurtful comments, that he withdraws from it altogether. Where a child constantly sits alone in school, never speaking to anyone unless spoken to, the teacher should not assume that his behaviour is an inevitable concomitant of his handicap, but rather, that the child may need help. I encountered such a child, a boy so fearful of being stared at, that he could not recognize or interpret signals of liking or approval which he received from other members of his class. He could not recognize them, because he never really saw them, interpreting every glance as 'staring'. In such a case a child can be helped, first by learning, in a secure setting, to read the non-verbal signals sent by others, and next, to practise the initiations of social interaction himself. This may be done in the one-to-one situation initially, perhaps with the pupil transferring to a group when he is ready to try out the newly-acquired skills on his peers.

Again, a pupil may court rejection by means of 'touchy' behaviour or aggression, when he feels that his handicap is being drawn to attention, whilst another child may seek to divert notice from a disability by assuming a 'clowning' role. The latter example is often deceptive since it can bring the child a measure of popularity with his classmates. Nevertheless, in this, as in the other

154

modes of behaviour, his interactions with peers are unrealistic, because he has not acquired the skills necessary for easy social intercourse.

The pupil who lacks such social competence may have had a limited background of experiences in which to learn such skills. He may need to be taught how to begin and maintain a conversation, how to help a friend in trouble, or how to approach a potentially threatening new situation. In addition, he has to acquire strategies for coping with other people's reactions to his disability. Handicapped children dislike being stared at, asked tactless questions, being talked about in their hearing, and being 'helped' more zealously than they would wish. Yet all of these things happen, and without coping strategies the child will continue to suffer.

The children in my study (1977) found it easier to answer questions about their handicap when these came from other children rather than from adults. Several suggested that to explain as simply as possible the nature of the disability was the best solution. This strategy is likely to be most effective with younger children who tend to lose interest once their natural curiosity has been satisfied. The adolescent is less likely to ask direct questions, but his curiosity will be apparent. This is harder for the handicapped boy or girl to cope with, although if he or she is able to break the ice with a casual or joking reference to the handicap, his peers are likely to be as relieved as he is. Certainly the children in the study felt that this was an effective ploy. For the very self-conscious child, it may not prove easy, and he could well benefit from the opportunity to role-play it in private first.

The denial of a handicap presents another obstacle to the achieving of social competence, and as Wright (1960) suggests, can severely limit the pupil's chances of ever learning to cope with a disability. In Rogerian terms, experiences which are seen as inconsistent with the organization of the self are perceived as threatening (Rogers, 1951). Thus, when handicap is not accepted, the pupil may angrily reject any reminder of it. He may refuse to use special aids for his condition even though he needs them, and may set himself goals which are unrealistically high. Since he can never learn to cope with that whose existence he denies, he is caught up in a time-consuming and finally self-defeating process. Sometimes, therefore, it may fall to the pastoral care worker to help a handicapped adolescent, firmly but with compassion, to face the reality of his situation. Extreme depression, sometimes accompanied by rage, is likely to result from the first stage of the process, and the pupil will need much supportive counselling to help him through his uncertainties towards the beginnings of self-acceptance.

Certainly the handicapped school-leaver cannot afford to face his future, still retaining unrealistic ideas about himself, and this must always be borne in mind when vocational guidance is given. If, as Ginzberg believes (Hopson and Hayes, 1968), for most young people vocational choice implies compromise, then for the handicapped adolescent, the degree of compromise may be very great – indeed, for some, there may not even be the possibility of compromise. Whether he wishes to pursue a course of higher education, or to begin work at once, he will encounter difficulties and discouragement. The choice of a first job is particularly crucial, since as Kershaw (1974) points out, the young disabled worker can ill afford a period of initial failure. Not only will his self-esteem suffer, but other prospective employers are then likely to view him as a doubtful prospect.

For the most severely disabled, the only employment available may be in a work centre or sheltered workshop, with just enough remuneration to provide pocket money. There is little prospect for them of ever achieving financial independence from parents. For any handicapped pupil, the realization that his vocational aspirations are unlikely to be fulfilled will be a cause of anger and depression, sometimes accompanied by a defensive retreat into unrealistic fantasy which may prevent him from utilizing those strengths and abilities which he does possess. Teachers need to be aware of this.

Using the school curriculum

One of the tasks of the pastoral care team may be to create awareness of those areas of the curriculum where work may be done that is of particular relevance to the handicapped. It is felt that such work, in addition to benefiting the handicapped pupil in some way, should seek also to promote in other pupils an understanding of and sensitivity to the position of the handicapped person in society. This means that the subject of handicap will be brought out openly rather than discreetly pushed to one side, thereby encouraging a healthier approach to it by both staff and pupils.

It is suggested that the following areas of the curriculum could be used to advantage: the list is selective, and readers will certainly think of many more possibilities!

Vocational guidance cannot begin too early for the handicapped pupil. Morgan (1974) believes that personal counselling should begin at the pre-adolescent stage and should continue throughout the pupil's school life. Parallel with this must exist a constant process of assessing and reassessing his skills, abilities and interests. As he approaches school-leaving age the pupil's mobility needs must be estimated, and advice given on obtaining a mobility allowance or other forms of aid. There must also be contact with a careers specialist who is familar with the requirements of the handicapped school-leaver, and who can advise on local job opportunities for the pupil, and can provide specialized knowledge of any colleges or universities offering courses or facilities particularly suited to the pupil's needs. It is assumed that, along with such individual help, the pupil will receive the same careers lessons as other pupils, and therefore, the lessons could include material relating to the handicapped. Other elements of a careers programme, such as decision-making exercises and the use of self-concept instruments may help the pupil towards a better understanding of himself.

DRAMA: MUSIC AND MOVEMENT

It is suggested that the handicapped pupil be encouraged to participate as much as possible in these lessons, since he can probably do more than he and other people think.

Where the disabled pupil is able to join in physically with peers, he is likely to gain confidence in his physical abilities and improve his body-image. Slade (1971) records how mentally-handicapped girls seemed to acquire a new grace and sense of ease when they took part in a series of free improvisations. The pupil who is able to walk, albeit with difficulty, can gain confidence and satisfaction from activities such as the 'solid rock' exercise. Here, pupils arrange themselves in whatever position they feel most secure, whilst another pupil attempts to dislodge them, usually without success. Pupils confined to wheelchairs can learn to use their upper limbs more expressively, through mime. The wheelchair itself, used imaginatively, can become many things; a machine, a car, a bus, a cinema seat – whatever the improvisation requires. Many handicapped pupils can acquire better co-ordination and the confidence to move more freely through drama. Music and movement also can help them to achieve this, and is especially useful to the blind or partially-sighted child, who is in need of developing an improved rhythmic sense (Bowley and Gardener, 1972). In most circumstances there is no reason why these activities should not take place in the context of a class drama or movement lesson.

The drama lesson can also provide opportunities for role-taking, a valuable exercise for the handicapped adolescent who may find it difficult to put himself in another's place. It may be added that the ordinary pupil too can benefit from the experience of, for example, being 'blind' for five minutes. Again, drama offers the handicapped pupil the chance to practise in 'pretence' those social skills he may hesitate to use in reality.

ENVIRONMENTAL STUDIES

A class could carry out a project on the relative accessibility for the disabled of public places in the locality: cinemas, libraries, shops, etc.

SOCIAL EDUCATION

There might be involvement of handicapped and ordinary pupils in community projects that give the experience of interacting with, and helping, others in the wider community. In the process, handicapped pupils could, where feasible, become better acquainted with public transport, and learn how to handle money effectively, since often they have little experience of this.

HOME ECONOMICS

Handicapped pupils may learn more effective self-presentation, flattering modes of dress, etc. A sense of independence can be promoted where domestic skills are learned. Many disabled children are not actively encouraged to acquire such skills in the home. A wheelchair-bound pupil is perfectly able to use cooking equipment if it is adapted to his needs.

For the individual disabled pupil, the English lesson offers the chance to improve his skills of self-expression, both written and oral, and it is felt these skills are vital. A handicapped person, more than most, needs to be articulate and to express himself succinctly, because as an adult he often faces problems concerned with obtaining his social and legal rights. He may well have little *economic* status with which to impress others, therefore he desperately needs the ability to make himself heard and noticed.

One function of the English lesson should be to encourage awareness and tolerance of individual differences amongst all pupils. Thus, teaching materials could be included which illustrate the achievements of handicapped people, as in the story of Helen Keller, or in *Reach For The Sky*, the filmed biography of Douglas Bader. Pupils should be encouraged to examine their own and society's attitudes towards minority groups, the handicapped among them. Literature can be used as the starting point for the examination of stereotypes held about minorities: 'Othello', Shylock, 'Richard III', and Katy, the too-good-to-be-true crippled heroine of Susan Coolidge's classic *What Katy Did*. However, the teacher should approach this type of work with sensitivity, taking care that he is not reinforcing the stereotypes under scrutiny. This type of lesson is probably best done with older pupils, perhaps at fifth- and sixth-form level.

SPORT

As with drama, the handicapped pupil should be encouraged to take part in some kind of sporting activity wherever possible. Not only will it build up his confidence in his physical abilities, but will also provide the exercise which he needs as much as anyone of his age. Moreover, his physical co-ordination can often be helped through such activities. A visiting physiotherapist may be able to suggest alternative exercises to those usually provided in the PE lesson. Where the pupil is quite unable to participate in activities with his class, either another sport should be made available – for example, wheelchair archery – or some other meaningful activity should be provided. It is demoralizing for the pupil to be told to sit on the sidelines and 'watch' his classmates, as is so often the case.

TUTORIAL PERIODS

Where these periods are used specifically for pastoral care purposes, they can be of great help to all pupils, handicapped and non-handicapped, when they explore such topics as; identity, the self-concept, self-presentation, decision-making, social relationships, the concept of 'normality'.

8

Integration of Handicapped Pupils into the Ordinary School

Margaret Hart
(Formerly Deputy Head, Northumberland Park Comprehensive School)

THE PHILOSOPHY BEHIND INTEGRATION

I am particularly concerned with what the Warnock Report terms functional integration (Warnock, 1979, 7.9) – 'the fullest form of integration which is achieved where the locational and social association of children with special needs with their fellows leads to joint participation in educational programmes'. Warnock points out that functional integration makes the greatest demands upon an ordinary school, and yet firmly supports the aim of many children with special educational needs eventually receiving full-time education in an ordinary class. The Warnock Report also draws attention to the urgency of improving teacher training as a prerequisite for progressive integration of the handicapped (Warnock, 1978, 19.12). In the current climate the school may have to undertake training for itself.

It is important to emphasize the need to avoid exaggeration of the *differences* between handicapped and non-handicapped pupils, and to stress and focus on the *similarities*. Equally important is the need for acceptance of their condition, both by the handicapped and those in contact with them, and above all, for learning ways of coping.

161

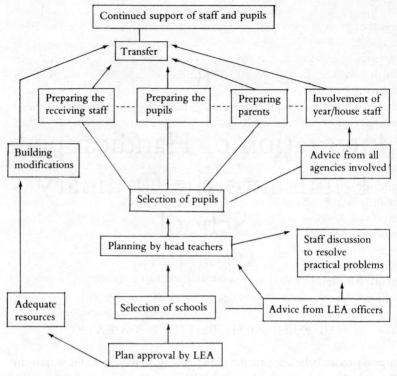

Fig. 8.1

PLANNING AN INTEGRATION SCHEME (fig 8.1)

Once the LEA agrees the philosophy and has the resources to implement a scheme of integration, the head teachers of the schools involved can begin planning, in conjunction with advisers from the authority. Their main task will be not only to convince their staffs of the philosophy of integration into ordinary school but that it is *practically* possible.

Selection of pupils

Any child selected for an integration scheme must be thought capable of benefiting from it both socially and educationally. One should also be able to indicate how the integration will equip him

162

to cope more successfully in later life. Certainly the pupil will find the change at sixteen plus less traumatic than if he had been entirely educated in a special school. Educational and social attainments are obviously important, but the child will only be able to benefit from an ordinary school if he can – with help – cope physically with its demands. In the schemes with which I am familar decisions about the 'readiness' of a pupil for integration were taken by the head teachers of the special schools following case conferences at which agencies and people involved with the child were present. In the early days of the scheme it was evident that only children who were educationally 'able' were considered for selection – multiply-handicapped children were not thought possible transferees at this stage. After four years, however, some of the schools involved are now looking at the possibility of transferring children who are not only handicapped physically or with a hearing defect but who are also in need of *intensive* remedial help, that is children with learning disabilities. Next, schools should carefully assess how many children can be transferred and into which year groups. There will be constraints – many of which are outlined in the practical section following – but I feel it is important for a school to take a few children and succeed with them before expansion.

Commencing integration at primary/secondary transfer stage appears most beneficial to the child. Every first-year child is new to the school and involved in making new relationships, thus the handicapped child is in many ways in the same situation as his peers. It is more difficult to enter a second- or third-year group where peer relationships are already formed – not only is the handicapped child new but also 'different'. When transfer occurs later in adolescence, thorough preparatory work is needed by the receiving school before transfer.

Preparing the pupils

A useful plan might be as follows:

1. Selection.
2. Preparation by his own teachers, and involvement of friends and family.
3. Visit to open evening at the new school in February/March.

4. Formal interview at new school. Opportunity to talk to pupils and teachers.
5. A week's placement in the new school in July.
6. Admission in September.

Often the handicapped child himself will be the most reluctant to move schools. Here he is: an eleven-year old, in a safe environment since he was five; believing he will stay where he is known, familiar with his surroundings and his teachers, for the rest of his schooldays. Suddenly his world is upturned: a deaf child is confronted with the challenge of moving into a hearing society, a physically-handicapped child is confronted with a mobile world; no close friends are there; but hundreds of children instead of the known few; different lessons; new teachers, fewer technical aids.

There must be no insistence that the child has to transfer – it must be a suggestion to be looked at as a possibility until the child gains confidence to believe that it is practicable. The child needs access to his teachers to talk out his worries, and to his new school and new colleagues. He will also depend on the support of his parents and friends.

Our scheme progressed as follows. In February/March the children visited the 'new' school on an open evening. They saw work exhibited and met teachers. Preliminary interviews were arranged in May with the head of year/house. They were shown round the school by pupils, who talked to them about the school. We found this to be valuable in dissipating fears and increasing confidence. It was also possible for some of the handicapped children to spend time in the school in July prior to entry. This was a worthwhile experience as the children had a realistic 'taste' of what the school would be like and thus were more confident that they would cope in September.

Mary:
... liked having a week in my new school. Before I went I was frightened that I wouldn't be able to get around on my sticks, its such a huge place, or to carry my books and things, but I made lots of friends and everyone helped me with my bag and the lift. I enjoyed the lessons and different subjects. When I started in September I was all right. You know you'll get on once you've had a week there.

Preparing the parents

Parents need as much support and information as their children before integration. Sometimes the child is confident that he/she can cope but the parent is full of doubts about the venture. If the parents can be fully involved in discussions with the special school, especially during assessment, and also with other involved agencies, their fears can be alleviated. They need to be assured that should the 'experiment' fail the child may return *at any time* to the special school. They need to have access to the head of the special school, or the social worker, to express their anxieties – the position of the person is irrelevant, but it must be someone they trust.

Once a decision has been taken about transfer it is vital that the parents see the ordinary school at work and meet the people who will be most closely involved with their child. The parents are probably accustomed to a small, informal school and may find the enormity of a large secondary school very threatening. It will help if they can see how the school will cater for their child: for example, toilet arrangements, the dining hall, the special rooms which the child will use and the facilities available. They need the opportunity to talk to the pastoral staff about their child's special problems, and will be relieved if the head of year/house shows some knowledge of the child's handicap and thus can talk specifically about his medical and emotional needs as well as his education. The terminology of the curriculum may cause confusion, as may talk of 'tutor groups', 'sets', 'periods', etc. All these need a word of explanation from the pastoral staff. Individual arrangements for the child need to be explained, and thus the school will show clearly its structure and personalize its approach so that its sheer size does not detract from the individual approach which can be offered to the parents and to the child.

Preparing the staff

Staff meetings and departmental meetings will iron out many of the practical problems at the 'drawing board' stage, but some members of staff may still feel threatened or worried at the thought of teaching a handicapped child in their class, yet unable to voice their fears.

The following ideas may be used in preparing the staff:

1. Visits to the special school to meet the children before transfer.
2. Informal discussions with the special school staff.
3. Information about technical aids used by the children.
4. Awareness of material resources available to the staff.
5. Knowledge of the staffing support services available.
6. Information about building modifications and reasons for them.
7. Medical information – simple explanation of various handicaps and how they may affect a child.
8. Staff involvement in curriculum planning for the children.

Teachers need to know clearly who is responsible for the day-to-day administration of the scheme in the school (preferably a member of staff other than the head teacher) and to whom they can turn for help. Above all, positive leadership and encouragement from the head teacher is needed to maintain the high morale of the staff.

THE PRACTICAL SITUATION

The building

If handicapped children are to be educated in ordinary schools, minor building modifications will probably have to be made. Warnock indicates (1978, 7.26) that the school premises are a major determinant of the effectiveness of special educational provision in ordinary schools. General considerations, for example, the degree of open planning, contribute to the viability of the scheme for children with impaired hearing. Physically-handicapped pupils in wheelchairs will be aided by ramps and by a lift if the building is more than one storey high.

Toilet facilities

Toilet facilities need careful examination. It will be necessary to build or adapt some of the toilets into ambulant toilets with handles, and to provide a changing room with a plinth (a high, narrow table) for pupils who cannot use a toilet. Some schools are fortunate in having specially built facilities, but it is more usual for the ordinary school to designate one toilet block for pupils with special needs and for minor adaptations to take place. A sluice is preferable to small hand basins and a plinth is preferable to a bed, but the lack of ideal facilities need not prevent an integration scheme from beginning provided that the welfare assistants feel the facilities are adequate. Some schools have a large medical suite and are able to allocate part of this for the use of the handicapped. It is obvious that toilet arrangements must be thought out long before a school takes handicapped pupils. Staff need to be informed of children who could be late to class because of toileting between lessons, and arrangements made for informing teachers – for example, by a duplicated form – when this occurs.

Physiotherapy and hydrotherapy

Many physically-handicapped pupils need regular physiotherapy. For some this means attending a clinic or returning to the special school for treatment, but the majority probably do not need special apparatus or facilities and could have their treatment session in a PE lesson or during the lunch hour if it is possible to provide a spacious, quiet area – an empty room, a corridor or foyer, free from interruption by other pupils or staff – where the physiotherapist and child can work.

Many physically-handicapped children are helped by swimming sessions in a specially heated pool – a hydrotherapy session. If transport can be provided it is possible for these sessions to be continued during games lessons (or at other times having regard to the curriculum). We found that not only did our physically-handicapped pupils enjoy returning to their special school for these sessions, and retaining contact with their old friends, but on occasions the games staff gave permission for one or two new friends to go with them – a learning experience for all concerned.

Classroom arrangements

Arrangements within the classroom are the concern of the teacher involved. Many children will fit naturally into the group, without any physical alteration of the room. Others may need a small, movable table at the front of the class for some lessons. Alan's wheelchair, for example, would not fit behind the normal desks, so special tables were left in the rooms he used which his friends helped to place in position at the front of the class when he arrived. In the science laboratories a small table was kept for him in a prep room. Other children needed higher tables in some lessons, so blocks were made. In one school I visited, a group of children had spent several evenings after school in the workshops making ramps and blocks to help the wheelchair-bound pupils move around the school. Here I am indicating the help which peers can give to a handicapped child to ease the physical constraints of a school.

It is important that teachers delegate responsibility to the class after making initial arrangements at the beginning of term. It may be best to make a particular child or group of children responsible for helping in practical lessons where mobility is necessary. Often it will be possible for the handicapped child to collect his/her own materials, but at other times friends can help.

Susan, for example, is damaged by cerebral palsy. She is rather unco-ordinated in her movements, although she moves around school unaided. In the home economics and science lessons her friend, Ann, collects materials for her and works with her, but Susan is always prepared to do more than her share of washing up and clearing away – which she does slowly after the end of a lesson when the room is less crowded. It seems important that the handicapped pupils are not oversupported but are allowed to do their share.

Staffing arrangements

Probably the most important resource of the ordinary school for any scheme of integration is the staffing available to it. At least one welfare assistant is needed to deal solely with the physically-handicapped pupils and a liaison (or link) teacher to work with the staff. The welfare assistant is responsible for the physical needs of the children, and the liaison teacher is primarily responsible for their educational programme.

Fig 8.2 gives some idea of the work undertaken by the welfare assistant.

We were fortunate that our link teacher was a member of staff of

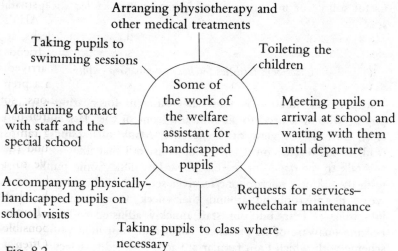

Arranging physiotherapy and other medical treatments

Taking pupils to swimming sessions

Toileting the children

Maintaining contact with staff and the special school

Some of the work of the welfare assistant for handicapped pupils

Meeting pupils on arrival at school and waiting with them until departure

Accompanying physically-handicapped pupils on school visits

Requests for services– wheelchair maintenance

Taking pupils to class where necessary

Fig. 8.2

the special school and knew the pupils well. She was able to advise the staff on a suitable curriculum for each child and then help the pastoral staff to monitor progress and evaluate the programme. She maintained close contact with the two schools and was a vital link for the members of staff and the head teachers. In the early days of the scheme she was placed in a counselling role by the staff – not only was she able to give information and help to teachers but she also listened to the problems they encountered with pupils and helped to devise ways of coping with them. Initially she spent time in the ordinary school every day but gradually was able to reduce this to half a day each week. Not only were the staff confident, but the physically-handicapped pupils had quickly established a routine which enabled the scheme to run smoothly. Some schools unfortunately do not have a link teacher. Many have appointed a member of their own staff to act as liaison teacher. This can be very effective if he/she is prepared to undertake some in-service training, and to spend time in the special school learning about the specific disabilities of the children and how these may affect their educational progress. The brief of the liaison teacher must be to act as a source of information and help to the staff, as well as to monitor closely the progress of each child and thus assist the pastoral team. Medical and educational information needs to be available to all staff involved with these pupils; and often the link/liaison teacher will remain in contact with the child's family – a useful source of information and point of contact for the pastoral staff.

Classroom facilities for hearing-impaired pupils

The practical situation is somewhat different for hearing-impaired pupils, who will need to sit near the front of the class and have a clear, unrestricted view of the teacher. Many such pupils will lip read, so the teacher must always be conscious that they are present, and talk to the *class*, not the blackboard or desk. Some pupils work with the aid of a microphone/receiver set, and teachers may need to wear the microphone around their neck – this can be a little inhibiting at first, but our staff quickly adjusted to it and most became unaware of its presence. All hearing-impaired pupils in the scheme with which I am familar are accompanied to selected lessons by their support teacher – a qualified teacher of the deaf who was appointed to work individually with the pupils in the scheme. She attends some lessons – sitting with the child and helping where necessary. This situation requires much sensitivity and perception on the part of the support teacher – *and* the class teacher – for although hearing-impaired children need help, the attendance of a special teacher in class draws attention to their disability and may affect the relationship of the child with his/her peers and class teacher. In some cases we found it better for the support teacher not to *attend* the lesson but to discuss follow-up with the teacher before working individually with the child. Many 'teachers' find the presence of another teacher in their class to be threatening and inhibiting, and however unobtrusive the support teacher is, her presence will undoubtedly affect the performance of some members of staff. It would be easy to disregard the feelings of teachers in our attempts to ensure that the integration scheme works, but this would be self-defeating. It is the responsibility of the pastoral system to help teachers in this situation.

Teachers of hearing-impaired children will be aware that often the child's speech is affected by his hearing loss, and it may be difficult to understand what he is trying to say. Often great sensitivity is needed on the part of the teacher – particularly in oral work – to include such pupils in class discussion and to allow them time to express themselves without either being hurried or ridiculed because they cannot be understood.

The role of the support teacher for partially-hearing/profoundly-deaf pupils is a crucial one. He/she must view this integration of these pupils as an individual scheme for each pupil. The needs of each child will be very different, the lessons from which they are withdrawn (usually a second language) may differ and the timetable of the support teacher will be drawn up according to the needs of each child. Demands on the support teacher will increase as pupils reach the fourth year – not only in terms of subject content but in terms of time – and if the system is to continue in the same way it may be necessary at this stage (that is, when option courses begin) to appoint a second support teacher to the scheme if more children are to be integrated. Not only does the support teacher play a vital role in terms of the curriculum, but he/she has much to offer the pastoral team and will work closely with the pastoral staff to help the child adjust to his new school or course. Her role in relation to the child is crucial – the child needs help, but also needs to develop relationships with his peers – and a balance is not-always easy. The following example illustrates this point.

Michael:
a partially-hearing boy, resented his support teacher's presence in French, Maths and Science, but had difficulty in making good relationships with his peers. He therefore had the support of neither his teacher nor his friends in these lessons – until his difficulty was realized and the form tutor and support teacher worked together to help both in terms of work and relationships.

SPECIAL PROBLEMS

Every week brings a new practical problem for someone to solve: a machine breaks down, a child returns from hospital temporarily in a wheelchair to find it is too large to fit in the lift, the lift breaks down and children work downstairs – away from their class – until it is repaired, a microphone fails to work and a crucial lesson is spent in silence, and so on. These situations are a nuisance but can usually be resolved quickly and easily. It may be useful to outline here some of the problems which appear insurmountable without major expense, or are recurrent and beyond the control of the school, and to indicate ways in which some schools have dealt with them.

Fire practice

Many of the schools with which I have had contact are concerned about arrangements for evacuation of handicapped pupils should there be a fire. Most schools are confident that *all* pupils can be evacuated speedily but arrangements do not always fully satisfy the local fire services. LEA's are involved in discussion to ensure that the legal safety requirements are met without great expenditure on chutes and external lifts.

My own school wrestled with this problem, eventually making plans which enable all children to be out of the building speedily. In classes with hearing-impaired pupils the teacher and children ensure the handicapped child knows why the room is suddenly being evacuated and makes sure this child is *in the middle of the class line* as it leaves for its appointed route to the playground. Physically-handicapped pupils who can walk also leave with their group – a friend helping the handicapped child on the stairs and the teacher checking that the whole class is present in the playground. Physically-handicapped pupils in wheelchairs present the greatest problem if they are not on the ground floor at the time of the fire drill.

Alan and Andrew could be 'bumped' downstairs if great care was taken. In the first and second year this was fairly easy as tutor groups were taught together and therefore a 'team' of four strong volunteers were 'trained' by the welfare assistant and link teacher (or pastoral head) to bring a wheelchair down the stairs. Training took place in tutorial time early in the school year. When the fire practice occurred the 'team' took the wheelchair to the top of the nearest stairs, waited until all other classes had passed, and then quickly and efficiently brought their friend gently down – two acting as brakes in front to stop the chair falling, whilst the others gently lowered it down each step – the teacher of the last group keeping a supervisory eye on proceedings until all were safely down.

There can be a danger in using children to help if all members of staff are not fully briefed and aware of the procedures and exit routes to be taken – an important point to remember where a school has a temporary change of staff, or supply teachers are needed. The following incident illustrates this danger.

Andrew:

was being taught on the *ground* floor in a room which had a fire escape staircase through the window. The designated route from this room was down the corridor and out of the main doors, but the new teacher took the class out via the escape window, instructing Andrew and team to follow the class next door down the corridor and to meet again outside the building. Andrew decided this was not on, he was going through the window with his class and his team saw to it that he did – much to the amusement of the rest of the class and the surprise of the teacher.

Although in this case the child was safely evacuated, the staff realized the potential danger and revised instructions. Third- and fourth-year sets and option groups presented a problem. The team was not always together in class. We decided that our system was dependent on chance, so the welfare assistant and pastoral head trained all the boys in the year group (group by group during tutorial time) to bring a wheelchair downstairs. Thus when the fire alarm rings any teacher can delegate four boys to take a chair down and they will know what to do.

A further complication arises where either a wheelchair is too heavy to bump down or the child would possibly be injured by such a method. John was such a case – he cannot support his head alone and has to be carried downstairs. He is light in weight and can be carried easily by most adults, but it was agreed (in a staff meeting held to discuss this problem) that he would leave the room with his group but wait with his teacher at the top of the stairs in the safety area behind the fire doors until everything had cleared, and a male teacher would be sent to bring him down. This system has worked on the few occasions it has been necessary to use it.

Breaks and lunchtime provision for handicapped pupils

This is another area where problems can arise unless anticipatory plans are made. Many physically-handicapped pupils are unable to cope with very cold or damp weather – they need to be indoors, but it is not sufficient to let them wait together in a corridor, foyer or cloakroom: this can discourage integration unless their friends can join them. To counteract this situation it may be possible to allocate a room to be staffed by the pastoral team on a rota basis in place of normal break duty. At lunchtime in the school where this system operates the house staff have formed a voluntary rota with the welfare assistant, liaison teacher and some sixth formers. Any handicapped pupil may come to this room with a few friends to play quiet games, read, talk or work. In another school pupils are allowed to use the library at these times. I personally feel the first facility is the better – the handicapped pupils are not separated from their peers and can use their time as they choose.

Transport

The transport situation in some areas can be extremely trying to schools which are attempting to provide a balanced curriculum for the handicapped pupils and offer extracurricular activities. It is rarely possible for such pupils to stay after school – transport arrangements are rigidly timetabled to bring all the special schoolchildren to and from their schools and it is difficult, if not impossible, to bring more flexibility into the system. This inevitably has an indirect effect on the curriculum of some pupils. It may be impossible to provide transport during a games lesson to take the handicapped pupil to hydrotherapy, or the handicapped pupils may not arrive at their schools on time each day (many special schools have a later start than ordinary schools and one bus may deliver pupils to both schools). A child may miss registration, or assembly or form period (tutorial time). The pastoral team should be aware of the effect this can have on the integration of that child into his/her group. Many handicapped pupils leave home very early if they are the first to be collected by the LEA transport, and arrive home late. This puts a great physical strain on the child, but staff should also realize the effect this can have on a child's work. Alan's situation illustrates this.

Alan:
was collected at 7.30 a.m. each day from home reaching school at 8.35 a.m. – the bus having toured the area collecting others en route. After school he had to wait for transport for over 45 minutes, arriving home very late. In Alan's case it was possible to alleviate the situation using private transport, but many children are not so fortunate.

174

Patrick:
used to arrive home at 5.30 p.m. as he was the last to be dropped off. He arrived home tired, irritable and in no state to start homework – all he wanted to do was sleep. Now, to enable him to reach home an hour earlier, he leaves on the earlier school bus and has to leave class five minutes before the end of lessons each day. Although this sometimes presents problems for his teachers they appreciate the necessity for it and recognize that Patrick's work has improved.

Detentions

Another problem – linked to the closely timetabled transport situation – is that of detentions. It is obviously impracticable for handicapped pupils to remain after school for any reason, if, by doing so, they cannot get home. When a class has detention, therefore, and one child is excluded, other pupils feel the situation is unfair and this can cause friction in the group. It is possible to set special detention work for the handicapped pupil to be done at home, although this may still be regarded as a 'let-off'. Andrew belonged to a group frequently in trouble. For two years he did work at home whenever the class was detained, until one day he caused so much trouble that a particular teacher refused to exempt him from the class detention – Andrew had to return for fifteen minutes every night (the time available before his bus arrived), until the detention was completed. Few of us realized what this meant to him, but on the Friday following he was heard excitedly telling a visitor that he had detention *with* his class and did not have work to do at home. He felt at last that he was accepted and was being treated like everyone else. We have much to learn!

THE CURRICULUM

Any ordinary school taking children with serious handicaps must be prepared to offer some flexibility in its curriculum and modify both materials and teaching objectives where necessary (Warnock, 1978, 11.10). The child's educational needs must be met, but they also need to be planned and timetabled together with services provided by area health authorities (Warnock, 1978, 11.39 and 11.41). The

Warnock Report draws attention to the significance of the organization of a school for slow learners or children with moderate learning difficulties and suggests where mixed ability groupings are in operation the curriculum will need special attention – particularly in relation to selection of aims and materials – if these children are to make useful progress (Warnock, 1978, 11.10).

If special educational provision is viewed in a much wider framework than the statutory concept, aims and objectives need to be examined for each and every child. Warnock concludes that one child in five will at some time during their school career require some form of special educational provision (1978, 3.17). Many of these children are not permanently or severely handicapped and can be taught in ordinary schools. Therefore the curriculum must be geared to meet the needs of these children. Once the main curriculum has been decided, the curriculum for the handicapped child should be built up as closely as possible to the tutor's timetable. Modifications will have to be made according to the individual needs of each child. The support teacher for the deaf, for example, will look at the needs of each child and decide which lessons the child can be withdrawn from for individual tuition; at which lessons the support teacher's presence will benefit the child; whether the child can manage alone in tutorial period/registration and assembly; when is the best time to arrange a speech lesson, etc.

Having structured a timetable to commence in September the support teacher must be prepared to alter this if at any time the child's needs alter.

Michael:
in the second year, needed minimal support in Science and Maths lessons. Therefore his timetable allowed him to go alone to these lessons, the support teacher following up work later in the week when necessary. During the spring term, however, topics were being covered in these lessons which Michael found difficult. The support teacher rearranged his timetable – and her own – so that she came with him to lessons to help him through this period.

Profoundly deaf pupils obviously need more help – both in class and individually – from their support teacher if it is thought they will benefit from education in an ordinary school. Their curriculum may be more limited than that of partially-hearing pupils, because they require more individual work in a one-to-one situation, and therefore it must be very carefully structured to meet the interests and skills of the child yet sufficiently broad to provide a good general education.

Physically-handicapped pupils may be constrained by their particular disability and it is frequently in practical subjects where limitations occur. If it is at all possible for the child to take these lessons than I believe they should be given the opportunity to do so, and only where their disability is likely to endanger them or to present too great a challenge should the timetable be modified.

John:
has minimal arm movement and virtually no strength to lift. He can write and hold a brush providing his arm is supported: he does not take woodwork, metalwork, cookery or textiles but his timetable allows him to join other sets for art and design when his own group go to the heavy craft lessons.

David:
needs intensive physiotherapy each day at a hospital unit. His schedule has had to be organized around this and it has been possible to arrange for him to omit a second language and games from the curriculum. The hospital helps enormously by arranging his appointments to coincide with the school timetable – an excellent example of co-operation between the two services.

Most of the physically-handicapped pupils in schools I have visited do not participate in games or PE lessons with their peers, but return at this time to their special school for swimming or wheelchair games (if transport can be arranged) or are timetabled for a library period or their physiotherapy. I feel it is important that whatever the modifications decided for each child they need to be made after consultation and discussions with the special school staff and *before* the timetable is given to the child on the first day of school. The structure needs to be clear from the start and should only be altered if serious difficulties arise; otherwise the child may be confused and attention will again be drawn to his handicap.

THE WORK OF THE PASTORAL TEAM

Some of the work of the team may be summarized as follows.

1. Liaison with special school before and after transfer.
2. Meet, interview and give continued support to children.

3. Personalize school to family and maintain supportive relationship.
4. Selection of tutors, tutor groups and support for staff involved with child.
5. Maintain effective records and disseminate information to staff.
6. Prepare child's timetable and monitor child's progress.
7. Maintain daily contact with link/liaison/support teachers and welfare assistant.
8. Maintain professional contact with outside agencies and arrange case conferences when necessary.
9. Evaluation of child's progress – educationally and socially.
10. Counselling of child and parents, both ongoing support and in crises.
11. Mobilize resources of community when needed, eg career advisers.
12. Attend in-service training courses and encourage others to do so.

The pastoral team is centrally involved in any scheme of integration, initially in ensuring a smooth transfer from special to ordinary school. Later, they have the care of each child to consider and this involves liaison with other teachers, the family, outside agencies and all support services. The process of monitoring and evaluating each child's progress to ensure he/she is deriving benefit from attendance at ordinary school is particularly important.

Pastoral staff must be capable of counselling the child and its family – not only in times of crisis, but to ensure new situations are not traumatic or threatening and to provide information and support, particularly when important decisions have to be made, for example, at option choice and exam entry; for career choice, etc.

Many pastoral heads are eager to attend appropriate in-service training courses on working with handicapped pupils and encourage their colleagues to read widely. The Warnock Report makes pertinent comment on the training of teachers and content of such courses. If integration schemes are to expand short courses (Warnock, 1978, 12.35) are urgently required to prepare the classroom teacher in ordinary schools.

THE FUTURE

One of the aims of educating handicapped pupils in ordinary schools is that at the end of their school career they will have increased opportunities for their future. If this is to be achieved the school and community must continually assess the needs of these children as their education proceeds. Good vocational counselling and guidance is needed at a very early stage, that is, the option choice (in the third year), and at this time a specialist careers adviser, the school careers teacher, and other professionals in contact with the child should be involved (Warnock, 1978, Chap. 10). This involvement will be an ongoing process over the next two years.

People who have had experience in placing handicapped persons in suitable employment or on further education courses are increasingly concerned about the lack of provision available. Whilst it is important to encourage these young people to aim high and to believe in their ability to succeed it is equally our responsibility to help them to realistic perception of the world outside.

To close, I quote from the Warnock Report (1978, 10.4): 'It is in society's own interest to invest more in opportunities for education, training, and other forms of support for these young people in order to minimise their disadvantages.' If this can be done then we can justifiably work to raise the expectations of children with special educational needs and increase provision for them in ordinary schools.

9

Disruptive Pupils

Jim Askins
(Counsellor and Head of Careers, Billericay School)

ROOTS OF DISRUPTIVE BEHAVIOUR

To examine the 'causes' of disruptive behaviour is not necessarily productive. The factors that have given rise to habitual modes of behaviour often lie in the earlier childhood of the pupil and are no longer open to change. To look for causes can carry the risk of allocating blame or simply labelling a pupil or his background. We need to concentrate most attention on the factors that may be open to change in the pupils' present situation. The factors below increase the risk of a pupil's becoming disruptive.

1. Insecurity. The pupil may feel threatened and be reacting defensively. These threats are commonly those to his social competence, masculinity, status or his sense of emerging maturity.
2. Background. The pupil's home and neighbourhood may convey a picture of a hostile and threatening world. The pupil may see violent and aggressive individuals succeed or may have learned such behaviours himself and obtained things he wants in this way.
3. Cathartic. The pupil's behaviour may act as a release for inner tensions.
4. Frustration. The pupil may be unable to achieve goals by legitimate means, and his frustration leads to demonstrative behaviour.
5. Self-concept. The pupil may see himself or wish to see himself

as tough or daring and actively demonstrate and defend this picture of himself.

6. Threshold of arousal. Some pupils will be more easily stimulated by others, by the media, or by stress or excitement to behave in extreme ways.

7. Relative strength of inhibition. Some pupils are less able than others to check their behaviour or are less open to control by others in a situation.

8. Dominance. A pupil may attempt to control a situation by 'getting in first'. The pupil, rather than wait for a situation to develop that he may or may not be able to cope with, instigates behaviours that are familiar to him.

9. Behavioural skills. Many pupils have not had the opportunity to learn the skills of behavioural control and have learnt few alternative ways of expressing themselves.

Those pupils who are attracted to disruptive behaviour may start to participate in disruptive activity and eventually achieve the reputation of being a 'trouble-maker'. Hamblin (1975) traces the steps through affinity, affiliation to conversion and signification very clearly. The pupil attracted by disruption at some point chooses to participate in the behaviours involved. The conversion to a disruptive identity progresses as he sees himself as different and the others, the 'snobs' and 'scholars', negatively. Return from his new identity is made less likely by the public remarks of teachers, their overt disapproval and punishments. The adolescent finds an identity confirmed by others when he is least sure of himself and eventually can no longer gain rewards in school other than those that his reputation for being difficult bring him.

In looking into the background of disruptive behaviours it is more productive to ask what is maintaining the behaviour than to guess at the causes. The pay-offs, or what the pupil 'gets out' of his behaviour, are more open to change than his past. The setting in which disruption occurs and the responses of others to it may be the important aspect for the teacher.

ANALYSIS OF DISRUPTIVE BEHAVIOUR

The aim of the analysis of a pupil's disruptive behaviour is to produce an explanation of the behaviours that will provide the basis

181

for the strategies adopted to change these behaviours. Rather than merely label a pupil as aggressive or maladjusted, we should try to determine the meaning that the behaviour of which we disapprove holds for him. Labels are categorizations that incorporate expectations and tend to be prescriptive rather than descriptive. Our main question is what maintains the behaviour rather than what causes it. Causes are rarely open to any modification, so our focus is on the behaviour as it operates within specific settings. Analysis should emphasize three elements: the pupil, the situation and the behaviour.

The pupil's characteristics have to be studied to allow us to adapt the processes of behaviour change so that they are appropriate to him. Our major concern is what strengths the pupil possesses that may be built on (interests, skills, potential and actual abilities), and what weaknesses need to be strengthened (language skills, perceptions, attitudes). The background of the pupil may help us to understand how some behaviours are learned and maintained. The family presents a model of the world to the pupil, and for many pupils the unintended outcome of communication in the family is the creation of a hostile world in which only the tough survive. As a result the pupil may be interpreting the messages and behaviours of adults and peers so that he perceives threat in situations where none is present. He then reacts to this supposed threat in aggressive ways. The neighbourhood may confirm a picture of a threatening world and present models of anti-social behaviour which the pupil adopts. In the context of his social contacts we need to know who supports or sanctions his behaviour and who he wishes to be like. Once we have a clearer idea of these things, strategies for modifying his behaviour can be developed.

The situations in which the pupil behaves badly or well need to be identified and understood. The timing of disruptive behaviour may offer a guide to effective intervention. Troublesome behaviour may occur at different points in a lesson; during structured or informal activities, while the pupil is engaged in new or routine tasks or at other times. The timing may be a guide as to the occurrence of 'triggers' for the disruptive behaviour. We also need to examine the pupil's expectations of the situation and what expectations of his behaviour are already held by others who form part of the situation. The pupil may be reacting to what he sees as threats to his self-esteem or fulfilling the roles sent to him by others. He may be fulfilling a function within the class as a 'clown' 'martyr', opinion-leader, cynic or reacting to expectations – it does not matter whether his perceptions are accurate or inaccurate. The hard fact is that they shape his behaviour. It is only common sense to identify the situations which precipitate breakdown in behaviour and to anticipate the pupil's reactions.

Incidents of bad behaviour can be analysed within the setting, identifying 'triggers' that set off the incident and the significance of the other people present as follows.

1. What are the relevant characteristics of those involved in the incident?
2. How do those involved perceive the situation? What motives, intentions and justifications do they hold with respect to the situation?
3. What were the relationships between the participants? What do they believe to be true of each other and what do they expect of each other?
4. What was at issue? What differing beliefs about the issue do the participants hold? What threats did they perceive?
5. What was the significance of the audience? What did the participants believe were the expectations of the audience? How do the participants believe the audience were judging the incident?
6. What was the actual outcome of the incident? What were the intended outcomes from the incident?

The disruptive behaviour itself needs to be accurately described. Variations in the behaviour, and not only consideration of what initiates, but also what concludes bouts of disruption need to be identified. The behaviour that gives concern needs also to be described in terms of its frequency and intensity. The pupil can sometimes be persuaded to co-operate at this stage by recording his own behaviour in a daily diary whilst teachers can use simple report forms to record instances of disruption. These initial records are important as they form the basis for evaluating any change brought about by processes in which the pupil participates. Pupils find their own and teachers' reports useful. Their own records are particularly useful in helping them perceive change although I have found they need initial help in knowing how much to record. Many girls are avid diarists and for them the recording of detailed incidents is very full and most helpful to them.

The relation between different situations and behaviour can also be considered in terms of what initiates and what maintains the behaviours. In what situations is the pupil disruptive? In what situations does he behave well? In each case, what rewards this behaviour (what is the *pay-off*)? In comparing good and bad behaviour, what factors trigger or initiate it? What maintains the pattern of behaviour?

The 'pay-off' or rewards the pupil receives for behaviours must be identified. Rewarding positive behaviour increases the likelihood of it reappearing while the reinforcement of disruptive behaviour has to be prevented. 'Pay-off' gives meaning to behaviour. This concept moves the diagnosis from labelling behaviour as 'attention-seeking' or 'showing-off' to looking at the purpose of the behaviour from the pupil's perspective.

The analysis is a shared activity with contributions coming from many sources including the pupil, his teachers and his parents. The teachers involved with the pupil have a major contribution to make. They not only can observe the pupil in many settings but, if behaviour change is to occur, their involvement is vital. Initially it is helpful to invite written or spoken comment on the pupil that can then form the basis for a conference with the subject teachers and the pastoral teachers concerned.

The case conference is intended to allow discussion and clarification of the problem, eventually leading to a summary of the pupil's relevant strengths and weaknesses and the organization of a programme of behaviour change. More than one meeting may be needed but it is important that sufficient time is given to allow negative feelings about the pupil to be expressed and subsequent suggestions for action to be developed in an atmosphere of positive concern. The organizer of such meetings needs to ensure that the meeting moves towards less rigid labelling of the pupil and an increasing clarity as to possible meanings of his behaviour. The analysis should provide a clear picture of the skills that the pupil possesses that are to be built on and encouraged, the skills he needs to learn and the system of rewards and constraints that will be utilized for him. The pupil will meet care and concern combined with firm control and consistent demands. An example of the type of simple analysis is shown below.

Preliminary skills analysis for a 14-year-old disruptive girl

Skills possessed	Skills needed
Can become interested and involved in school work	Accept correction without reaction
Good at practical tasks	Cope with frustration at failure to progress
Can work well on her own	Learning skills to allow progress
Can be polite and well-mannered.	Co-operation with others

Other factors: responds well to praise.

Constraints	Rewards
If she starts a lesson badly she should leave and return when the rest of the class is settled (she understands that she can settle better when there are fewer distractions).	She will be allowed to work in the pottery room on days when she is behaving elsewhere.
Correction should be kept to a minimum and she understands that she will leave the room if she responds aggressively.	Some of her practical work will be displayed in the library.
	As far as practicable she will receive attention whenever she is working quietly and quiet encouragement for this.
Her behaviour will be recorded by herself and her teachers and reviewed daily with her form tutor.	All examples of co-operation with staff or fellow pupils will be noted on her report card.

A BASIS FOR CHANGE

Change of behaviour is not an event but a process. Instant and effective means of behaviour change for disruptive pupils as yet are undiscovered. We can arrange supports, controls and teach new skills, but even the most co-operative pupil will need time to change. Unrealistic expectations of a metamorphosis, rather than a growth in behavioural terms, are dangerous. The pupil is unlikely to drop a maladaptive, habitual mode of behaviour until he has mastered a new adaptive way of coping with difficult situations.

Our attempts at facilitating behaviour change are not to be seen as a total onslaught on the pupil's behaviour, but a slow, careful approach, starting with the smallest steps in those areas where success is most likely. Only when the pupil has started to discover that he can manage his behaviour may it be possible to work on the more complex and more extreme areas. Staff need to appreciate this, which means they have to be involved in the process.

Attitude change

Attitudes as an integral part of behaviour need to be considered in any attempt to facilitate change in disruptive pupils. I have used two basic concepts from attitude theory; the concept of attitudes as functional and work on cognitive dissonance. Attitudes can be seen as functional, helping an individual's attempts to gain rewards or avoid unpleasant experience. Dissonance is seen to occur when two elements of a person's beliefs are contrary to one another. Dissonance is particularly strong when a person carries out an act which is at variance with his attitudes. The result of such an act is frequently an attempt by the individual to find support for his actions thus changing the attitudes. A pupil who dislikes a subject may receive good marks for some work and then justify this in terms of the subject being important for him and thus modify his original rejection of the work.

Attitudes represent a readiness or predisposition to act in a particular way. They affect the manner in which situations and persons are perceived. To cope with a new situation we have to understand them. Initially we can only do this by imposing our meanings based on what we consider to be significant about the people or situations we meet. This is a frequent occurrence and based on our previous experience we rapidly categorize people in order to behave towards them in appropriate ways. This categorization is liable to many inaccuracies, particularly when it is based on a very limited amount of information. It can become a source of difficulty if we do not continue to build up a picture of others and hold rigidly to our first impressions. Categorization can extend to the familiar 'halo effect' if crudely applied. A person exhibiting some characteristics of a 'type of person' is assumed to possess the other qualities we attribute to that 'type'. We expect bank managers to be similar and mechanics to be alike and assume quite erroneously that individuals of either group will conform in many respects to the picture we hold of them. A pupil who is disruptive is often assumed to be delinquent, dishonest, hostile, unreliable and disturbed, and our erroneous expectations produce what we suspected when in fact it was far from the true reality of the picture. Similarly the category 'teacher' for some pupils carries unfortunate assumptions about the person concerned.

The functions of attitudes in furthering aims and defending against threat may be extended. Rewards reinforce attitudes: if an attitude means that a pupil gains approval from others whose opinion he values, he is more likely to persist in that attitude. Defences against threat would include those attitudes that are evident when a pupil fears being 'shown up' or 'losing face'. Girls particularly may hold very aggressive attitudes to teachers who use sarcasm, ridicule or seem patronizing. Attitudes that are used to defend will be strengthened by threats, thus confirming a pupil's view of those threatening him as hostile to him. Attitudes that maintain a pupil's view of himself are also important. If a pupil values toughness, daring, standing up for oneself or aggression, it will be unlikely that he will wish to behave differently until he experiences dissatisfaction with himself. A pupil's attitudes extend to other pupils and teachers as he gives meaning to his experiences in school. He develops from his own attitudes an explanation of other's intentions, motives and behaviour. Adolescence is also a time of change: the young are self-critical and attitudes may well be questioned, particularly as coping with entry to employment comes closer.

The following factors may be considered as heightening the chance of attitude change occurring:

1. A pupil participating in an activity that is at variance with his attitudes. Initially this may be less threatening if a pupil is introduced to the required behaviours through role-play or simulations where he can experience different standpoints. These can be very simple. A pupil can be asked with respect

to a particular incident: 'How do you think a pupil who wanted to do well would have reacted?'

The ideas can be role-played with the pupil trying the new behaviour and the teacher's position in response to it. Situations of a young worker seeing a supervision over lateness or similar situations give opportunities for learning new behaviours. These activities can then be carried into the classroom setting. The pupil as an active participant actually carrying out new behaviours is the most powerful element in behaviour change.

2. The pupil's less extreme attitudes are far more likely to change than those he holds most strongly. This is taken into account and the process of change starts from small, easily-achieved steps rather than a threatening attack on the pupil's total behaviour. A pupil who valued toughness is not likely to be 'good' in class but a boy like this responded well to help with revision for tests and organization of his homework in order to promote his career chances. He did not cease to value toughness, but also valued competence in school work. Eventually he dropped much of the behaviour that he saw as unnecessary, accepting that if he needed continually to prove his toughness, he demonstrated that he was very unsure of it himself.

3. Support for change will enhance the likelihood of the pupil re-evaluating his attitudes. If the teachers that he likes display desired attitudes, it will help towards change. Peers are important in this respect: the stress on group work later in this chapter recognizes the importance of the other pupils in facilitating or inhibiting change. Change can also be supported by helping the pupil to understand the links between attitudes and behaviour. The pupil can learn how to examine the costs of his attitudes and to assess alternatives (an example is given on p. 189, fig. 9.1).

4. A feeling that previous attitudes were of little worth is likely to maintain a change in attitude. We can help a pupil who is changing to evaluate his previous attitudes in this way.

5. New attitudes that are seen as a positive part of the self are more likely to be maintained. We can reinforce this by providing information to the pupil that confirms his positive value and shows how his new actions support this view.

Attitudes can be modified, not by exhortation or threat, but by the involvement of the pupil in activities that will create dissonance and support for attitude change towards positive and worthwhile directions. To say of disruptive pupils, 'their attitude is all wrong', contains some truth but they are unlikely to change without help in acquiring the skills of managing their behaviour. It is simple to help a pupil explore his attitudes to a subject, as fig. 9.1, used in one interview, shows.

Behaviour change

Programmes of behaviour change for disruptive pupils will aim to help them accept responsibility for their actions and understand the part they play in what happens to them. The pupil will be an active

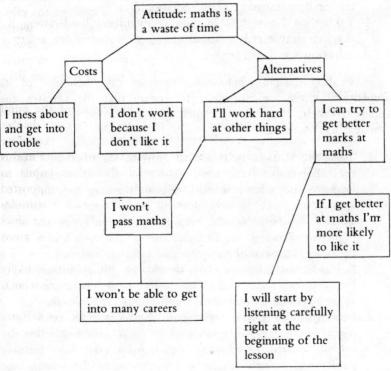

Fig. 9.1

participant in developing appropriate behaviours directed towards the attainment of worthwhile goals. The pupil will learn to initiate positive experiences and to develop self-control. The skills learnt can be transferred to other settings and will be an important contribution to the pupils' future careers.

Programmes of change need initially to give the pupil the idea that he can succeed. Small steps early in the process are ideal, they bring rapid results. From the initiation of single examples of co-operative behaviour that are easy to achieve, we can build further steps toward change, rather than attempting the unrealistic target of instant modification of an entire behaviour pattern. Examples of these initial goals pupils have attempted include:

1. Arriving at lessons on time (avoids initial bad impression).
2. Greeting teachers pleasantly (sets a new pattern early in an interaction).
3. Refraining from comment when instructed to do something (rather than initiating a confrontation).
4. Taking on a new task in school, organizing fund-raising for charity, simple redecoration, etc. (a new outlet for assertive behaviours and energies).

Rewarding desirable behaviour increases the likelihood of its repetition, while we also need to ensure that the rewards for disruptive behaviour can no longer operate. Success depends upon the teachers ensuring:

1. The behaviours to be rewarded must be identified and within the capabilities of the pupil. The pupil is not just asked to 'improve' but what is wanted – e.g. only asking questions in an appropriate way (clearly defined) – is specified. The task should also be achievable. An initial step may be to ask a pupil for silence in the first five minutes of each lesson – not the unrealistic step of complete silence in all lessons.
2. Rewards for improvement should be given immediately. Every teacher will need to know the 'target' behaviours and, as far as possible, reward the pupil as quickly as possible.
3. Rewards need to be appropriate. In most cases with older pupils realistic praise, quietly given, that does not invite the ridicule of the peer group seems most effective. Younger pupils will often respond well to house or form points or similar token forms of reward that can be accumulated.

4. Rewards need to be consistent early in a programme. Pupils who attempt change often feel their efforts are unnoticed and early recognition of their efforts may prevent abandonment of the attempt by those pupils who have not yet learned to look for longer-term rewards.
5. Negative behaviours should be ignored as far as possible. In order for 'ignoring' to be used, the pupil must know what is being ignored and that ignoring a behaviour is rejection, not acceptance of a behaviour. The pupil also must not be allowed to exploit the ignoring of a behaviour and still must face the consequences of his actions if he persists with them.
6. Standards should increase as the pupil progresses. The pupil, as he masters simple behaviour control, should extend this to more areas and to the positive directing of his behaviour to his goals in school and in the future.

Models of appropriate behaviours are of great value in teaching pupils positive ways of coping with situations where they experience difficulties. The models should be people with whom there is no easy communication. Tape-recordings, or even videotapes of pupils showing successful ways of coping with situations, and expressing positive attitudes, are not difficult to produce and the 'models' invariably benefit from the experience themselves. The opportunity to join in groups, work with suitable models and a school system that allows for older pupils to play a helping role with younger ones, also facilitates this technique. I have found older pupils keen to produce modelling material. They are often beginning to find disruptive behaviour immature, and the imminence of entering employment is already forcing many of them to re-examine the costs of attitudes and behaviours that have prevented success in school. Ex-pupils who have started work, or even those experiencing difficulty, often want to advise other pupils and provide attractive examples. Taped discussions with young workers has produced comments like, 'I wish I'd done more to get a job and wasted less time trying to be "famous", and 'We might have laughed at the "scholars", but they're laughing now'.

Role-play is an active and effective way of teaching new behaviours and finding out the effect of one's behaviour on others. It should not be simply a chance to express aggression, but the pupil, by taking different standpoints, should begin to learn to anticipate the reaction of others. I often initiate role-play by saying to a pupil who has been telling me of a negative encounter, 'Let's see if I've got it right, I'll be you and you be the teacher.' This is followed up by seeing how they felt as the teacher and then perhaps experimenting with different approaches. Familiar situations, as in complaining about poor goods or incorrect change in shops, or coping with false accusations, provide a way for the pupil to learn positive ways of asserting themselves and, by taking the other's part, learn how to handle criticism and how to apologize in a meaningful way. This technique is invaluable when used to help pupils anticipate situations and prepare a variety of ways of coping with them.

The peer group is important to adolescents. They are an important source of ideas and approval during the development of identity during adolescence. The opinion-leaders of these groups, the sociometric 'stars', are important and can have a powerful influence on disruptive groups. Work aimed at behaviour modification with groups will need to start with these pupils. The individual pupil who is attempting to change his behaviour can be helped enormously by peers. Friends are a useful source of information on behaviour and by participating with the individual in recording his behaviour, act as a check on impulsive reactions in the classroom setting. Friends' support and encouragement during change will be a more valued reinforcement of behaviours than much that teachers could offer by way of rewards. For friends to help, they may need to learn to give positive feedback on behaviours, and ideas for this are included later on work with groups. Many disruptive pupils are rejected by their peers and teaching them to develop friendly, co-operative patterns of interaction may be an important part of facilitating change. I have found pupils who have experienced difficulties keen to help others and with support, often working in small groups, they have proved most successful at helping individuals.

The peer group can prove a hindrance to behaviour change: they may resent a pupil's efforts to change and coerce him back to his former behaviours, or they may be cynical of his sincerity and of his ability to succeed. We must help the pupil to anticipate the reactions of other pupils, both positive and negative and help him devise means of utilizing the former and coping with the latter.

Parents remain a major influence on most adolescents, and can prove helpful in the process. The encouragement to 'stand up for yourself' and not to 'be pushed around' is often interpreted by the son or daughter in a very aggressive way. Parents often are willing to examine the communications with their sons and daughters for messages that are interpreted in unintended ways. They can help to explain that self-assertion need not be aggressive. Parents can also help to understand the stress and difficulty of changing behaviour, offering realistic praise and belief in their children's ability to change. Parents can help each other and I have found groups of interested parents enjoy learning about adolescence and its difficulties. These groups have appeared as a result of a request from a parent teacher association to talk about adolescence and also have been most useful when a friendship group amongst the pupils starts to get into trouble. Many parents are coerced into permitting activities for their children which they are unsure about because 'everyone else is going'. In a group they can work out their ideas of what they will encourage and what they will not permit.

The evaluation of the process involves checking on the pupil's progress. Clumsy checking can lead to resentment and resistance, while monitoring that involves the pupil can further the aims of the programme. The pupil will understand that the recording of his behaviour is temporary and in the initial stages we need to evaluate the programme as well as giving the pupil a measure of his emerging control. The staff involved with the pupil can note the frequency of both positive and negative behaviours or assess the change in intensity of a behaviour. This also reminds them that the pupil is involved in a developing process, not an instant conversion. The staff can use simple record sheets either carried by the pupil or retained by the staff and then collated by the form tutor.

'On report' systems, where the pupil has a blank timetable on which the staff comment at the end of each lesson, are common. These often help a pupil to explain to his peers that he 'has' to behave, thus reducing the likelihood of their scorn as he attempts to be 'good'. Self-set targets for particular lessons with forms of self-checking are also effective. Pupils can be encouraged to keep a 'behavioural' diary recording their feelings as well as their behaviour. In some circumstances friends can act as monitors and their presence in this role can help as a constant reminder of the pupil's targets. Whatever strategies are employed in evaluation it is important that the pupil understands their real purpose and that eventually, as he accepts full responsibility for his own actions, external measures will become unnecessary.

The way in which setbacks, where the pupil reverts to former disruptive activities, are dealt with is crucial. The pupil may immediately feel he cannot manage to change. The response at the time should convey disapproval of the behaviour, but belief in the pupil's ability to make continued progress. Later analysis of actual incidents with the pupil can help to show how the breakdown occurred and what alternatives are possible in future similar situations. An example of this type of analysis drawn out with a fourteen-year-old girl is given in fig 9.2. The events were role-played to clarify the situation, to explore feelings on both sides and particularly to experiment with alternatives. An analysis of this type could have been portrayed in a 'comic strip' form, or other diagrammatic presentations (see fig 9.3). The suggestions for alternatives were worked out with the pupil and it was she who set her next target of learning to apologize, practising through role-play and then actually apologizing to the teacher concerned.

The maintenance of change can be facilitated by continuous reviewing of progress and ensuring that staff continue to reward the new ways of coping appropriately, even though less frequently. Support from friends proves invaluable as the following example shows.

Jane and Gill worked out a useful way of supporting Jane's attempts to keep out of trouble. Jane was given ten 'points' for each lesson and Gill subtracted points for each interruption. At the end of the week they would both go out if Jane had more than 100 points. With 200 points they would go to a nearby town; with 100 points just to the youth club.

Group work

Group work has the twin advantages of economy and effectiveness. A greater number of pupils can be worked with in a given time, and effectiveness is increased due to the help pupils can give each other, the variety of viewpoints available to each pupil, the opportunity for immediate feedback on the effect of an individual's behaviour, and the increased opportunities for role-play, discussion, exercises and simulations.

Starting group work with disruptive pupils needs careful preparation. The group should have a clear purpose and be led in such a way as to provide control that ensures the safety of the group. We may expect the group initially to be restless as they get

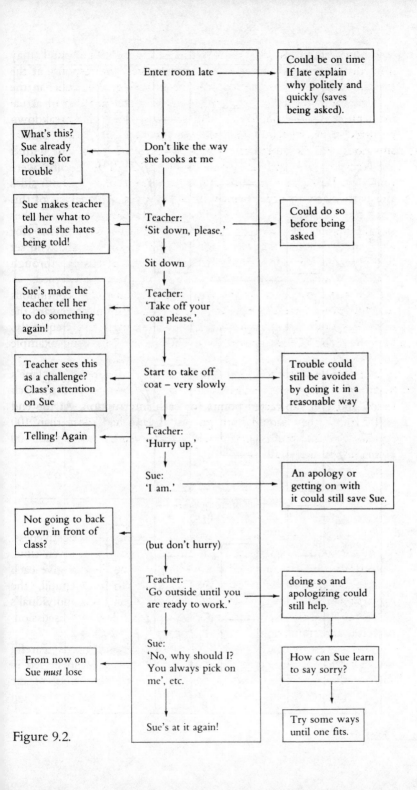

Enter room late → Could be on time If late explain why politely and quickly (saves being asked).

What's this? Sue already looking for trouble ← Don't like the way she looks at me

Sue makes teacher tell her what to do and she hates being told! ← Teacher: 'Sit down, please.' → Could do so before being asked

Sit down

Sue's made the teacher tell her to do something again! ← Teacher: 'Take off your coat please.'

Teacher sees this as a challenge? Class's attention on Sue ← Start to take off coat – very slowly → Trouble could still be avoided by doing it in a reasonable way

Telling! Again ← Teacher: 'Hurry up.'

Sue: 'I am.' → An apology or getting on with it could still save Sue.

Not going to back down in front of class? ← (but don't hurry)

Teacher: 'Go outside until you are ready to work.' → doing so and apologizing could still help.

How can Sue learn to say sorry?

From now on Sue *must* lose ← Sue: 'No, why should I? You always pick on me', etc.

Try some ways until one fits.

Sue's at it again!

Figure 9.2.

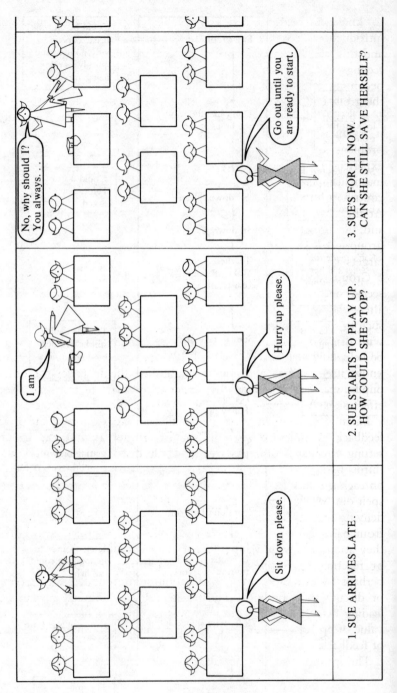

196

to know each other and co-operative exercises form a useful introduction. Conflict may occur as frustration or rivalry emerge and this will need careful handling as success in coping with these feelings is one of our aims. The group needs also to guard against becoming too insular and clear goals that will be aimed for outside the group setting need to be the main work of the group.

A group of this nature is more likely to be productive if initially it is small (about six to eight pupils), single sex (avoiding the problems of adjustment to the opposite sex that many adolescents experience) and not composed entirely of difficult pupils. The inarticulate, very aggressive or highly manipulative are unlikely to contribute much and can distort the positive aims of such a group. At the start, the work should be carefully planned and structured and the limits of what is expected and accepted defined. As the group learns to work positively together it can begin to set its own targets and develop its own programme.

Groups do not need to be set up as special or different. I have seen concerned teachers use the setting of a lunchtime or after-school club, careers sessions, discussion groups and projects such as fund-raising as a chance to develop meaningful group work with disruptive pupils. Friends often wish to help a pupil and can be helped to form a ready-made group that does not need to 'get to know itself'. Once a group is established the inclusion of other pupils who could be helped is easier to evaluate in terms of their effect on the group and the likely reaction of the group to them.

Initially a group may need help in learning to accept and give feedback. Simple exercises in smaller groups within the group setting can help. In threes, two pupils can discuss an issue while the third observes the impact their speech and non-verbal signals have on each other. The sort of activities the observer is looking for are spelt out with help from the group and should include interrupting, denying or ignoring what others say and preventing another person from participating. This can be shared and then places changed as they attempt to state their point of view without arousing hostility or reacting aggressively. These exercises need to be short – of perhaps two or three minutes' duration before pupils change places or discuss their findings. The teacher can, by joining in, and by leading discussion, keep the tone positive, helping pupils to see the value of criticism. They also see the immaturity of defensive denial of feedback.

The group can use simulations and exercises, role-play and

discussion, to explore situations that are familiar and that demand skill in handling. We begin with relevant, although indirectly related situations, containing the core of a problem that occurs within another setting. Role-play exercises can include simple outlines of making a mistake at work, complaining about unfair treatment from a supervisor or being falsely accused of saying something about a friend. The opportunity to experience all the roles in a situation teaches the pupils to understand the standpoint of others and the feelings they experience. Simulations that start to give more information about participants and more complex situations help to extend behavioural learning and the group can learn to share ideas about constructive ways of coping. A small group can be given the problem of young workers being picked on by a foreman or supervisor, a group falsely accused of vandalism, workers facing closure of a factory or friends who want to organize a holiday with different ideas and constraints on what they can do.

The holiday: a simulation

Bill, Joe, George, John and Garry are leaving school and want a short holiday before they start work. They must obviously choose something that is possible and will be acceptable to them all. They have limited amounts of money.

Bill   He has little preference over the type of holiday, but wants to go to Brightsands, a small seaside town. He has been there before and liked it and doesn't want to risk going somewhere that he might not like.

Joe   Joe would like a camping holiday. Ideally he would like them to use their bicycles and see how far they could get in a short while. He doesn't want to waste his time sitting around on a beach.

George   George wants to go to a big seaside resort where there is a lot going on, particularly in the evenings. He does not want, in his words, 'to get soaking wet and eat cold beans in a draughty field for a week'.

John   John's parents worry about him and are rather strict. They have said unless they know exactly what he is doing they will not let him go. John wants to go to college and his parents may not let him if he upsets them over this holiday. He wants to join the others very much indeed.

Garry   Garry wants to have fun. Planning tends to spoil things for him. He likes the unexpected and enjoys a laugh. He is the only one with a motor bike and is determined to take it wherever they go.

(Each pupil takes a card with just one description and starts to decide what to do as that person. They change cards after a set period and the teacher can introduce new ideas, like one of their uncles offering them a working holiday on a farm, George getting the offer of a job starting half way through the holiday, etc.)

It is important that the simulations and exercises are short and that the pupils can change places within the situation to experience more than just one standpoint. The simulation should aim at co-operative and constructive behaviours so that the pupils learn how to use new behaviours in flexible ways.

Discussion and activities should relate to familiar situations: being told off in class; deciding whether or not to skip a lesson; choosing between going out or revising. The pupils can share ideas and work out ways of coping with situations that prove difficult. It is particularly useful to examine actual or simulated situations in the group, asking them to identity the 'triggers' that lead to a breakdown. Paper exercises where the costs and benefits of decisions can be worked out (see p. 200) help to stimulate discussion and the pupils can start to see how attitudes, behaviour and the reactions of others are linked.

Examples of attitudes that lead to antagonistic behaviour can be given. The group may be able to see from a simple example: a pupil who accidentally bumps into another is unable to apologize because he equates saying sorry with being soft and therefore ends up in an unnecessary conflict.

Models of productive methods of behaving can be presented to the group in ways outlined earlier. Older pupils can help with groups of younger pupils and at the same time provide positive models of behaviour. An older pupil or a small group are often willing to talk about their school experience and relate the costs of their attitudes and behaviour to their relative success. Pupils who have changed and enhanced their career chances as a result are particularly useful. The group can prepare questions for an interview and follow this with a discussion. Care is needed in introducing older pupils as, unless they are well prepared, their presence may inhibit younger members of a group from expressing themselves.

The group can after a while start to formulate solutions to members' problems and provide invaluable feedback on behaviour. In the technique of brainstorming the whole group suggest any possible solutions to a pupil's difficulty. The group can then select the most likely solutions and evaluate the possible consequences. The discussions surrounding any technique can start to build a simple prudential morality in which behaviours are chosen that are most likely to be rewarding and carry the least risk of negative consequences. The group may also start to evaluate the members' contribution to the work. The teacher can help to identify who leads under different circumstances, what skills they contribute and help in sharing these strengths.

Group experience carries risks. Focusing on negative behaviours risks reinforcing negative attitudes and stimulating hostility and aggression. Individuals in the group may need protection from the others if they start to be defined as a scapegoat, clown or in some other negative way. Alertness and sensitivity to the processes at work within the group are essential. The timing of a session needs attention so that it closes on a positive note. The pupils should be encouraged to recall what has been learned and search for ways of quickly implementing this in school. Reporting back to the group at the next session ensures that the behavioural changes the group work towards are carried outside that setting.

EXAMPLE OF A SIMPLE PAPER EXERCISE

Your friends want you to go to an important youth club meeting to which you had already arranged to go. You have a project to do and have been told that you will be in trouble if it is not handed in tomorrow. So far the project is good, but needs to be finished properly.

What are the likely results of going out?

How could you keep the bad results of this to a minimum?

What are the results of staying in?

How can you explain to your friends if you stay in?

What other solutions can you think of?

10

Towards a Constructive View of Alcohol and Young People

James Cowley
(INSET, The Open University)

The use of alcohol is increasingly becoming a normal part of the experience of maturation for many young people. This statement can inspire a range of reactions from a quiet acceptance to a semi-paranoic state! To commence a review of this theme and the subsequent pastoral response in schools, I intend to try to overcome some of the emotion that surrounds the theme and to reduce it to being another aspect of adolescent behaviour.

One of the major problems in this area is that the press, the local community, some parents and possibly some colleagues are only too willing to sensationalize the drinking behaviour of young people, rather than to see it as an integral part of the business of growing up in our society. We occasionally find ourselves in a situation where young people are talking freely to us about the type of socializing that they do and the part that alcohol plays in it. At other times we may find that the main evidence of drinking comes from the occasional pupil returning to school having been drinking at lunchtime: the age-old phenomenon of the end of term lunchtime drink (which the press seem to have suggested is a 'new' phenomenon sweeping through the adolescent culture!) and the disco, where a small group turn up with bottles of alcohol or slip out for a drink at the local.

These comments are not intended to denigrate the difficulties caused by these types of incident, or the skill that is required in any teacher who has to handle them. They do pose difficulties, but the majority of schools handle them extremely well. They do, however, serve to illustrate that often we see alcohol and young people in terms of 'problems' related to the few young people who we can easily observe, rather than the more general awareness of the way in which the majority of young people may be using alcohol. This is not to say that all young people are having problems with alcohol, rather to suggest that if pastoral care is the system of support offered to all young people as they grow up, then the same support should be available to help them to talk through their developing drinking habits.

Pastoral care concerning drinking is then exactly the same as pastoral care over any aspect of adolescent behaviour. It is not primarily about the problems that a few children have, but a means of giving support, opportunity to talk, opportunity to explore practices and beliefs and giving this opportunity to all normal children.

Fundamental to this is the acceptance that we are living in a multisocial and multiracial society, in which alcohol will have very different meanings to different social, ethnic and religious groups. The pastoral teacher needs to be careful that he does not assume that everybody drinks in the same style as himself or that alcohol has the same meaning that it does for him. A teacher who is actively against young people drinking alcohol is unlikely to be of any help to those young people who have been brought up in an environment where regular drinking is an acceptable practice. Equally, the more usual case of a teacher who assumes that everyone in the group drinks and phrases his talking in such a way that it assumes a societal norm of social use of alcohol will not be supporting individuals from particular ethnic groups or from certain religious backgrounds. Sensitivity in this area is necessary to the highest degree.

HOW DO YOUNG PEOPLE USE ALCOHOL?

It is extremely important to read publicized research figures and reports carefully as there has been a tendency for some ill-found conclusions to be drawn in the past from research into young people's drinking habits. The result of this is that we can be looking out for those children with serious drinking problems and missing the much larger number of children to whom we could be giving effective advice and support as they developed their drinking style.

Of major assistance to us is the research carried out by Ann Hawker into young people's drinking habits where she questioned over 7,000 young people between the ages of thirteen and eighteen and provided a sound basis for drawing at least a partial picture of what type of drinking occurs among young people (Hawker, 1978). She surveyed many aspects of young people's drinking but for our purposes I will look at a small number of her findings. She carefully worded her questions to discriminate between those who had just tasted alcohol – for example, at a wedding reception – and those who had consumed an alcoholic drink. Table 10.1 (Hawker, 1978) shows the age at which young people reported they had their first proper drink.

It is important to recognize from this that during teenage years the majority of young people commence drinking. However, the *context* of that drinking would seem to be extremely important in determining whether we are concerned or not about it. For instance, surreptitious early drinking behind the off-licence is likely to be far more worrying than drinking a glass of watered-down alcohol with the Christmas dinner.

Table 10.2 (Hawker, 1978) shows the response to her question about the place of the first drink.

It is extremely important that we note that a large number of those questioned commenced their drinking at home. However, a significant number showed that they had commenced drinking in a pub, disco/club, at a friend's house, at a party or somewhere else, which would lead one to suspect that in these contexts they were a lot less likely to receive the degree of supervision of early drinking that the good home may provide.

It is also important to note that by the age of sixteen, 98 per cent had tasted alcohol in some context but 7 per cent had not continued to take it and considered themselves not to drink alcohol. This is extremely relevant to the way we talk with *groups* of young people about their drinking.

These results are borne out by other research into young people's drinking *consumption* and patterns (Davies and Stacey, 1972).

The pastoral teacher, unlike the 'moral reformer', cannot just take results like these to signify a particular type of problem that has to be helped or corrected. The pastoral teacher has the extremely difficult task of finding out what this use of alcohol *means* to young people. What is the social context for their drinking? What part does it play in giving them identity in the setting in which they find themselves? How do *they* see it? Unless we are able to see the

Table 10.1

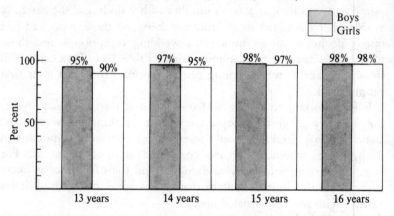

Q.27. "Have you *ever* tasted an alcoholic drink?"
% answering yes
Boys (n = 3427)   Girls (n = 3464)

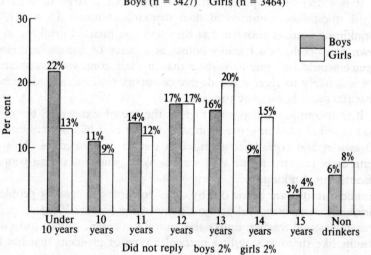

**Q.28. "How old were you when you had your first alcoholic drink?
Not just a sip – a real drink?"**
Boys (n = 3427)   Girls (n = 3464)

Did not reply   boys 2%   girls 2%

204

Table 10.2

Q.30. "Where were you when you had your first alcoholic drink?"
Boys (n = 3427)   Girls (n = 3464)

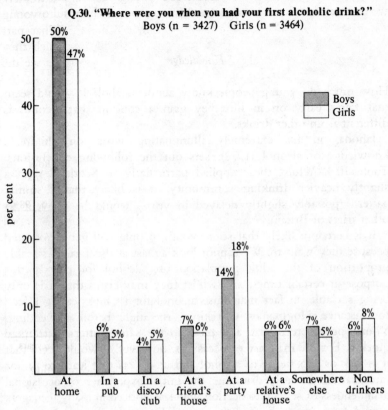

drinking as *they* see it, rather than as adults looking on with our own perceptions and preconceptions then we may fail to be able to give constructive support.

AN ANALYSIS OF SOCIAL BEHAVIOUR

One way I have found to be extremely helpful in attempting to gain at least a partial insight into the way young people perceive their behaviour is to analyse with them those factors which may mould that behaviour. In most aspects of social behaviour we can normally identify the following influences: knowledge; attitudes and values; previous experience; expectations of others; parental views; the media; situational constraints; the law. This gives us an insight

205

into what the use of alcohol means to a young person, and thereby we can start to assess whether his drinking may be harmful or not.

Knowledge

How much do young people know about alcohol? It would seem that fairly early on in life they gain a concept that alcohol is different from other drinks.

Jahoda, in his extremely illuminating work on children's knowledge of alcohol (1972), sets out the following conclusions: Table 10.3. Whilst these applied particularly to Scotland with a slightly heavier drinking community, it is likely that a similar pattern (possibly slightly delayed in years) would be relevant to other parts of Britain.

It is certainly likely that some young people will get intoxicated because they want to. We cannot look aghast at this fact. A sizeable proportion of the adult population use alcohol for exactly this purpose at certain times, and whilst they may claim that it is only being sociable, in fact many use alcohol for its intoxicating effect: for instance, Hogmanay, Christmas, the night before a wedding. Young people recognize and pick up the same pattern extremely quickly. For the majority of occasions, however, it would seem that it is lack of experience of alcohol and its effects that leads to minor intoxication. In early drinking, the initial experience of occasional drunkenness or semi-intoxication which is noticed in many teenagers would be seem to be due to an inability to know when to stop drinking. Alcohol has the peculiar effect of building up in the body. A young person stops drinking when he feels ataxic (swaying around), but the blood alcohol content in fact will rise for some time after that.

Certainly young people hold a number of myths about alcohol which the good pastoral teacher may be able to illuminate informally in group discussions: coffee as the immediate sobering agent; beer as far less alcoholic; two pints as the safe amount to drive with. All these are simple but extremely effective myths which we can dispel. Unfortunately we do still spend a lot of time in the more formal side of pastoral care, in social and health education, making sure that young people know every illness caused by alcohol and exactly how it is made, when perhaps there only are a very few major facts to be communicated.

Table 10.3

		Ages				
		4	6	8	10	14
Cognitive		Learning about specific drinks		Operational alcohol concept	Beginnings of verbal concept	Concept fully established
Personal influences	Parents	Serve as models, but little if any specific teaching		Provide some negative information (little factual) and exhortations, often contradicted by behaviour; some children in extreme drinking or abstaining groups begin to react against parents		Decline of parental influence
	Peers	Negligible until adolescence				Peers exert pressure towards alcohol; offer of first drink
External social influences (presumably including school, church, mass media)		No discernible impact		Learning of negative evaluations of alcohol and drinking on the part of authoritative persons and institutions; no trace of media effects		Negative evaluations from authority sources discounted; mass media support for drink
Resultants	Expressed attitude to drink	?	Neutral	Increasingly negative		Positive, with residual guilt?
	Declared intention about drinking in future	?	High: will do as everybody does	Substantially declining		Majority drink

207

The attitudes that young people adopt are extremely important and the pastoral teacher has a good opportunity to discuss with young people how they see alcohol. Going back to our influence upon social behaviour, it would seem that young people very quickly develop attitudes about drinkers and non-drinkers. In our society we tend to perceive the drinker as strong, masculine, sophisticated, sociable, whereas we see the non-drinker as weak, unsociable, unsophisticated. Young people to tend to see drinking as a symbol of sociability and manliness or adulthood. This acts as an extremely important predictor of their social behaviour. Take for example the young man who has taken his 98cc motor bike to the pub. When he meets up with his friends they will be buying a round of drinks. We may assume that he will not drink and drive, that he knows the facts and, knowing him, that he is an extremely careful road user. However, he has a strongly held view that the non-drinker is anti-social and weak. If he refuses the offer of drinks he has to assume this unattractive role for himself, and he will expect others to see him in this way. According to all the evidence we have available he will probably still drink alcohol in this context.

Perhaps one of the most significant sets of attitudes held in our society is the distinction between drinkers and non-drinkers. It has arisen from a long history of argument between the moderate drinkers and the abstainers but has come through to the majority of the population as an ambivalent and confused message. One of the most helpful ways that we can support young people is to discuss with them their views towards *all* different patterns of drinking, from non-drinking to heavy drinking (for instance, in cultures where this is determined by the work pattern, such as mining) and to attempt to help them to recognize the crucial importance of letting people at any specific time have complete freedom in what they drink (Cowley, Caruana and Rutherford, 1978).

Unfortunately our drinking culture is ambivalent and incongruous. There are many pressures on young people to drink, and many constraints upon them telling them not to drink. If we can at least encourage hosts always to provide an attractive range of non-alcoholic and low alcohol content drinks, we may begin to develop a society in which people are allowed to choose their drinking behaviour on a particular occasion.

Expectations of others

Expectations of others mould behaviour considerably. This is very similar to the previous point but concerns more the external pressure put on a young person by others within a group rather than just the way he perceives himself. We often hear about peer group pressure as a determinant of drinking, but one suspects that most young people are not actually pressurized into drinking. It is more that the group conclude that it is the natural thing to do in a particular setting. If the off-licence is there, then one or two members can probably persuade the others to buy some alcoholic drink. We can help young people to come to terms with the way that the group may mould their behaviour, and to decide how to handle cases where one or two members have an undue influence.

Previous experience

If the young person has unpleasant memories of drinking, he may take them into account next time. If, however, he enjoyed being intoxicated, he may want to do it again. People do not necessarily learn from experience; and many adolescents find it difficult to understand causal relationships: if I am violent on the way to a football match, it has nothing to do with my drinking. Pastoral care is concerned with helping young people, by discussion, to reflect on the nature of their behaviour and the factors that cause it. The good pastoral teacher will be able to use language in such a way that the young person does not feel that previous behaviour or experience is being judged, but that they are being helped to reflect upon it.

Parental views

Parental views will affect a young person's drinking. It is highly likely that young people go through a period of 'rebellion' against the values and practices of their parents but in the end return to behaviour patterns which reflect modified forms of their parents' positions. The work on early socialization of children indicates that the main 'patterns' for life are laid down in the first five years, not in the teenage years.

It is fair to assume, however, that if a child comes from a home where heavy drinking is acceptable they will often accept this as the norm. If they come from a home where parents' drinking affects their own security, self-image and emotions, then they may well reject the drinking patterns later in life. If a child comes from a teetotal home, where the parents ostracize them if they decide to drink, then this will probably produce surreptitious drinking. The crucial factor seems to be not so much the drinking patterns of the parents but rather the type of relationship they have with the young person.

The media

We do not know how much the media affects young people's drinking. Authorities are contradictory. Some suggest that the advertizing and the models of drinking offered in popular programmes increase consumption. Others suggest that advertizing changes the type of alcohol consumed not the amount.

We can draw a number of conclusions. Whilst drinking is a product of numerous social factors, an image tends to reinforce the norm. The ideas of manliness, enjoyment, sophistication, sociability are likely to be reinforced as being linked to drinking. The young person will be developing his identity as a young adult during adolescence and part of that identity will be determined by pictures of adulthood presented to him. This will affect his social behaviour.

Situational constraints

If we sit in a bar in a large group, and refuse another drink, we may feel 'out of place', particularly if we find socializing difficult. We have nothing to pick up at regular intervals, to 'break up' the fact we are just sitting there: fig 10.4. A person in a group needs to feel at ease. Having something in his hands or something 'to do' can fill awkward silences. This is particularly noticeable in young ex-offenders or inarticulate young adults of low ability. They have difficulties with alcohol. Much of this uneasiness is a product of the fact that in a social setting they do not have the language skills to participate in some groups. They therefore tend to drink faster and more regularly in small sips. In fig 10.4, a, the relaxed hand in pocket, stretched out, indicates that the person is relaxed and

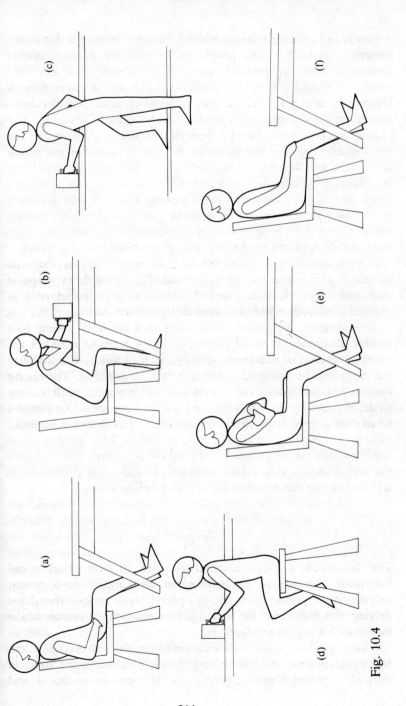

Fig. 10.4

211

sociable. In b, sitting relaxed, leaning forward, holding a drink or a cigarette, seems to make people fit in with the group, possibly because it is the 'aggressive' pose in body language and gives the image of confidence in the situation. In c and d the person is leaning or sitting at the bar with a drink in hand, while e and f shows the person sitting at a table without a drink.

It is easy to see that in b–d the person will – extraneous circumstances apart – feel secure as they are behaving in a way that is sociable, and they have a method of interspersing other behaviour by drinking. Watch someone assuming position a, and without a drink they do not appear to be ill at ease. It is one way for some people to feel at ease within a group without necessarily having some object which will ease inter-personal relationships. This, however, depends on the seating and space available.

If a person has completed his limit of drinks, he may have to assume e or f without a drink, particularly if he feels even less at ease with a non-alcoholic drink. In this position, a young man in particular will often feel ill at ease and may have another drink just to overcome it. In position c or d without a drink the person feels acutely ill at ease.

Other situational constraints involve such factors as the way that the environment predicts a particular type of social behaviour. An example of this would be that a pub environment produces the norm of drinking alcohol, whereas a party environment may have a variety of norms, from drinking alcohol, to not drinking alcoholic drinks, to smoking marijuana (Dorn, 1976). The good pastoral teacher assists young people by helping them to come to terms with the way that they respond to social groups and social environments and by helping them to develop ways of feeling at ease.

The law

The law, and a person's observance of it, will affect social behaviour, determining the amount of drinking or drinking and driving. If the person has a strong opinion concerning drinking and driving, this may affect the way that he drinks, or the circumstances he allows himself to be placed in.

I have spent so much time examining the determinants of social behaviour because we see young people's drinking through *our* eyes, *our* experience and *our* perception. This may mean that we can do little to support and advise those who are slowly trying to develop a positive and relatively safe style of drinking. Whenever we have to deal with a drinking incident in school, or advise young people, we need to spend time finding out what their drinking pattern is like, how *they* see it and what factors determine the drinking style. An over-earnest counsellor of alcoholics found a group of intoxicated youngsters. They said that this often happened, that they felt the need to drink, and that they often drank to alleviate tension or problems: the classic statements of alcoholics. It was easy, but a mistake, for the counsellor to think they were alcoholics: he was looking at the group through adult eyes and with an adult's view of problem drinking. Yes, they were regularly intoxicated, but they were fully capable of controlling when they wanted to be and when they didn't (just like most adult society). Yes, they felt they needed to, but what they meant was that it was socially correct to do so. Yes, they drank to overcome tension or problems, but what they meant was that they used it as a social lubricant. We so often create problems for young people in the way we perceive their behaviour. The good counsellor asks what a particular social behaviour like drinking *means* to *them*.

ENJOYMENT, HARM, DEPENDENCE

A fairly high majority of the population enjoys alcohol as a social beverage. A percentage like to use it occasionally, a small percentage do not use it at all. The line between enjoyment and harm is an extremely narrow one. The line between the adult encouraging the young person to modify their drinking and the young person feeling he is being 'got at' is equally extremely narrow. Young people seem to expect *some* adult disapproval for their drinking although increasingly they do receive parental approval. One of the most important tasks of the pastoral teacher is to develop in young people the recognition of the point where enjoyment stops and harm begins. A number of indications of harm are listed below.

Harm to others

Young people find it difficult to assess how far they offend others when drinking, and due to normal adolescent egocentrism, they

213

may not behave responsibly as we see it. They may be noisy particularly in groups, and so alarm adults. If we can increase their sensitivity to the feelings of others and to the effects of their behaviour, we may encourage a reasonable drinking style. Equally, we must help young people to recognize that they may harm others by pressing them to drink or to drink more than their limit.

Drunkenness

The good pastoral teacher can help young people by discussing their drinking. They may regularly get drunk because they want to, or because they do not know when to stop or how to control social pressures. If it is the first reason, then we have to assess whether the degree to which they become intoxicated is likely to produce further harm or whether it is a passing phase. If the second reason, there may be an urgent need to help them assess a reasonable limit for different drinks, and in different contexts. One limit may apply in pubs, where the volume of drinks is carefully measured; another limit at parties where measures may be larger. It might help to suggest ways of pacing drinks: for example, by alternating soft drinks or shandies with other drinks, or halfs with pints. Young drinkers may need help in developing social skills, in learning how to behave in groups.

If the young person regularly gets drunk, we need to assess whether alcohol is being used to 'drown sorrows' or possibly to cope with socializing. In these instances, they are at risk, and the counsellor must spend time helping them to consider and come to terms with the underlying problems. Often the drinking is given primary attention, at the expense of underlying causative factors. A reversal of this process is more likely to offer a productive and realistic approach for the pastoral teacher.

Road accidents

This is one of the most serious effects of young people's drinking. In 1974 one in three deaths in driving accidents occurred when the driver had over the legal limit of alcohol in his blood. Half of all male deaths in the 15–24 age group are due to road accidents and of these alcohol is the single most important causative factor (HMSO, 1976).

There are two major problems related to young people drinking and driving. First, they may not believe that there is a maximum limit, or even that alcohol affects their driving. Second, in adolescent groups, if someone is driving, they are still often encouraged to drink. We might expect the constant advertizing of data to affect the drinking and driving habits of adolescents. This is to some extent the case in the top social classes, probably partly because certain groups have greater access to such information, and more developed concepts of causality. Many health educationalists would suggest however that knowledge is unlikely to change behaviour in this instance. Stricter and enforceable legislation on drinking and driving is known to be effective, but if used specifically with this age group, or increased overall, it may damage relationships between public and police.[1]

Good group counselling may well go a long way to helping young people in this aspect of drinking and related harm. If we can encourage groups to discuss their difficulties in travelling to and from places of drinking, including taking girlfriends home, then we may help them to recognize the need to choose one driver each evening who does not drink alcohol. We may also show them how to support that driver socially through the evening by supplying non-alcoholic drinks. This is naturally a difficult point to make below the age of 17, but the teacher or youth-tutor may manage some helpful group counselling.

Pregnancy

Girls are often said to become pregnant while under the effect of alcohol. There may be some difficulty proving this, apart from telling anecdotes; but even if it is only sometimes true, it is the harm caused by the short-term effects of alcohol. The pastoral teacher may be able to support and help young people to come to terms with their sexuality and personal relationships, through group counselling, and this may be the best place to help girls to recognize the consequences of lessening their social inhibitions and controls through the influence of alcohol.

[1]The Road Safety Act 1967 produced an immediate 11 per cent drop in casualties. This has been offset by increased difficulties for the police in apprehending offenders, in bringing about convictions, and a parallel massive rise in consumption generally in the country.

For a certain group of young people we must accept that alcohol may be one cause of crime and violence; but we cannot conclude that it is the sole cause. It does seem to precipitate and influence other factors. People who are aggressive, become even less restrained. Counselling about alcohol is unlikely to *decrease* the person's criminal behaviour or violence. It may however be useful to analyse with some young people the contexts in which they become violent. Some may regret their behaviour, and wish to modify it. In this instance, the part played by alcohol in determining their behaviour needs to be analysed carefully, so that they can at least recognize its influence. The pastoral teacher can help by setting in context claims by the media and pressure groups that drinking leads to crime. Whilst this may be partly true, it is also an opiate for our social conscience, allowing us to ignore the complicated intermeshing of factors which cause the high incidence of adolescent crime and violence. Alcohol is only one of these factors, and in some cases may be a product rather than a cause.

Dependence

The short-term effects of alcohol cause harm, which can be suffered by anybody who drinks: for example, drunkenness, leading to overintoxification, leading to death. The categories of harm are the *major adverse conditions* that we are likely to be able to help young people with.

Dependence on the other hand is to do with the long-term effects of alcohol and with patterns of drinking that have long-term consequences. Many teachers worry about teenage alcoholics. But it is far more productive to pay attention to the majority of children and how they form normal drinking patterns, than to spend too much time looking for the rare case where an older teenager has developed early dependence.

Where a school-age person does become dependent on alcohol, it is likely to be a psychological dependence. In other words, when they start to drink, they will not be able to say that they can completely control the amount of their drinking, or whether they could stop at a particular time.

Some of the suggested danger signs are:

drinking taking precedence over other activities
drinking in order to relieve tensions
drinking regularly and heavily to perform adequately in a social context
memory blackouts
drunkenness during daytime, morning drinking
loss of appetite/neglecting needs
suicidal thoughts (Hassall, 1968).

We have to be extremely careful about such lists, however. They give factors observed in young people dependent on alcohol. They are factors noticed in the young dependent drinker. This does not mean that the same factors are present in the drinking of non-dependent drinkers. In other words, suicidal thoughts and drinking in order to overcome some slight social inhibitions may be present, but this does not mean that the person is necessarily dependent on alcohol.

In the rare event of a teacher recognizing that a young person does not seem to have control over the way that they drink, they should not immediately refer to an alcoholism treatment body. Except on the very rare occasion, it is highly unlikely that a regional council on alcoholism, an Alcoholics Anonymous branch or a psychiatric unit for alcoholics will be able to help a *young person* in the early stages of alcoholism. It is far more likely that they will perceive the young person's drinking in adult terms, as they work most of the time with adults. They are also likely to introduce the school-age person to young adults in their early twenties, with whom they will identify, and this may possibly exacerbate the problem.

Where a teacher feels that there is a need for outside support it is far more appropriate with *school-age* young people to seek advice from a youth counselling service (for example, Off the Record; Open Door) who will know specific individuals who may understand the factors affecting teenage drinking. The school psychological service is another source of help as they are likely to have contacts who work from the basis of understanding child development and adolescent culture, rather than from a medical or treatment standpoint. The parents naturally are another source of help and assistance.

If the young person is actually requiring help, then the teaching of social skills, teaching of drinking skills, helping them cope with

217

causative problems or helping them to cope with group pressures are all ways of aiding the young dependent drinker. Experience has shown that in general the medical services have great difficulty in understanding the social determinants of adolescent behaviour, although there are some developments recently with more attention being paid to social psychology rather than psychiatry. It is therefore acutely important they any person to whom a young person is referred understands both the condition *and* adolescents. If medical help is then needed, it is far more likely that they will know the right member of the medical profession to approach. They will approach someone who has learnt to adopt the counsellor role and who can relate to young people, rather than one who still has the traditional treatment role. The pastoral teacher has an extremely difficult responsibility here, if he decides to refer to outside help. The teacher should, however, never fear calling upon special expertise: the choice, however, must be made wisely, without undue attention to the label others have of being 'expert'. The over-riding quality necessary in any person referred to must be an understanding of adolescents, and if relevant an ability to relate to them.

A DIAGNOSTIC APPROACH

1. *If an incident occurs*:

children come to a school disco with alcohol.

GENERAL QUESTIONS

(a) What caused it?
something at school?
something happening to the young people?
chance?
mistake?
other?

(b) Why did 'it' come into school?
because they 'trusted' the school?
rebellion?
symbolic behaviour (we are now adults!)?

showing others they have rebelled?
other?

(c) From where did the alcohol come?
   pub?
   home?
   supermarket?
   other?

Is there any action necessary – by the school to stop/change source?

(d) Do the children need discipline? Do they need support? or both?

2. *If discipline is needed*

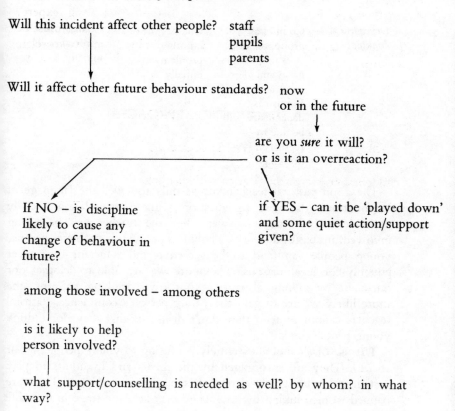

Will this incident affect other people?   staff
                                            pupils
                                            parents

Will it affect other future behaviour standards?   now
                                                     or in the future

are you *sure* it will?
or is it an overreaction?

If NO – is discipline
likely to cause any
change of behaviour in
future?

if YES – can it be 'played down'
and some quiet action/support
given?

among those involved – among others

is it likely to help
person involved?

what support/counselling is needed as well? by whom? in what
way?

3. If support is needed

This can be a development from discipline in the incident (as above) but it can also apply if you are in a situation where you are just lending support to a young person through pastoral care.

Pattern of drinking?   frequency; types of drink; contexts; subsequent behaviour?

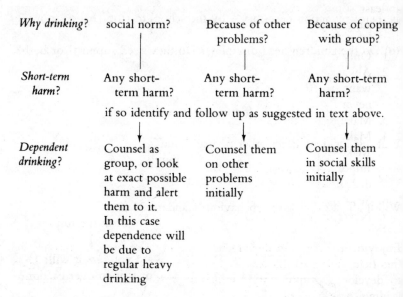

Why drinking?	social norm?	Because of other problems?	Because of coping with group?
Short-term harm?	Any short-term harm?	Any short-term harm?	Any short-term harm?

if so identify and follow up as suggested in text above.

Dependent drinking?	Counsel as group, or look at exact possible harm and alert them to it. In this case dependence will be due to regular heavy drinking	Counsel them on other problems initially	Counsel them in social skills initially

The good pastoral teacher knows only too well the language of 'negotiation', the way to question without stimulating socially desirable and defensive answers. For the teacher just becoming involved in pastoral work, alcohol is an extra problem because young people can tend to be secretive and reluctant to answer possibly for legal reasons. The more we are able to 'clothe' our questions by talking also about our own drinking patterns, the more likely we are to gain the young person's confidence. Pastoral teachers cannot pretend they don't drink, or that they don't think young people drink.

The use of alcohol is extremely confusing to young people in our society. They are encouraged by the media and by adults to play certain roles in which alcohol has an important part. They are banned from drinking by law. They may at some stage in their life have the 'manly image' of the drinker reinforced by a sports teacher; they may be disciplined for drinking by the school. The British culture has been described as ambivalent on alcohol. It has been said to have a split morality and conflicting values over alcohol's place in society. The pastoral teacher can only help young people to accept this ambivalence, and somehow to arrive at a drinking style that is relatively safe, but which accepts the different styles of others. Enjoyment of alcohol may therefore mean adopting at least some of the following stances which different authorities have suggested:

1. Only drink with meals/snacks.
2. Always accept the other person's right to choose what they want to drink, always provide non-alcoholic alternatives, never frown on people asking for alternatives to alcohol.
3. Make drunkenness unacceptable.
4. Make drinking and driving non-acceptable.
5. Make *respect* of other people's drinking choices crucially important: i.e. discourage drinkers who frown on non-drinkers; discourage non-drinkers who frown on drinkers.
6. Set a limit before starting a drinking session.
7. Never drink alcohol alone.

Enjoyment, harm and dependence are very close to one another in this field. The pastoral teacher can help the ordinary young person to develop a drinking style which at least has a higher chance of leading to enjoyment.

SECTION THREE: EVALUATION

11

Pastoral Care in a Local Education Authority

Ken David

(Adviser with special responsibility for Personal Relationships, Lancashire Education Authority)

As one of the first advisers appointed in the field of pastoral care I can speak with appreciation of the opportunities I have had, first as a tutor–adviser in personal relationships in Gloucestershire from 1966 to 1971, which is described elsewhere (David, 1971; 1972) and from 1971 to the present time in Lancashire. Lancashire in 1971, when I was appointed as a county adviser for schools, with special responsibility for personal relationships, was a very large authority with some 1,600 schools. Apart from demanding general advisory duties with a district of schools, one was given a free hand and good financial support for in-service training in a very loosely defined area of 'personal relationships'. The personal interest of Conrad Rainbow, then Deputy and now Chief Education Officer, illustrates the accident of such advisory posts, for no other LEA had made a similar appointment before.

The purpose of education is twofold – to provide opportunities for learning and gaining qualifications and to socialize pupils. 'Personal relationships' are obviously linked with the latter aim, and with the task of preparing youngsters for living in families, at work, in communities, and living with themselves as healthy autonomous individuals. This in turn involves a concern with curricular matters and with the effect of teachers on their pupils through their teaching methods, their duties and their attitudes. This offers a fascinating range of interests, but in severely practical

225

terms it reduces to two curricular concerns – specific courses in health, relationships, personal development and similar themes; and the co-ordination of such themes in various subject departments – to the leadership and ethos of schools and to the pastoral and tutorial function of teachers.

'Pastoral care' or 'education for personal relationships' is an appropriate general title for such objectives, which have provided a fundamental and continuing core to one's work. But 'pastoral care' may be considered to have a further connotation, associated with structures and establishments, staffing points, records, attendances, order, welfare and many bread-and-butter parts of school life. At a time of great educational change in Lancashire, it seemed appropriate to link pastoral care policy in the authority with such easily understood matters, associating them firmly with the support of efficient learning. There was an obvious danger of a dichotomy between pastoral and academic work, and an emphasis on their inevitable relationship was essential. Pastoral care is primarily about efficient learning, which does not take place without such care, and most pastoral care problems in schools are closely linked with learning and teaching. The first priority of pastoral care, therefore, is to support and encourage efficient learning; counselling, tutorial groups, welfare and referral systems are to do with the efficiency of a school as a place where people learn. The second priority must be interwoven with the first, but it is the more difficult to explain and achieve, and it is concerned with helping families to socialize children, and to develop attitudes which will support and improve society.

In planning an overall advisory strategy one has to balance other problems with the fundamental aims. Schools as institutions have their own life. One considers how the tone and ethos of different schools, the widely differing styles and qualities of leadership by head teachers, and the organizational structures chosen by head teachers and their LEA contacts can give emphasis to affective or cognitive aims. Many views of pastoral care can develop. The influence of the head teacher's personality is a major consideration, but so is the influence of dominant personalities on the staff, the prevailing attitude to examination success, the pressures from parents, the type of environment, and, of course, the general quality of the staff. The flexibility and relevance of the curriculum has to be considered, as it affects pupils in more than cognitive ways; themes chosen in English lessons can profoundly affect pupils' attitudes at times, and geography lessons can be about the quality of pupils' lives, as well as about examinations. One does not have to have separate lessons about personal relationships, if the choice of curriculum and the balance of the timetable give thought to the personal development of pupils as well as to their examination successes.

After some months of planning, a policy letter outlining the authority's advice on pastoral care matters was sent to all secondary schools in 1972. The letter had been reviewed by administrators, advisory colleagues and by teachers in advisory committee, and had been checked with a number of head teachers before being approved by the chief education officer and the education committee. So a 'county policy' was circulated to secondary schools and an important first stage in a pastoral care strategy decided. An alternative approach would have been to delay such a policy statement until much later, letting it evolve eventually from teacher working parties and from practice in schools, but for a number of reasons I chose the direct statement at an early stage. Comprehensive reorganization was producing changes in many schools, including new pastoral structures and appointments. Many of those appointed to pastoral posts appeared confused in purpose, and needing a lead and support. Experience in Gloucestershire had shown what was possible in schools, and which mistakes to avoid. There was an urgent need to establish centres of excellence among secondary schools in the first place, in colleges of further education in the second place, and in primary schools at a later stage, so that good practice could be illustrated and encouraged. Secondary schools were a priority because of obvious rapid change, colleges were urgently seeking advice and support in student counselling, and primary schools necessarily had to come third in priority for advisory support. Another urgent necessity was to encourage in-service training within schools, and delay in starting the training of trainers within staffs would be regrettable.

The policy statement was, in fact, generally welcomed in schools. It emphasized the need for co-ordination of pastoral work and affective education, and explained the repertoire of in-service training available. It offered advice in certain controversial areas, such as sex education, and gave the authority's views on counselling and liaison with other agencies. The translation of such a suggested policy into the life of schools then depends partly on effective and regular written communication, chiefly in the influence spreading

227

from extensive in-service courses, and often on the effectiveness of an adviser's contacts with head teachers and principals. A vital factor also is the communication of one's confidence and enthusiasm by taking every opportunity to talk to staffs and groups of teachers.

SECONDARY SCHOOL PLANS

At an early stage in Lancashire's development of pastoral work a series of day courses for secondary head teachers was initiated, and deputy heads were included in later years. At these courses there is consideration of leadership, of pastoral management, of health and EPR programmes and their co-ordination, and of staff relationships, as well as discussion on counselling, tutorial work and referral to other agencies.

Advisory visits to schools reinforce these contacts with head teachers, and additionally they are regularly invited to attend the last afternoon of the county EPR residential course, at which members of their staff are present. There are also a number of opportunities to talk to various local gatherings of secondary head teachers. Topics which regularly arise in such contacts include the merits of various forms of pastoral teaching, the vertical house and the horizontal house systems as well as the division of schools into lower, middle and upper divisions. The question of balancing pastoral and academic staffing points commonly arises, as does the management of staff relationships, discipline, liaison with other agencies, and problems of communication and administration in schools. It is also not unusual for head teachers to discuss with some frankness how they can best survive the stress of their demanding jobs.

The county residential EPR course for secondary teachers has been the main contribution of the LEA in the development of efficient pastoral care in schools. For six years since 1972 there have been two courses a year, each of about fifty teachers, and these have regularly been oversubscribed, for teachers quickly accepted the courses as practical and relevant. For the first three years the courses were of ten days duration, divided into four days in the autumn term, three in the spring and three in the summer terms. In later years economies required the reduction of the courses to two parts in the autumn and spring terms. In the 1978/79 session, the training has been reduced to one course in two parts totalling five days of residential training. A parallel new residential course has been introduced as an additional and alternative form of training, and is described later.

The county EPR courses have aimed to give an intensive basic training in pastoral administration, counselling and group work, and education in personal relationships. The majority of secondary teachers attending have been deputy heads and teachers with pastoral posts, though in recent years an increasing attendance by heads of academic departments has been an encouraging development. Head teachers have not been accepted, deputy heads and educational psychologists are always accepted, and a proportion of young teachers are often included. On occasions further education teachers have been accepted, and also youth workers, though separate training is available for FE colleagues, as described later. If the demand for places by pastoral staff from schools had been less, one would have welcomed a more interdisciplinary mixing of those attending.

A typical recent course programme is as follows:

Wednesday	2.00 p.m.	Assemble and introduction to course.
Autumn	2.45	Tutorial groups for discussions.
Term	4.30	Techniques of discussion work.
	7.30	Working with groups, a survey of group dynamics.
Thursday	9.15 a.m.	Tutorial groups.
	11.00	A review of secondary school pastoral systems.
	2.15 p.m.	Childhood and adolescence.
	4.30	The role of the form tutor.
	7.30	Tutorial groups.
Friday	9.15 a.m.	Counselling and interviewing methods.
	11.00	Co-ordination of health education and EPR in schools.
	2.15 p.m.	Tutorial groups.
	3.30	Final form for discussion.

Monday Spring Term	9.30 a.m.	Assemble and revision of pastoral principles.
	11.00	Personal and group counselling methods.
	2.30 p.m.	Specific areas of health education: homosexuality, contraception, abortion, VD, alcohol and drugs.
	4.30	Moral education.
	7.30	Tutorial groups.
Tuesday	9.15 a.m.	Co-ordinating a health/careers/EPR programme: evidence from selected schools.
	11.00	Friendship and loneliness.
	2.30 p.m.	Discipline, authority and aggression.
	4.30	Tutorial groups.
	7.30	Simulation exercise: presenting arguments to head teacher and colleagues.
Wednesday	9.15 a.m.	Referral agencies representatives attend.
	11.00	Relationships in a school context.
	Noon	Final forum.

The content of the courses is based on a series of lead talks, each with a detailed handout of information, which are then followed by extensive discussion in groups of ten or so members. A major feature of the training has been the carefully planned use of group work. Tutorial groups are formed with a balance of men and women, and senior and junior posts, and with teachers from different schools and districts. The staff tutors have become a very effective team over the years, and consist of college and education staff, a secondary head teacher and deputy heads, curriculum development officers, adult education staff and marriage guidance tutors. All have had considerable experience of group work, sometimes having attended national training in group work at the invitation of the authority. They aim to develop the groups to a level of trust and honesty so that members learn how they appear to each other, and how to clarify their attitudes on a great many topics. A sensible level of frankness in discussion enables people to learn more of themselves through the interaction of the group as they discuss important and often controversial themes in human relationships. To discuss is often to clarify, and the ability to help young people in counselling and discussion is facilitated by teachers listening, talking and learning in such groups. The extremes of 'T' group hurts are avoided, and the large majority of teachers who attend enjoy the experience and support of these tutorial groups. The staff tutors safeguard individuals carefully in case exchanges of views get too heated – our aim is to challenge thinking and let people glimpse how they appear to others, but not to confront or distress, for that would serve no purpose.

Further details of the content of the course are as follows:

1. *Pastoral administration:*
   communication within a school;
   assessment, records and reports;
   discipline;
   legal aspects;
   liaison with parents;
   staff team management and relationships;
   learning and study skills.
2. *Counselling and group work:*
   different styles and levels of counselling;
   confidentiality and legal aspects;
   different levels of teacher involvement;
   referral, and limits of counselling;
   interviewing;
   group dynamics;
   discussion techniques.
3. *Education for personal relationships:*
   childhood and adolescence;
   love and marriage;
   loneliness and friendship;
   aggression and violence;
   sex and sexuality;
   family life;
   intolerance;
   work, leisure and authority;
   morality and religion;
   freedom and responsibility;
   health education, including smoking, drugs and alcohol;
   themes of controversy in society:
   contraception, abortion, VD, and
   homosexuality.

231

To cover all these titles in detail is impossible, but one can remind teachers of the extent of human relationships themes. Young people in schools are not withdrawn from society, and are not insulated from the range of stress met by adults. So counselling and group work can help youngsters to understand themselves and the human condition, and then to be able to learn. The teachers' discussions serve both to illustrate the subjects of many pupils' problems and to clarify the teachers' own attitudes and feelings about these themes.

By having the course in two parts there is an opportunity for teachers to reflect and consider ideas in their school setting, before returning for the second part of the course. Reading is provided, and local meetings are often held in different parts of the county to provide a link between course members.

The authority's programme also includes a number of day courses, intended to be complementary to the residential training. Recent day courses have included the following for secondary teachers:

(a) *Sex and family life education* in secondary schools, emphasizing the link with science departments.
(b) *Refresher conference on counselling* in Lancashire, taken by a visiting speaker of national standing. 'Counselling and achievement' was a recent theme.
(c) *Teachers and social workers* meeting in local seminars.
(d) *Drama and pastoral care* in secondary schools.
(e) *Making choices and decisions in the middle years* of secondary education.
(f) *Induction programmes and tutorial work in the first year.*
(g) *Schools Council Health Education Project.*
(h) *School management tasks*: staff appraisal;
job analysis and job description;
staff recruitment and selection.
(i) *Materials for social, personal and careers education.*

For the last two years a new residential course has been held in the spring term, and again has been fully subscribed. This is a three-day course entitled 'Academic and Pastoral Roles in the Secondary School', and it is intended to offer an alternative form of pastoral training for senior staff, including head teachers. A recent programme was as follows:

Wednesday	4.30 p.m.	Personal excellence and potential.
	7.30	Pupils' individual needs, and tutorial and teaching roles.
Thursday	9.15 a.m.	Tutorial groups to discuss 'The integration of social and academic knowledge and experience'.
	11.15	The management of learning.
	2.30 p.m.	Tutorial groups to discuss selected themes.
	4.30	Active tutorial work and affective education.
	7.30	Co-ordinating health education, EPR and social education pro-grammes: evidence from three secondary headteachers.
Friday	9.15 a.m.	Problems and possibilities in the future in pastoral work. Taken by a speaker of national standing.

It is interesting to note that the majority of teachers attending new course have been deputy head teachers and heads of departments, showing the need to offer alternative entries into in-service education in pastoral care. The new course allows a deeper reflection on the form tutorial period and the form tutor's role, and gives an opportunity to look harder at the processes of learning. It has enabled the authority to strengthen the argument that academic and pastoral work must be seen as essential partners in the development of pupils.

A large number of local courses have been arranged in various parts of the county, and these have effectively reinforced the central training and have offered in-service work for teachers who do not seek the commitment of longer courses. The extent of these courses is illustrated by the fact that in the past year seven courses each involving six to eight evening sessions have taken place, with an involvement of about 200 teachers.

School-based conferences have been increasingly useful in the last three or four years. They are usually taken by the county adviser, assisted sometimes by pastoral staff from different parts of the county, and involve the closure of the school to enable all the staff to spend several hours considering their tutorial responsibilities. Some of these conferences have led to other courses being arranged in the school for interested groups of teachers who wish to study counselling and group work skills more carefully. Several schools have produced excellent staff handbooks on guidance and tutorial work, following such conferences, and liaison with other agencies has often improved considerably by their officers attending the conferences with the teachers. Heads of contributory primary schools often attend, as do members of the board of governors and local clergy.

The following introductions to three such handbooks on school guidance, chosen from many, indicates a common approach to such work with staffs.

The welfare and guidance of pupils are not new concepts – teachers have always cared for their pupils. Today, the pressures of society on young people are immense and the support, care and guidance given to pupils by their teachers is even more necessary and vital than ever before.

The basic aim of guidance in school is to help pupils to establish themselves as individuals, and for teachers to recognise them as such. Each child will need to develop his or her talents to the full and to learn to understand self, family and community and the society they will enter as young adults. Guidance is linked with educating the whole child.

Success of the curriculum relies heavily on the relationships between teacher and learner, both needing respect for their feelings and dignity. Staff will be committed not only to their subject teaching but to the total welfare of pupils in their charge. Guidance in school will aim to give support, care and control and to ameliorate or to prevent behavioural and educational difficulties. Academic work, educational and pastoral guidance go hand in hand and it is hoped that teaching will be synonymous with caring. We want the pupils to accept the school as a caring community to which they belong as important members, whilst at the same time developing and establishing themselves as individuals.

This is the first in our programme of Staff In-Service Seminars. We have chosen as our theme the work of the form tutor and his crucial involvement in the developing relationships in his form – both as members of form and year groups, and also as individuals during the difficult progress through adolescence. We shall also

234

set our work in the context of the community and its various agencies which help the school-child in so many different ways.

I hope the shared discussions will lead to continuing development and greater effectiveness in our work in the future.

While I feel it is presumptuous of me to attempt to preach to well qualified fellow professionals and to colleagues, the vast majority of whom instinctively carry out their pastoral role with professionalism and common sense, nevertheless, a statement of our policy has to be made. It falls to me to make that statement and I hope that you will bear with me.

It will at least serve to inform recently qualified and as yet inexperienced staff of our pattern of caring and to reaffirm that 'no man is an island' and that we all depend on the help and support of one another.

The help is there for all of us and for all the children in our charge if only we know where to look for it when we feel inadequate at a particular time.

It happens to us all, hence this document.

Many schools hold parents' evenings on aspects of education in personal relationships, particularly on the theme of adolescence. Such a theme can enable a school to interpret to the parents what it is endeavouring to do in pastoral work, and to seek co-operation. The evening can sometimes be linked to work being done by pupils in their tutorial work, thus encouraging a better dialogue with their parents.

National courses in counselling, youth work and careers education have contributed to the development of the county's aims in pastoral work, largely by strengthening the staffs of secondary schools with teacher-counsellors. The authority does not encourage full-time counsellors in secondary schools, but it welcomes the recruitment of teachers with deeper pastoral training, who can teach and act as trainers and support their colleagues. National curriculum development projects also give impetus to pastoral care, and the Schools' Council Health Education Project 5–13 has been of particular value, for the wide view of health education in this work matches well with the interests of Lancashire schools in personal relationships. A number of day courses in health education have been very well attended by primary school and lower secondary school staffs. The need for liaison between primary and secondary schools in health matters has been usefully emphasized, and a number of secondary schools have incorporated the material in their own guidance programmes.

In order to assist pastoral staffs with information, a county pastoral work bulletin is issued to secondary schools and colleges two or three times a year, summarizing a variety of information gleaned from many sources. A county booklet 'Pastoral Care and Education in Personal Relationships in Lancashire Secondary Schools' was produced in 1978 (Lancashire LEA, 1978). It has restated the authority's policy, and provided a great deal of background information. Sales have been extensive outside Lancashire and a second edition has now been printed.

FURTHER EDUCATION AND SIXTH-FORM COLLEGES

The authority formed a county working party on student counselling in 1972 and this has been a most effective instrument for influencing pastoral care in colleges. The membership has included full-time student advisers, LEA staff, and a number of vice-principals and other college representatives. All pastoral care ideas have been channelled through the group, which has included a number of enthusiastic and efficient activists in pastoral care, several of whom have become trainers and tutors on training courses. At an early stage a statement of policy on student counselling was hammered out in extensive discussions, and this has formed the basis of work in most colleges. The statement recommends different types of counselling services within colleges, and endeavours to state a simple policy to underpin the work of full-time student advisers, teachers who do a proportion of counselling duties, staff with tutorial responsibilities, and college staffs generally.

During the last year the working party has produced a handbook, 'Student Counselling in Lancashire' (Lancashire LEA, 1979) which incorporates the policy statement and reference and background material. Contributions are also included from a number of staff in colleges, illustrating a varied array of pastoral care approaches in different settings.

This approach differed from that used in secondary school developments. It has been a slower development than with secondary schools, in fact, but this was probably inevitable. The practical and vocational nature of much further education work produces a practical view of life among many staff, and attitudes may be closer to the world of work than is the case in schools. There can be limited sympathy for preparing students for anything other than their vocational life, and a robust view of how personal problems should be dealt with. Young people themselves have contributed to this more impersonal view of education, for they are learning to be independent from family and teachers. The professional training of staff has varied, and many have entered from industrial backgrounds, with practical instruction and factual lecturing as their models. They have also worked in clearly-defined and often very independent departments, in a seeming adult world where reference to a student's personal life could be seen as intrusive.

Sixth-form colleges and tertiary colleges are closer in outlook to the secondary school pastoral attitude, but most colleges dealing with sixteen-plus and eighteen-plus students have tended to treat students as more mature than they are, and have presumed an adult student attitude in coping with college and personal problems. There is often a presumption that study skills have been dealt with in secondary schools, that vocational guidance has been dealt with by admission to a college course, and that young people are capable of separating their personal and work lives easily. While a secondary teacher often presumes immaturity, further education teachers are sometimes too optimistic about the adulthood of their students, and impatient with pastoral and learning problems. These generalizations have been debated with many further education and sixth-form teachers, and can, of course, be disproved in many colleges. Students themselves are changing some of these things, for personal relationships are important and valued by young people, who seek different relationships with staffs.

As with secondary school head teachers, much depends on the value attached to guidance and counselling by college principals and their departmental heads. The influence of the LEA can be questioned and disregarded more perhaps in further education than in secondary settings, and one's work with college teachers has been closely channelled through the working party, and at a modest pace. Considerable changes in the view of pastoral care as a practical way of increasing a college's efficiency are taking place, particularly in the role of tutors, and counselling and guidance facilities are developing well. The appointment of full-time student advisers can be argued for in large colleges, and there is a demand from colleges for such appointments which the authority is unable to satisfy fully because of financial economies. Full-time appointments are increasing, and should then provide a support and incentive to improve the counselling and tutorial skills of the staff generally. One deplores student advisory work becoming a specialist enclave for experts to take over problems from staff. Difficult cases may require this, but one wishes to strengthen the concern of all staff in student guidance and support.

A gradual increase in the number of full-time student advisers is necessary because of the size and complexity of colleges, and because group tutors and departmental teacher-counsellors cannot be expected to deal with more than 'first-level' learning and personal problems. Accommodation problems can be considerable, there is a great deal of work in helping overseas students, and there are new demands from the increasing population of 'open sixth' students who do not have regular qualifications and ambitions. A new world of counselling work is likely to develop as unemployment diverts more young people into colleges.

The more adult nature of the college population requires more of a self-referral system than in secondary schools, though we regularly overestimate the sophistication and maturity of students. The appointment of selected teacher-counsellors in different departments and divisions of colleges has been useful in providing a simple counselling service on a part-time basis. Their availability as a first line of counselling reference, complementary to the work of all staff, has been advertized in some colleges by student union publicity, and other advertizing methods. The best form of such advertizing, is, of course, a mutual referral system between all colleagues on a staff, so that the most appropriate person helps a student. The most appropriate person can be a class teacher, a group tutor, or one of the counselling team, and students like to be able to 'shop around' for the person they find they need.

Most colleges now have an internal training system for staff in counselling and guidance themes, and the departmental teacher-counsellors often form a college pastoral care committee to advise and support their colleagues. Such committees are often chaired by a vice-principal or head of department with special responsibility for student advisory services, and full-time advisory staff are, of course, a major source of advice for such groups. A number of seminars have been held in which all the college staff consider tutorial and counselling roles, and regular in-service work and confident leadership are gradually bringing recognition of the value of tutorial groups and counselling support as aids to an efficient college.

County residential courses have been provided for further education and sixth-form teachers, and youth workers have attended as well. The colleges have recommended selected staff to attend, usually to act as departmental teacher-counsellors, though many staff have attended to study their role as group tutors. In all cases the authority regards those attending as potential trainers of their colleagues back in college. The courses have been similar in style to the secondary teachers' courses, but there is greater attention to individual counselling and the problems of the sixteen to nineteen age group, as well as work with older adult students. A typical programme is as follows:

Thursday	10.30 a.m.	Assemble. A survey of college guidance systems
Autumn		
Term	2.15 p.m.	Counselling concepts
	4.30	Discussion techniques
	7.30	Attitudes and prejudices
Friday	9.15 a.m.	Liaison and referral systems
	11.15	Moral education
	2.15 p.m.	Attitudes in counselling
	4.30	Tutorial groups for discussion
	7.30	A study of group work
Saturday	9.15 a.m.	Listening techniques
	11.15	Case studies
	2.15 p.m.	Counselling and guidance in the community
Wednesday	6.30 p.m.	Support – an LEA and college viewpoint
Spring		
Term		
Thursday	9.15 a.m.	Different types of problems
	2.15 p.m.	Tutorial groups for discussion
	4.30	Difficult themes in counselling: abortion, drugs

	7.30	Difficult themes in counselling: contraception, homosexuality, VD, violence
Friday	9.15 a.m.	Case studies
	2.15 p.m.	Methods and content in discussion work
	4.30 p.m.	Tutorial groups for discussion
	7.30	Methods and content in discussion work
Saturday	9.15 a.m.	Learning and motivation
	11.00	An overall view of guidance

Members of the county working party provide staff to act as tutors with groups, and an emphasis on group work continues. Reference is made to the way in which college counselling teams can mutually develop in-service work in their colleges, and the struggle to improve tutorial services is emphasized. County curriculum development officers arrange local courses for college teachers wherever possible, and a number of further education and sixth-form teachers attend the secondary teachers' residential and day courses. The authority is slowly developing local support groups for secondary and college counselling staffs, to provide better liaison and support in counselling tasks.

PASTORAL CARE IN SPECIAL SCHOOLS

Since the whole nature of special education is linked with pastoral care there has been little extra provision for LEA in-service training in the pastoral care and education for personal relationships programme, though special school teachers have always been free to attend courses aimed at other types of school. Pastoral work has continued with advisory visits to head teachers, often in conjunction with sex education and health education, in addition to the extensive advisory support these schools receive from special education advisers.

A county working party has spent some time considering ways to extend the Schools' Council Health Education 5–13 Project into special education. This Health Education project has, in fact,

240

provided a helpful impetus with special school staffs, and several day conferences have been held to consider personal relationships and health education topics. The isolated and specialized nature of special education teaching has perhaps resulted in less attention to staff development in the area of health education and demand from teachers for more in-service provision may develop.

PRIMARY EDUCATION

There are a great many small and denominational schools in Lancashire, and the task of supporting and influencing some 700 primary schools in pastoral matters is a daunting one. The nature of primary education, however, makes it child-based and caring in style and there is less urgency with subject teaching and examinations than in secondary schools. Primary teachers are normally on one's side already in reviewing the pastoral nature of teaching, and all primary advisory work is linked in one way or another with pastoral care it seems. As with secondary schools one has noted primary schools with particular efficiency and success in pastoral care and developed them as 'centres of excellence'. By concentrating effort on such schools one can represent ideas to many of their neighbouring schools.

For many years there has been a regular series of day conferences for primary head teachers and deputy head teachers, 'Pastoral tasks of primary head teachers', to consider the role of the head teacher, staff relationships and the development of pupils in social and personal relationships. Working through head teachers in this way is the only practicable way of disseminating ideas. In recent years an additional day conference has been developed. Working with a team of advisory colleagues we have gathered the head teachers of each Lancashire district in turn for a day conference under the title 'How we influence children'. It was felt that many schools were not challenging their teachers' thinking sufficiently with various recent educational research findings, and there has been a session when county psychological staff have listed useful research which can have practical application in schools. The effect that teachers' personalities and school rituals can have on the development of pupils is considered, and there are discussions on moral and religious education, and health and social education. Whilst the day can only be a superficial reminder of these matters it is hoped that many head teachers will continue the topics in discussions with their staffs. A number of school-based gatherings of primary teachers have followed these day conferences, and there have been requests for advisers to provide follow-up work.

County day courses are also held for primary teachers, under the heading of 'Health and family life education', and other day conferences on the Schools' Council Health Education 5–13 Project have been well attended. Courses on sex education, an area of education in which one is dissatisfied with present standards in primary schools, are not popular, but it is hoped that a better understanding of a wide view of health education will lead to improvements eventually. There seems to be an innate conservatism in Lancashire schools about developing sex education with children, and a failure to realize that children do not live in innocence of sexual matters until an ill-defined 'appropriate' time. Denominational schools, in particular, are cautious about suggestions that we have a duty, preferably in parallel with parents, to interpret such matters in the setting of family life and caring relationships. More planned health education programmes, in which sex education will have a part, seem the most likely future development.

OTHER DEVELOPMENTS

The authority's concern with pastoral care extends to very useful liaison with other agencies who can contribute to the efficiency of schools and colleges in this work. A recent development with the Lancashire Area Health Authority has been the development of health education teams in different areas of the county. This scheme, still in the experimental stage, plans to have groups of health and education staff with particular interest in the subject supporting and developing health education in their particular areas, with particular reference to the new Schools Council Health Education 5–13 Project. Additional health education officers are being appointed by the Area Health Authority and there should be a great improvement in the support offered to schools with materials and resources, speakers and local training facilities.

Liaison with the Lancashire police is good, and the recently formed Juvenile Bureau has been helpful in schools. The Lancashire police juvenile liaison scheme has always been highly valued by schools, and it is regretted that the freedom of action previously given to these excellent officers has been reduced of late. The co-operation between these officers and school pastoral staffs has often meant that young offenders have been salvaged from a criminal career. One can recall many cases where the influence of the teacher has been reinforced by the juvenile liaison officer in a pupil's home setting, and where the early warning system has caused offenders to pause for thought.

Work with the social services department has been strengthened by holding local conferences of secondary school and college pastoral staffs with senior social services officers, and it is hoped to continue these. There is also an arrangement for teachers and social workers to attend each other's in-service courses, though this has yet to be developed more fully. Schools are encouraged to form 'youth liaison groups', where representatives from a variety of agencies meet with school pastoral staff periodically, and social services training officers have been helpful in organizing similar local seminars.

Educational psychologists and educational welfare officers are valued colleagues in schools, and schools are constantly demanding more support from them. Efforts are made to encourage school seminars at which psychologists can advise teachers on how to cope with pupil problems, rather than by extracting pupils to attend clinics. Many of the educational welfare officers are seen as full members of the school pastoral team.

The Teachers' Advisory Council for Drug and Alcohol Education in Manchester has been a useful ally in in-service training, and regular meetings of the Lancashire Council for Drug and Alcohol Education provides useful liaison. The latter council has representatives from a large number of statutory and voluntary bodies, and is funded largely by the Area Health Authority. A recent project has provided in-depth training for a number of counsellors from several agencies, including education, in drug and alcohol problems, and this strengthening of referral services will be useful.

The future holds many challenges in education, and inevitably, therefore, in pastoral care. Falling rolls and economies in education may lead to a concentration in secondary school pastoral appointments, and pastoral in-service training must concentrate even more on the role of all teachers as effective form tutors. The linking of secondary school academic and pastoral roles must be emphasized more as pressure mounts for improvements in academic standards and qualifications; there is much to be done yet in curriculum development and in civilizing examinations. The way society is developing requires much better planning of how we co-ordinate work in health and relationships topics in all types of schools. More attention must be given to study skills and learning problems.

When we link these educational tasks with the increasing demands of school welfare work, the needs of children from broken homes, the requirements of children from other cultures, and with the prospects of planning for different types of working lives, we have plenty of work ahead. Evaluation of pastoral care is difficult. An extensive survey of Lancashire's work in this field by Her Majesty's Inspectors has given clear approval to what we are doing, but in the end we are acting in faith that such work is in the best traditions of good schools and colleges.

12

The Evaluation of School-Based In-Service Training

Geoff Jones
(West Glamorgan Advisory Service)

Since the James Committee's recommendations were published in 1972, in-service training has received the full support of the teacher associations and the Department of Education and Science.

However, in recent years the assumptions underlying in-service training are being questioned. It has been claimed that the emphasis in training has been concerned with extending the teacher's knowledge rather than with helping him to deal effectively with problems which confront him in school. If the purpose underpinning in-service training is to improve what is happening in the classroom, then a major element in the process must be related to identifying problems facing the teacher and the promotion of innovation in teaching methods as part of the problem-solving process.

A training programme designed to enable a teacher to adopt new teaching methods can only be effective if the school is willing to accept new ideas. Criticizing traditional INSET, Bolam (1978) writes: '. . . it ignores the characteristics of schools as social systems and thus underestimates the problems encountered by individual teachers when they return from a course and try to implement their new ideas.' Evidence suggests that successful innovation usually necessitates the commitment of several people in an institution, together with considerable resources, over a period of time. School focused in-service training could, of course, satisfy such criteria for success.

The main aims in such a training structure would be to: specify goals to be achieved; mobilize resources within the school and, if necessary, from outside the school; design a programme of investigation and develop techniques for evaluating what has happened as a result of the programme.

Areas which promote most difficulty for those responsible for organizing programmes of in-service training appear to be:

1. Introducing objectives into the planning process.
2. The evaluation of course effectiveness.

OBJECTIVES

Objectives lie at the centre of the planning process and Davies (1976) argues that three types of planning can be recognized: systematic, expedient and piecemeal.

Systematic planning

In essence this approach involves defining ends or objectives to be achieved and then selecting procedures for attaining them. Although Davies sees much to commend systematic planning, in terms of practicability, he also makes the following criticisms of the method:

1. Means and ends are isolated as successive steps in the process, rather than being seen as the 'heads and tails' of the same situation.
2. The ends are seen as unchanging and not subject to radical re-definition.
3. It ignores the fact that ideas and ideals commonly evolve during both the process of planning and its subsequent implementation.

Expedient planning

This approach defines the means or procedures to be used but does not specify objectives. An example of curriculum development using the 'means' technique is the Schools Council Humanities Project. The developers suggest ideas for developing enquiry-based discussion and the procedures by which the teachers could adopt a neutral role when leading such discussions in the classroom. However, objectives are not identified by the developers. Reservations about expedient planning tend to fall into two areas:

1. That it is an irrational way of planning.
2. That it fails to clarify the nature of achievements.

Piecemeal planning

In this method a rough definition of the more important objectives are agreed before considering resources. After a consideration of resources the objectives are modified accordingly. A further examination of procedures will allow a more precise definition of objectives to be determined. The advantage of this approach, argues Davies, is that it forces all the specialists into constant interaction with each other throughout the life of the project, and, above all, it places the teacher in a central position in development work.

It is evident that without objectives priorities cannot be allocated and resources cannot be effectively concentrated. Objectives are also important guides for the training team who wish to find out what has been achieved. However, as suggested in the 'piecemeal' or what we shall term the step-by-step approach, objectives need to be set and sharpened within a total plan rather than to be viewed as a number of distant goals.

TRAINING EVALUATION

Training evaluation is clearly a complex matter. It is not a single act but the whole process. It involves determining needs, establishing objectives, conducting a programme and measuring results. It will also involve:

1. The trainees' assessment of benefits derived from the training experience.
2. The trainer's view of changes in the trainees.
3. The responses of colleagues and others to the training process after observing trainees employing new skills.

Kirkpatrick (1967), however, maintains that training evaluation changes from a complicated generality into clear and achievable goals if broken down into four logical steps:

REACTIONS   How well did the trainees like or dislike
                   the programme?
LEARNING   What principles, facts and techniques
                   were learned?
BEHAVIOUR   What changes in job behaviour resulted
                   from the programme?
RESULTS   What were the tangible results of the
                   programme in terms of reduced cost,
                   improved quality, etc?

These logical steps form the essential framework on which a training team can build course objectives and procedures. They allow questions to be raised which give method and meaning to the process of course evaluation and it will be argued that such an approach may be applied effectively to school-focused training in pastoral care.

SITUATIONAL CONSIDERATIONS

Hamblin (1978) maintains strongly that year heads and house heads are not paid to do pastoral care. They are paid for management, co-ordination and for the in-service training of staff. Marland (1974) supports this view when he argues for a situation which involves the entire staff in pastoral responsibility with particular emphasis on the form tutor role. In what Marland describes as the tutor ascendant role, the responsibilities take the following pattern:

1. A tutor is afforded full access to all information on pupils in his care.
2. He has a vital part to play in the reception and induction processes.
3. Before a pupil is seen by senior staff management, the tutor's views are solicited.

In such a structure, the entire staff has a clear pastoral involvement, and evidence from the work of Richardson (1973) suggests that this approach leads staff away from an authoritarian discipline towards a personalized control based on relationships. However, if the role of the tutor is to be recognized as the logical point in planning an effective pastoral system, and not that of head of house or year, it would imply:

1. A clear job analysis which specifies what must be done.
2. A skills analysis which states how the task can be carried out.

TEACHER INVOLVEMENT

Success will depend, to a great extent, upon the willing co-operation of teachers in the school. This can be best achieved by involving them at the outset in the planning process. It will also ensure that the content of the training course will be relevant to the particular needs of the school. Meetings can be arranged to discuss tentative objectives and outline planning. At this early stage the tutors could be invited to submit, in writing, topics or areas of interest they would like to see included on the course agenda. Such a list often helps to illustrate the extent of knowledge and skills related to the effective role of the tutor. The number of topics will, of course, be related to the amount of time available for the training programme. Items receiving the most nominations would then constitute the course content. It is also important that feedback of information is prompt and well presented. This approach helps to maintain interest and demonstrates to course members that the course is being conducted in a serious and professional manner.

Using the step-by-step method of planning objectives, the modified list of topics agreed for the course could possibly read:

1. Communication skills
2. The disadvantaged pupil
3. Bullying
4. Motivation
5. Study skills
6. The role of the tutor
7. Coping with adolescents in difficulty
8. The effective tutorial
9. Aims of pastoral care
10. Links with parents

11. Interviewing
12. Keeping records.

During the process of clarifying objectives, in terms of course content, the training team would be mobilizing resources within and outside the school.

There is evidence to suggest that teachers favour collaborating with 'experts' in their own school. Vandenberghe (1978) invited primary school teachers in Belgium to classify, on a six-point scale, thirteen proposals concerning staff development activities of in-service training (1 – very little preference; 6 – very much preference). For each proposal the number of teachers who gave one of the three highest scores of preference (6, 5, 4) was recorded. Table 12.1 shows in descending order the ratio of approval of each proposal.

Table 12.1

No of teachers who responded *2 044*	
Order of preference	*% teachers having given the score* 6, 5, 4
1. Collaborating with experts in one's own school	76.1
2. Assisting at practice lessons and discussing them	63.8
3. Training skills intensely	62.7
4. Exchanging with colleagues one's experiences about a previously accomplished task	62.0
5. Watching demonstrations in one's own class	59.9
6. Listening to lectures followed by discussion	53.2
7. Doing researches in one's own class led by an educational psychologist	53.1
8. Visiting other schools	49.5
9. Visiting exhibitions of didactical equipment	48.8
10. Following courses via TV	46.5
11. Listening to lectures	28.3
12. Written courses on staff development	27.7
13. One or two teachers of one's school following staff development courses and informing the whole school team	20.8

This does not mean that the findings in the secondary school would necessarily be similar. However, experience at this level has shown that teachers will accept important others with special skills and training as leaders in discussion groups, seminars and workshops. These may include remedial department colleagues, tutors, counsellors, heads of year or house and senior teachers.

In the following discussion concerning a suggested approach to a school-focused training programme in pastoral care, the four steps nominated by Kirkpatrick (1967), reactions, learning, behaviour and results, are used as a framework. Reference will also be made to a study carried out with part-time youth workers. For clarification it may be useful if a brief statement is made about this piece of small-scale research.

The study concerned an investigation of changes in the knowledge and role perceptions of youth workers, induced by a part-time training course. The course was one of a series undertaken by an education authority and directed by an outside person involved in a training role in various counties in England, Ireland and Wales.

In order to study such changes, two underlying hypotheses were formulated for appraisal:

1. That there will be a change in the values and salience given to areas of work.
2. That there will be a change in the youth workers' perceptions of their expertise and adequacy of their knowledge.

The youth workers were expected to attend four weekend sessions, each of some twenty hours' duration. Six written assignments were submitted by each course member and each assignment was closely related to practical work with young people. The trainees concerned in the study were fifteen men and women aged from twenty-three to forty-eight years. Each was experienced in youth work, and had completed a basic training course in previous years which had comprised some twenty evening sessions of two hours and three residential weekends. They had been chosen from a group of forty-three youth workers who had applied to attend the course of training, and each had been recommended by a youth leader or an officer of the authority.

It was considered that changes in the knowledge and role perceptions of these trainees, if they occurred, would be significant because they had already been exposed to training. The procedures for evaluation will be mentioned during the main discussion.

AN APPROACH TO EVALUATION IN A SCHOOL-FOCUSED TRAINING COURSE IN PASTORAL CARE

Step 1: Reactions. How well did the trainee like or dislike the programme?

This level of the evaluation process raises a number of important questions for the training team. Is it important that the trainee should like the training experience? If someone does not like aspects of the course, should the programme be changed in order to accommodate? Is enjoyment a course objective? Will the question of like and dislike affect the chances of a course member learning or changing attitudes? Do reactions change as a course progresses? Can the course expectations of trainees influence their reactions? Questions such as these should be raised when designing a course and the implications considered in the planning of objectives.

To learn how people are reacting and feeling about a course, it is important that methods of obtaining feedback should be built into the training process. Personal reactions to lectures, tutorials, seminars or workshops could take the following rating scales method, based on a format used by Hamblin (1974). [See 12.2]

In order to gain the necessary feedback to refine and improve future training programmes the reactions of course members can also be sought after the course has been completed. The questionnaire could take the following form:

1. What do you feel are the most useful things that you have learned on the course?
2. Have you found the course to be valuable from a personal point of view?
3. What did you find to be the most important area of learning?
4. Is there any way in which the course has changed your job behaviour?
5. Can you think of any other areas in which your style of behaviour has changed as a result of what you learned on the course?

252

Table 12.2

Session ―――――――――――――――――――――― Date ――――――――

Name (optional) ―――――――――――――――――――――――――――――

Please rate the session you have just attended by placing a circle around one number in each line

Interesting	1	2	3	4	5	6	7	Uninteresting
Relevant to my work	1	2	3	4	5	6	7	Not relevant to my work
Easy to understand	1	2	3	4	5	6	7	Difficult to understand
Well organized	1	2	3	4	5	6	7	Disorganized
I learned a great deal	1	2	3	4	5	6	7	I learned nothing
Valuable	1	2	3	4	5	6	7	A waste of time

Any comments you may wish to make:

---

6. What are your general views about the course you have just completed?
7. Can you suggest ways of improving this type of training?
8. In which ways has the course proved to be particularly useful in your work in pastoral care?

Instruments of this nature concentrate the thinking of trainees about their reactions to a course which could make them more critical than they would otherwise have been. However, the training team must be prepared to change aspects of the course when feedback is negative or trainee frustration could prove to be destructive in terms of course success. This implies a willingness to adapt on behalf of the training team and a training programme which is flexible enough to meet changing needs.

253

Although reaction questionnaires are important measuring instruments for training organizers, an essential part of the process is to feed data back to course members. This ensures their total involvement in the evaluation process and, as has been mentioned, it demonstrates a serious and professional approach to the concept of training. There must also be a willingness on behalf of the training team to bring any negative reactions into the open and to initiate discussions for clarification and possible programme change.

Step 2: Learning. What principles, facts and techniques were learned?

Training is associated with learning and any attempt to evaluate a training course at this level may promote the simple questions: 'Have the course members learned anything?', 'In what areas has learning taken place?', 'Have new skills been learned?', 'Is it possible to measure this increase in knowledge?', 'Are the trainees resistant to learning in certain areas?', 'Can these resistances be broken down?' Feedback from the reactions level may help to answer some of these questions.

Any attempt to evaluate learning change is further complicated by the fact that training of the kind anticipated for a pastoral care course is open-ended and objectives are not formulated in measurable terms.

In a study of changes induced by part-time training in youth work, a method applied by Burgoyne (1973) was used with interesting and rewarding results. The aim was to obtain a subjective rating of the trainee's attitude or personal impression about his knowledge and skill.

A rating scale consisting of seven equal segments were arranged along a line labelled *No Knowledge* and *Thorough Knowledge* at the extremes. A separate scale was arranged for each of the twenty areas of knowledge and skills that were to be incorporated into the training course (Appendix 12.3).

APPROACH

The trainees were invited to complete *three* copies of the same instrument in the following order:

254

	Response Key
1. Before the course began the youth workers were asked to rate their existing knowledge on the scales.	B1
2. At the end of the course the youth workers were asked to reassess their knowledge on the scales, as they now saw it, *before the course began*.	B2
3. Also, at the end of the course, the youth workers were asked to rate their knowledge as it was now, at the end of the course.	A

(In order to gain some insight into what might have happened to the experimental group had it not been involved in the training course, a carefully matched control group was set up.)

The findings revealed:

1. (B1 – A) That the youth workers' perceptions of their expertise and adequacy of knowledge had increased in each of the twenty items on the instrument.
2. (B2 – A) In nineteen items the youth workers' perceptions of their expertise and adequacy of knowledge showed a greater increase than was demonstrated in B1 – A. In one item the degree of increase was the same.
3. (B1 – B2) In each of the twenty items on the instrument the trainees' reassessment of knowledge and skills decreased in relation to that given before the course began.

These results supported the findings of Burgoyne (1973) who found that the ratings of his group of trainee managers tended to be lower on the second assessment than on the first.

This would suggest that the trainees' opinions of their level of knowledge and skill, as it had been when they came to the course, became *less* favourable as the course progressed. Burgoyne describes this as a change in the trainees' beliefs about themselves. He goes on to argue that this could be described as partly an attitude change, and partly a change in the trainees' knowledge of their own limitations and capabilities. It could also be interpreted as a new awareness of what there is to be learned in relation to a body of knowledge.

255

The data accumulated during the training course for youth leaders suggested that the experience for the trainees was valuable and worthwhile. The findings also suggested that it was possible to gain an insight into the value of a training course by use of a controlled experiment of this nature.

It is felt that such an approach to the learning level of the evaluation process could be used to advantage in a school-focused training programme concerned with pastoral care.

SUGGESTED OUTLINE PROCEDURES

The instrument, rating existing knowledge on a seven-point scale, could be applied in the same way as for the youth workers. The twelve items agreed for the content of the proposed course could be incorporated (Appendix 12.4).

Analysis of responses
1. Individual change scores.
   This allows an examination to be made of individual shifts in perceived knowledge. Recognizing that the distance between each step on the seven-point scale can be interpreted differently, it could be argued that group average shifts have little or no meaning. Hamblin (1974), however, maintains that *a consistent change in one direction* by a large number of trainees represents a significant attitude change. It is possible to increase accuracy by determining the change score of each trainee. In this way the 'distance' between the steps on the scale are confined to the perceptions of individuals.

Example (From youth worker study)
Item: *Sexual development of the adolescent*

Trainee	A	B	E	F	G	I	K	L	M	N	O	P	Q	R	S
B1	3	5	4	5	5	5	4	3	6	6	5	5	4	6	4
A	5	5	6	6	5	5	6	6	6	4	6	4	7	7	4
Change score	2	0	2	1	0	0	2	3	0	−2	1	−1	3	1	0

Total change score $15 - 3 = 12$

Average change score per trainee $\dfrac{12}{20} = 0.8$

The results showing the average change score per trainee (each item) for B1 – A and B2 – A are shown in Appendix 12.5.

2. Visual interpretation of data.

A mass of words and figures can be both confusing and frustrating when trying to analyse just what has happened on a course. Diagrammatic interpretation of data can prove to be easily understandable and rewarding to trainer and trainee. Again it is important that such data concerning course findings should be made accessible to all participants.

(a) *Individual responses*

This method allows a visual study to be made of individual shifts in perceived knowledge regarding each item on the instrument. The technique was employed by Burgoyne (1973) in his investigation of managers in training. Individual responses in the youth worker study supported Burgoyne's findings and they reflected the following pattern:

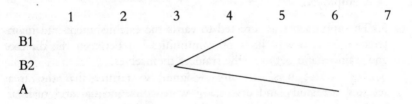

(b) *Frequency rating scales*

Carefully scaled bar diagrams allow easy recognition of:

(i) The number of people who chose a specific rating regarding an item on the instrument.
(ii) The general shift in the knowledge and skills perceptions of the trainees (Appendix 12.6).

That the youth worker experimental group perceived their knowledge to have increased significantly during training can be attributed, to a large extent, to the teaching skills of the course director. The techniques employed are worth noting as useful guidelines for any proposed course on in-service training:

1. Stress was made on the practical application of ideas and skills presented for consideration.

2. The approach throughout was to relate new concepts to familiar areas in the job situation and to relate new learning to that already known.
3. Motivation was encouraged by means of variety and challenge; e.g. discussions, role-play, activity sessions and simulations.

4. The use of feedback: meaning the information by which the learner determines what is going on and how well he is doing. Techniques employed:

   a. Rewarding the trainee by recognizing his contributions to the session or activity. By validating that the trainee is interpreting material correctly and by identifying the additional knowledge or skill needed to enhance his value as a youth worker.
   b. By a flow of signals, verbal and non-verbal, by which the trainee is able to determine that he is progressing.
   c. The positive and encouraging manner in which feedback was employed.

5. The approach was directed towards the establishment and maintenance of two-way lines of communication between the director and trainees and between the trainees themselves.
6. The course was carefully designed to ensure that the areas selected for study and discussion were consequential and realistic. Problems were posed that would represent familiar situations and that would develop coping strategies that would help in future job challenges.

Step 3: Behaviour. What changes in job behaviour resulted from the programme?

The problem of evaluating whether learning gained on a course is transferred to behavioural change in the classroom is impossible to solve by means of applying a simple test. Evaluation of this nature would require careful observations of, and discussions with, the teacher, before and after the course. It would also require the observations of colleagues, his superiors and children in his care. Even then it would be extremely difficult to define criteria in order to measure with any degree of accuracy where benefit had been achieved.

258

Some indication of change could, of course, be obtained from after-course discussions with a group of teachers who had been involved in school-focused training. Working together in the same milieu would allow opinions of change to be refuted or supported. Yet there are dangers in drawing conclusions at this level. It is easy for someone to respond, 'Yes, I am more patient with difficult children as a result of attending the course.' This could mean that he *thinks* there has been a change. It could therefore be said that the course member has experienced a change in attitude during training, as a result of which, he views his own 'unchanged' job behaviour in a different light.

It could be argued, however, that if a teacher saw a change in the value and salience of his working role after training, then it is at least possible that a change in his job behaviour could follow. This line of thinking could raise important questions for the trainer which could be posed for discussion during the course: 'What are the role expectations of a teacher with responsibility for pastoral care?' 'Is he able to define his role?' 'To what extent do the expectations of management effect role identity and role concept?' 'What role stresses occur when working as a pastoral tutor in the school?' 'Is there conflict with the teaching role?'.

To obtain a subjective rating of the perceived role of part-time youth workers, a rating scale consisting of seven equal segments was arranged along a line labelled Unimportant and Important. The trainees were invited to complete two copies of the same instrument; before the course began and at the end of the course. A statistical test was applied to indicate the significance of any changes and similar procedures were carried out with a control group. The findings enable the course director to ascertain:

1. The roles considered to be most important by the trainees.
2. Whether perceived role importance had changed after the course and in what areas.
3. The average change score of each trainee.

This approach could be applied to assist in the evaluation of a school-focused training programme in pastoral care. The results would most certainly help clarify teachers' views about their role in the pastoral care team. In focusing thinking on this important area, it could also influence a change in the attitude which could, in turn, effect positively a change in job behaviour.

The rating scale could be applied in the same way as used in the youth worker study. A suggested instrument for examining the perceived role of the form tutor is shown in Appendix 12.7.

ANALYSIS OF RESPONSES

1. Individual change scores.

Example (From youth worker study)
Role: *To continue the work begun in school*

Youth worker	A	B	E	F	G	I	K	L	M	N	O	P	Q	R	S
B1 (before course)	2	2	2	2	4	2	3	5	7	4	3	6	2	3	3
A (after course)	5	5	2	2	5	7	5	6	6	5	7	4	6	6	3
Change score	3	3	0	0	1	5	2	1	−1	1	4	−2	4	3	0

Total score $27 - 3 = 24$

Average change score per trainee 1.6

Step 4: What were the tangible results of the programme in terms of reduced cost, improved quality, etc.?

The work of Kirkpatrick (1967) was very much concerned with the organization and evaluation of training in industry. In this field evaluation at the results level can be measured with some accuracy in terms of cost benefit. However, in the open-ended training envisaged for a course in pastoral care, measurement at the results level is far more difficult to quantify. Yet school-focused training does allow some possibility of gaining an insight of this stage of the evaluation process. For example, it could be that the teachers in a school agree, in the main, that a problem area exists. Following a course of in-service training, it may also be generally agreed that positive elements of change are seen to have occurred in dealing with the problem. Although it may not be possible to obtain measurable evidence to support this viewpoint, it can be argued that the opinion of teachers regarding the solution of a problem facing them in school must carry some weight in the evaluation of training results. An evaluation procedure of this nature could take the following pattern:

1. At the initial planning stage it may be generally accepted that a long-term objective in the proposed training course is to reduce truancy in the school. In order to clarify the problem as it exists, information is gathered and tabulated concerning the number of pupils involved, age range, pattern of truancy, etc. Obtaining such information in itself may raise problems for the training team because to assess the extent of truancy with any accuracy is extremely difficult. However, such complications will assist the team to appreciate the extent of the problem and may help in the formulation of a meaningful and effective training programme.
2. During the training course and after it has been completed, the trainees will be encouraged to introduce relevant coping procedures and techniques into the day-to-day work of the school. Regular pastoral conferences will be held to work out ways of helping pupils and to ensure consistency of approach.
3. After a suitable period of time the training team can once again gather information concerning truancy in the school. This can be compared with data collected before the course began and evaluated in terms of results. The data comparisons should, of course, be made available to all teachers in the school and a meeting held to discuss the implications of the findings.

The crucial stage in the process is the transfer of training into the work situation. Teachers may willingly attend a course, contribute positively when participating, and yet fail to change their teaching approach sufficiently to affect work positively in the classroom. Teachers who attend external courses often fall into this category. A major reason for the failure to transfer new learning and skills may be attributed to the resistance of colleagues and management to new ideas and methods.

School-focused training, however, has a major advantage in meeting any such resistance. A team of teachers, involved in programme design, dealing with problems relevant to their school situation, sharing experiences and supported throughout by management have the freedom and support necessary for effective teaching innovation.

CONCLUSION

School-focused training is an important ingredient of good management. However, to make such training truly effective, evaluation must be seen as an essential part of the process. The approach to evaluation recommended in this paper can be said to be unsophisticated in terms of research. Yet, for management who intend to take the first important steps in training method, it will provide a useful foundation. The data obtainable may influence a reappraisal of a training course, which on the surface appears to be meeting the needs of the trainees and the school. It can lend objective support to mere feelings that methods and procedures are proving to be effective. It allows an opportunity to tease out areas in which trainees show little evidence of movement in attitude change, learning or application of skills.

The force of thinking about training is expressed by Hamblin (1974): 'the control of training is, in effect, the management of training: the process of collection, analysis and evaluation of information, leading to decision making and action.' In this short paper an attempt has been made to outline the importance of such control which, in turn, becomes a means of increasing the contribution and the job satisfaction of teachers in the classroom.

APPENDIX 12.3   KNOWLEDGE AND SKILLS ASSESSMENT

The following list is a summary of the components which can be found in a variety of advanced training courses set up for part-time youth leaders. Read carefully through this list and rate your *existing knowledge* on the following 7-point scale by placing a ring around one of the numbers.

For example, on the third line:

If you feel that you have a thorough knowledge about communication skills, ring (7).
If you feel you have a good knowledge, ring (6).
If you feel you have a fair knowledge, ring (5).
If you feel that you have neither thorough nor no knowledge, ring (4).

If you feel you have little knowledge, ring (3).
If you feel you have very little knowledge, ring (2).
If you feel you have *no* knowledge, ring (1).

Please remember that this is not a test. There are no desirable or undesirable responses. It is how you assess your knowledge of each area that is important.

	No knowledge				Thorough knowledge		
1. Sexual development of the adolescent	1	2	3	4	5	6	7
2. Aggression and violence in the adolescent	1	2	3	4	5	6	7
3. Communication skills	1	2	3	4	5	6	7
4. The adolescent in the family	1	2	3	4	5	6	7
5. Anxiety in the adolescent	1	2	3	4	5	6	7
6. Observing members	1	2	3	4	5	6	7
7. Getting to know members	1	2	3	4	5	6	7
8. Working with individuals	1	2	3	4	5	6	7
9. Working with groups	1	2	3	4	5	6	7
10. Principles of counselling	1	2	3	4	5	6	7
11. Suicidal behaviour	1	2	3	4	5	6	7
12. Coping with adolescents in difficulty	1	2	3	4	5	6	7
13. Group dynamics operating within the club	1	2	3	4	5	6	7
14. Using and making games for use with members	1	2	3	4	5	6	7
15. Interviewing young people	1	2	3	4	5	6	7
16. Role-playing	1	2	3	4	5	6	7
17. Community service	1	2	3	4	5	6	7
18. Small group discussions	1	2	3	4	5	6	7
19. Helping young people to make decisions	1	2	3	4	5	6	7
20. Adjustment to work from school	1	2	3	4	5	6	7

APPENDIX 12.4   KNOWLEDGE AND SKILLS ASSESSMENT

The following list is a summary of the components of the training course you have elected to attend. Rate your existing knowledge on the following 7-point scale by placing a ring around one of the numbers.

For example, on the sixth line:

If you feel that you have a thorough knowledge about the role of the tutor, ring (7).

If you feel you have a good knowledge, ring (6).

If you feel you have a fair knowledge, ring (5).

If you feel you have neither thorough nor no knowledge, ring (4).

If you feel you have a little knowledge, ring (3).

If you feel you have very little knowledge, ring (2).

If you feel you have no knowledge, ring (1).

	No knowledge					Thorough knowledge
1. Communication skills	1	2	3	4	5	6	7
2. The disadvantaged pupil	1	2	3	4	5	6	7
3. Bullying	1	2	3	4	5	6	7
4. Motivation	1	2	3	4	5	6	7
5. Study skills	1	2	3	4	5	6	7
6. The role of the tutor	1	2	3	4	5	6	7
7. Coping with adolescents in difficulty	1	2	3	4	5	6	7
8. The effective tutorial	1	2	3	4	5	6	7
9. Aims of pastoral care	1	2	3	4	5	6	7
10. Links with parents	1	2	3	4	5	6	7
11. Interviewing	1	2	3	4	5	6	7
12. Keeping records	1	2	3	4	5	6	7

APPENDIX 12.5 KNOWLEDGE AND SKILLS ASSESSMENT, EXPERIMENTAL GROUP. AVERAGE CHANGE SCORE PER TRAINEE

In order of greatest change:	B2 – A
Using and making games for use with members	3.46
Suicidal behaviour	2.46
Role-playing	2.20
Group dynamics operating within the club	2.06
Aggression and violence in the adolescent	2.06
Principles of counselling	2.00
Anxiety in the adolescent	1.86
Helping young people to make decisions	1.86
The adolescent in the family	1.66
Working with groups	1.66
Sexual development in the adolescent	1.60
Observing members	1.60
Adjustment to work from school	1.60
Coping with adolescents in difficulty	1.60
Small group discussions	1.53
Interviewing young people	1.53
Communication skills	1.40
Community service	1.20
Working with individuals	0.86
Getting to know members	0.66

This table shows the average change score per trainee calculated from reassessed ratings of knowledge before the course began (B2) and ratings at the end of the course (A).

APPENDIX 12.6 KNOWLEDGE AND SKILLS ASSESSMENT, EXPERIMENTAL GROUP

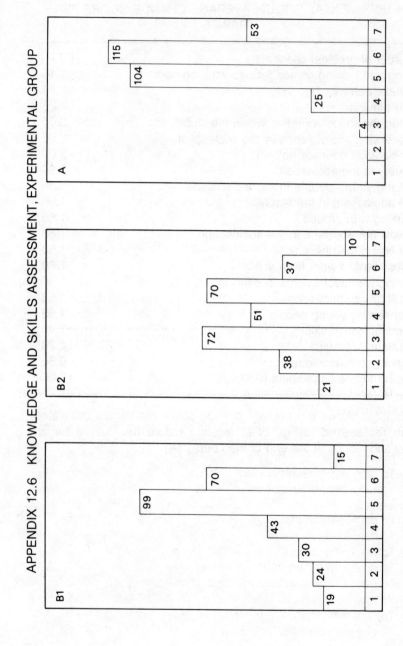

Base figures indicate the rating scale on the questionnaire.
Figures on the columns indicate the number of trainees who chose a particular rating.

APPENDIX 12.7   THE ROLE OF THE FORM TUTOR

On each line please put a circle around *one* of the numbers according to how you feel about the role of the form tutor.
For example, on line 5:

If you feel that to help pupils with personal problems is *very important*, ring (7).
If you feel it is *important*, ring (6).
If you feel it is *fairly important*, ring (5).
If you feel it is neither important nor unimportant, ring (4).
If you feel it is *fairly unimportant*, ring (3).
If you feel it is *unimportant*, ring (2).
If you feel it is *extremely unimportant*, ring (1).

Please remember this is not a test, but a way of finding out how you feel about the role of the Form Tutor. It is what *you* think that is important.

The role of the form tutor is:	Unimportant						Important
1. To have a disciplining function	1	2	3	4	5	6	7
2. To have an understanding of group dynamics	1	2	3	4	5	6	7
3. To have an insight into adolescent needs	1	2	3	4	5	6	7
4. To assist pupils to develop decision-making skills	1	2	3	4	5	6	7
5. To help pupils with personal problems	1	2	3	4	5	6	7
6. To help children with examination anxiety	1	2	3	4	5	6	7
7. To participate in induction courses	1	2	3	4	5	6	7
8. To help develop study skills	1	2	3	4	5	6	7
9. To teach the rules of the school	1	2	3	4	5	6	7
10. To deal with failure in homework	1	2	3	4	5	6	7
11. To get to know pupils in the form	1	2	3	4	5	6	7
12. To maintain a record system	1	2	3	4	5	6	7
13. To deal with truancy	1	2	3	4	5	6	7
14. To consult with parents	1	2	3	4	5	6	7

The role of the form tutor is:	Unimportant					Important	
15. To help pupils to make relationships	1	2	3	4	5	6	7
16. To have an understanding of communication skills	1	2	3	4	5	6	7
17. To work as a member of a pastoral care team	1	2	3	4	5	6	7
18. To instil standards of behaviour	1	2	3	4	5	6	7
19. To employ the use of simulations and role-play	1	2	3	4	5	6	7

13

A Framework for the Evaluation of Pastoral Care

Kate Doherty

(Head of Careers and Counselling, Enniskillen Collegiate Grammar School)

EVALUATION: THE STARTING POINT

It is arguable that many teachers have been discouraged by conventional approaches to evaluation which seek to assess the effectiveness of any educational innovation by examining whether or not it has reached the standards implied by its objectives. Perhaps they have been influenced by the same arguments as Stenhouse (1975), who has remarked that objectives have sometimes been used as a stick with which to beat teachers.

However, the reasons for not using the traditional 'measuring' approach to evaluation do not preclude an acceptance of the value of aims and objectives for the teacher. I would agree with Daunt (1975) that aims should express the highest-level objectives of a system and therefore, if a school has no stated aims and is failing to achieve its objectives, it will have no point of reference for redefining them. If the view is taken that aims constitute an ideal and give direction to educational activity, we may then use the terminology of Davies (1976) and see goals or intermediate objectives as necessary because they act as markers along the way and expose underlying assumptions.

There is however an alternative approach to evaluation – this is described as 'illuminative evaluation' and is advocated by Parlett and Hamilton (1972). The origins of this approach are found in the discipline of social anthropology and its aims are listed below:

To study the innovatory programme
1. How it operates.
2. How it is influenced by the various school situations in which it is applied.
3. What those directly concerned with it regard as its advantages and disadvantages.
4. How students' intellectual tasks and academic experiences are most affected.
5. To discover and document what it is like to be participating in the scheme.
6. To discern and discuss the innovation's most significant features, recurring concomitants and critical processes.

This approach to evaluation, which is not predetermined by ideas of success or failure and is concerned more with learning than measuring, is singularly suitable for the evaluation of pastoral care. Stress is laid on the fact that innovations cannot be separated from the context in which they occur, and, similarly, no pastoral care system should be viewed in isolation from the total social-psychological and physical environment in which staff and pupils work. There are many processes within and without the school that are likely to impinge upon pastoral activity. One example is the negative labelling of individuals or groups of pupils because they belong to particular families or a certain low-ability class. This labelling can call out from those pupils the type of reaction that is expected and then the pastoral team is asked to cope with the difficulties that result.

However this approach to evaluation is not without its critics. In a recent book Shipman (1979) criticizes illuminative evaluation stating that 'the lantern has replaced the slide rule' but I would argue that it is unnecessary to view the situation in such mutually exclusive terms – in fact Shipman himself implies that few aspects of school life actually lend themselves readily to the use of a 'slide rule'.

However later in the chapter, I will show that there is room for measurement within the illuminative approach, drawing upon the findings of an evaluation study carried out in a large comprehensive school: the 'slide rule' used on that occasion was a questionnaire administered to pupils. The results it furnished provided statistical backing for impressions gained through the use of other methods. In this case the questionnaire was custom-designed but in a different set of circumstances a published measure might have been used – what matters in each case is the relevance of the measure.

Shipman also assumes that the evaluator must, of necessity, be someone apart from the teacher, but since the illuminative approach utilizes information collected by means of observation as well as documentary and background information, it is arguably best used by 'insiders' who have a wide knowledge of the total school environment.

Furthermore Shipman maintains that there should be some planned visible reference against which the figures or judgements can be interpreted. It is necessary here to make clear, as does Marland (1974), that there cannot be a single pattern of pastoral care which can be universally applied and used as an external reference – each school must assess the relative merits of various systems bearing in mind variables such as pupil characteristics, teacher resources and the organizational constraints of the school.

The final defence of the illuminative approach is its adaptability. Here is no standard methodological package – it can be adapted to the situation in which the evaluators find themselves and it can take into account factors such as the time available for investigation, the level of co-operation within the school and the evaluators' previous experience. The fact that the individual school situation can to a large extent define the exact methods used would seem to be a considerable strength rather than a weakness of the illuminative approach.

EVALUATION AS INNOVATION

In many schools a conscious commitment to evaluation may best be seen as an innovation within the school, and in this situation the work of Poster (1976) and Gross et al. (1971) become relevant. The first vital task must be to establish who will be responsible for the innovation.

Who evaluates

This is obviously an important question since the positions of those chosen will influence the transmission of data to them, and their

271

values are likely to have some bearing upon the eventual findings. However, lest at this point the impression gained is one of total subjectivity in evaluation, it must be noted that the illuminative approach should include various procedures by which findings can be cross-checked and doubts about partiality combatted. Reference has already been made to one such procedure – the use of a pupil questionnaire.

Many skills are required by the evaluators and this is particularly so when evaluation is an innovation as far as the school is concerned. Judgement is needed as they choose samples, construct questionnaires, decide what weight to give certain information, select and present their findings in reports which will be discussed by their teaching colleagues. Interpersonal skills are obviously vital. Evaluators will seek co-operation but cannot demand it, and so they need tact, sensitivity and responsibility. They must be open about the scope and aim of the evaluation, seeking to maintain their own integrity and the trust of their colleagues.

In my view heads of year or house heads (whatever the pastoral system adopted by the school) should develop these skills and should be encouraged to do so by the senior pastoral head whose task it is to lead the pastoral team. This recognizes their position as middle management figures.

As far as the year or house heads are concerned this would mean that their role as an evaluator would coincide with the practice of accountability within pastoral care advocated by Hamblin (1978). Certainly, if no information is ever sought about the performance of form tutors by year or house heads, it would seem that some doubt is being cast upon the legitimacy of the pastoral tasks being carried out by those teachers. However the evaluator is *not* gathering information simply to assess tutor performance and this must be made clear at the outset. He will also be interested in the perceptions of tutors as to the pastoral work they are carrying out, and his overall aim will be to obtain a greater understanding of the complex realities surrounding pastoral care activity. Such understanding could surely be deemed essential in those whose task is primarily one of management and co-ordination. It should be stressed however that if form tutors and year or house heads approach the task with vastly differing perceptions of what evaluation will involve, the amount of real co-operation may well be minimal and a number of difficulties can be anticipated.

The hope would be that in-service training could focus on the skills needed for evaluation, so that individual year or house heads could approach the task armed with a framework for action. In practice, a starting-point is needed, and if, for example, the guidance programme for the sixth form was being evaluated, it might well be appropriate for the senior pastoral head and the head of sixth form to work together as an evaluatory team – they would then be able to share their experiences with other pastoral heads, and thus skills could be more widely disseminated.

Preparation

Thorough preparation is essential. Pastoral activity needs to be viewed in the context of the social-psychological and physical environment in which it is carried on and so the evaluators need to be well informed – they must understand the school's communication system and recognize the opinion leaders within the staff. There must also be a recognition of the various subsystems within the school and the nature of the transactions across the boundaries. One immediately thinks here of the curricular and pastoral subsystems which exist in most schools and the links there are between them.

Preparation also involves decisions about the scope of the evaluation. Shipman rightly points out that evaluation is time-consuming, and therefore should be concentrated where it will have most effect. Evaluation, like any other innovation, is best broken down into stages, and it would seem advisable to begin work in an area where co-operation is likely to be forthcoming. This principle of working from areas of strength allows the evaluators to gain skills reasonably quickly before proceeding to investigate areas where a greater degree of depth of information is required. The alternative is to begin in an area where there seems to be an acute problem and where most members of staff feel something must be done urgently.

The evaluators must be able to recognize the feelings of resistance and suspicion that some staff may have when evaluation is introduced. Ambivalence as well as opposition may occur whether or not staff are directly involved, which makes it all the more important to supply information about the evaluation process and discuss plans for implementing it. Staff must know why evaluation is being introduced, what its objectives are, and should have the

273

opportunity to discuss openly any reservations they might have. Stress needs to be put on the benefits of the evaluation for the staff themselves. These benefits could include the raising of pupils' academic performance through increasing the effectiveness of the study-skills programme or improving the relationship between staff and pupils through changes in the job specification of form tutors and pastoral heads. It may also be appropriate to suggest that the evaluation may throw up ideas as to how staff can become more effective through using time and resources more economically.

However, initial acceptance by staff will not be enough – problems are bound to arise as the evaluation proceeds. For example, form teachers might begin to feel that the evaluators are really only interested in scrutinizing their performance, and in such a case, there must be an opportunity for hostile feelings to be openly discussed. This emphasizes the importance of good feedback mechanisms which can operate throughout the evaluation.

Attempts to adopt a consensus approach assume the existence of some opposition – the hope is that with thorough preparation, real negotiation and careful monitoring at every stage, then the opposition will be kept to a minimum.

THE PRACTICE OF EVALUATION

The evaluation study described below was carried out over a period of an academic year during which I worked part-time in the school as a trainee counsellor. In this particular instance the pastoral care system in its entirety was under scrutiny.

Not having the advantage of being a long-term member of the school staff, background information about numbers on roll, the catchment area of the school and the rationale behind the particular horizontal pastoral system adopted, provided a useful starting-point, although most of the information used came from three main sources:

1. Interviews with staff.
2. Questionnaires administered to pupils.
3. Informal observation on a regular basis.

The variety of methods facilitated the checking of tentative findings, and removed the need for restriction in advance to fixed

274

areas: as the study unfolded, it was possible to focus attention on emerging issues.

Interviews with staff

The information being sought could be divided into two broad areas.

1. OBJECTIVES

(a) How pastoral care was viewed by the senior management of the school and by those directly involved in the pastoral system.
(b) What long-term objectives were being pursued and how far there was a consensus of opinion on them.
(c) What the short-term objectives for each year-group were; what procedures and methods were being adopted and the nature of the relationship between those procedures and the long-term objectives.

2. CURRENT FUNCTIONING

This involved an examination of the role specifications of those involved in pastoral care, bearing in mind the tasks carried out and the skills, hazards and barriers which affected performance of the role. There was, in addition, a consideration of the management function exercised by members of the pastoral team including such elements as co-ordination, communication and accountability. Finally, the link between the pastoral and curricular elements in the school was investigated.

The interviews were structured to enable comparisons to be drawn but all those interviewed had the opportunity to discuss other issues they felt were pertinent. The interviews proved to be a most useful source of information. A comparison of objectives revealed a consensus of opinion about the need for pupils to experience care and concern within the school, but there were vestiges of the idea that pastoral care is only required for certain problem pupils. This view was at variance with that expressed by others who considered that the function of the pastoral system is to enable the school to attain its objectives.

When more specific objectives were investigated, what emerged was a lack of differentiation between the long-term objectives of the pastoral system and the intermediate objectives for each year-group. There were numerous references to the words 'care' and 'concern' in the objectives quoted but little or no mention of specific ways in which that care or concern could be given a practical expression for year-groups facing differing adjustment problems – for example, there was no mention of help on study skills and examination technique which could have greatly benefited fifth-form pupils. However since it has often been noted that teachers are better known by what they do than by their statement of global aims, it was then necessary to focus upon the actual procedures and methods adopted by pastoral care staff before evaluating the relationship between those procedures and the objectives outlined earlier.

When this was done it became clear that the 'caring' aspect of the form tutor role, which was mentioned so often in the objectives, consisted mainly of attempts to engage pupils in informal conversation so that the form tutor 'got to know them'. Furthermore, personal observation during the year suggested that the extent of these conversations varied considerably from form to form.

Again there was evidence that some staff identified pastoral care with problem pupils but the sixth-form induction course, on the other hand, was an excellent example of an activity designed to help pupils cope with an important transition within school. This seemed to be an example of positive 'caring', enabling pupils to work for standards of excellence, and enabling the school to achieve its objectives.

THE OUTPUT OF PASTORAL CARE

Here the task of the pastoral team was analysed using the input-conversion-output model – this is a term taken from the industrial sector but one which can have meaning in a school context. This approach took into consideration the pupils coming to the school in terms of their socio-economic background, ability and attitudes towards school – this was the input as far as the pastoral team was concerned.

The idea of 'conversion' required information about the work

276

actually carried out by form tutors and year heads. Here it seemed vital to know where the balance of effort lay – how much time was being spent on preventive as opposed to remedial work with pupils? With regard to first-year pupils for example, it was necessary to assess the time and effort spent in anticipating the transition difficulties experienced by new pupils, detecting those who might be at risk and devising an induction programme which could provide the pupils with the necessary skills for adjustment, thus getting them off to a really good start in their new school. Set against this was the time spent by pastoral staff in dealing with new pupils who were experiencing serious adjustment difficulties or with pupils whose underfunctioning might be traced back to an inability to cope effectively with the adjustment crisis.

If the information gained suggested that more energy was being expended on remedial work with pupils in difficulty, then this would provide a basis for future decision-making about how to use staff resources most economically. As a result more emphasis might be placed on preventative work with new pupils which would seek to anticipate their difficulties and provide them with the means of learning the necessary adjustment skills.

If the output of the pastoral system is seen as synonymous with the objectives of the school, this raises questions about academic attainment, level of aspiration, self-image and social competencies of pupils (Hamblin, 1974). How can this output be evaluated? Apart from the external reference of public examination results in the area of academic attainment, quantitative evaluation seems out of the question. In the study being described note was taken of the number of pupils seeking help from the counsellor and the generalized nature of the help required, while attention was also paid to the subjective impressions of staff working in different curriculum areas.

In some schools where there have been curricular innovations, staff have been asked to involve pupils in activities like trust-walks which come under the aegis of creative drama. While no quantitative evaluation is possible, the input-conversion-output model could help to provide a framework for evaluation, with staff, not just those directly involved, being asked to consider what transfer of training has occurred. Whatever the activity, whether it be a study skills or a group dynamics programme, it can only be judged worthwhile if there is some agreement about its transfer effect.

A positive transfer effect requires, from both staff and pupils, an awareness of the specific skills being taught in the programme as well as a determined effort from the teaching staff to stimulate and develop those skills in the classroom. A study skills programme may fail because subject teachers are not involved in the planning of the programme and thus cannot encourage their pupils to develop further the skills they have learnt. This situation can occur in a school where there is a very distinct pastoral/curricular divide and so the approach taken by the pastoral team in such a school will be crucial.

ROLE SPECIFICATIONS

Any attempt to make objectives explicit must involve detailed role specifications, and in the study undertaken some attempt was made to bear in mind the three different aspects of a role. Perhaps this can be illustrated best by considering a specific role – that of a form tutor.

1. The prescribed role – what others expect the form tutor to do.
2. The subjective role – what the form tutor feels he/she should be doing.
3. The enacted role – what the form tutor actually does.

In the school being studied there was an absence of detailed job specifications, and this left a considerable degree of scope for personal interpretation of role. In the field of discipline there was some role conflict with some subject teachers abdicating their responsibilities. There also seemed to be an underlying implication that heads of year were really the servants of the academic staff, and this stemmed from a very clear academic/pastoral divide operating at the middle level of management within the school. Significantly too, there was a division of opinion as to how far heads of year should become directly involved with pupils. Should a head of year 'do pastoral care' as one form tutor put it, or should he see himself primarily as the leader of a team of tutors?

As far as the form tutors themselves were concerned, their interviews revealed feelings that a dual standard was being operated. On the one hand year heads stressed the importance of the form tutor's role but the tutors themselves felt that the treatment accorded to them did not correspond with this. 'It's a nothing' was one comment on the role of the form tutor while others described themselves as merely 'channels of communication' or 'recording machines'. The failures of the school's communication system, and the tendency for heads of year to deal with pupils directly were most often mentioned as reasons for this, and, of course, these are connected. Information can be used as part of the power struggle within a school – accordingly the degree to which heads of year see themselves as sources of information which may or may not be distributed to form tutors on request can be associated with their attempts to achieve staff recognition through direct dealing with pupils. This situation can of course operate in reverse, with form tutors withholding important information from heads of year, but there was no evidence of this occurring in the school being studied.

Much seemed to hinge upon the lack of a clear job specification for tutors which outlined the tasks and skills required. Where such a job specification gains acceptance and achieves legitimacy, one would expect procedures to exist which would ensure that the job was done at least at a minimal level. These did not operate except at a purely administrative level in the case of registers.

When the transfer of information between middle and senior management was examined it became clear that information was often passed to the school counsellor, rather than to heads of year, and this provided a further justification for an investigation of the counsellor's role within the pastoral system. In turn this raised questions about the role of the counsellor in relation to in-service training and the importance of the consultative role that might be adopted. These were issues that had not suggested themselves as worthy of investigation at the outset of the study.

When the field of careers guidance was investigated it emerged that some heads of year did not see themselves as responsible for any specific vocational guidance while others assumed limited responsibilities within this field. The resources available to the careers staff to carry out the task attributed to them seemed hardly appropriate. While a reasonably generous allowance was made as far as non-teaching time was concerned, much of this was taken up with the heavy burden of administration – preparing information sheets for careers officers, writing references for ex-pupils as well as the administration concerned with works visits, careers talks and careers officers' interviews. The allocation of only four careers lessons in the timetable was totally inadequate. Only some fifth formers had careers lessons, there was no direct contact between the careers department and fourth-year pupils and contact at the third-year level was limited.

This was evidence that much more needed to be done, particularly at curriculum level, if careers education was to assume central rather than marginal importance in the school. A comparison with the recommendations for careers provision made as long ago as 1973 in the DES *Education Survey 18* (Department of Education and Science, 1975), underlined this further and provided a factual basis for future decisions about developing careers provision.

Finally, interviews with staff were used to consider the processes within the school which impinged upon pastoral care activity and this is in line with the illuminative evaluation approach used throughout. Evidence was sought about the effects of the streaming and banding of pupils in leading to the 'labelling' of pupils, both as groups and as individuals, and the approach of staff to such problems as truancy, underfunctioning and disruption within the classroom was also considered carefully.

Here one is not assuming that the pastoral team should be able to 'solve' all the problems of the school, particularly when some of them at least may be either reinforced or created by the strategies adopted within the school. What is being advocated is an attempt at pastoral/curricular integration, which allows these issues to be a focus of concern for all those staff who do not feel that their task is simply that of teaching a subject but that of realizing their dual teaching and caring role.

INFORMATION FROM PUPILS

Schools are of course not limited to the use of questionnaires when they seek to find out pupils' reactions to pastoral provision, but in the wide-ranging study being described, their use seemed to be the most efficient way of acquiring information.

The questionnaire used is to be found at the end of the chapter and its general objective was to investigate pupils' perceptions of the function and purpose of the pastoral system as a whole. Subsumed under this general objective were a number of more specific objectives:

1. To make a comparison between the use made by pupils of sources of advice external to the school and the use made of the pastoral system.
2. To investigate the extent to which parents' advice is sought on difficulties which are school-based.
3. To investigate the extent to which pupils seek the help and advice of school staff if they have:
   (a) difficulties of a personal nature;
   (b) difficulties with school work;
   (c) difficulties associated with career choice.
4. To provide information on how far pupils use the formal pastoral system rather than seek advice from any available source within the school.
5. To investigate pupils' perceptions of the functions of role-holders in the pastoral system.

Some sections of the questionnaire asked pupils to answer a series of closed questions concerning the help they would seek if in difficulty. As a check on these findings, pupils were also asked to consider four practical situations and to suggest in each case the action they would take and the person they would consult. Other sections invited pupils to write brief descriptions of what the job of the form tutor and head of year seemed to be. An approach based on incomplete sentences provided a check on this information as well as widening the area under investigation. Thus issues and attitudes not recognized as important when the questionnaire was devised had an opportunity to emerge.

Obviously not all the objectives listed above will be relevant to every school, and indeed such a wide-ranging investigation of pupils' attitudes may not be necessary, or indeed desirable, when evaluation is begun. It was suggested earlier that evaluation might begin in an area where there is likely to be most co-operation so that the evaluators can gain skills reasonably quickly before proceeding to other areas of investigation where a greater degree and depth of information is being sought. With co-operation in mind then, staff reaction to pupil questionnaires must be investigated thoroughly and the ways in which they are introduced to pupils thought through carefully. Certainly this is a sensitive area, and if pupils are asked, for example, to comment on their perceptions of the role of form tutor and year head, the information gleaned must be handled in a thoroughly professional way.

281

However reservations about questionnaires should not discourage teachers from seeking out pupils' reactions to pastoral provision. The writer recently investigated pupil reaction to a newly instituted sixth-form induction course using a questionnaire at the time of the course and then following this up by a small-group discussion at a later stage. As a result, a number of changes regarding timing and format will be made in the course being arranged for next year.

In the main study being described some vital issues emerged when the questionnaires were analysed. Pupils were clearly anxious to seek help on educational and vocational matters from within the school although this was not the case with personal matters. Indeed, the small percentage of pupils who stated that they had discussed a personal matter with a member of the school teaching staff raised questions about the availability and privacy of the sources of help within the school although it may simply have been that pupils did not view staff as appropriate sources of help on personal matters, however these were defined.

Of course, those pupils who see learning as something that is imposed upon them by an external source and accordingly view it negatively may well see any form of personal guidance as a threat to their autonomy. If this is the case, attempts to foist guidance on personal matters upon such pupils will be foredoomed to failure and this would need to be borne in mind when decisions were made about future provision. The introduction of a structured guidance programme for each year-group seemed to provide the best way forward – this could anticipate difficulties and teach new skills while at the same time making sources of support visible and available to those pupils who wish to avail themselves of their provision.

Obviously sixth formers have had more experience of the pastoral system than any other pupils and their responses were given particular attention. In fact one part of the questionnaire was completed only by them. In general there was satisfaction with the amount of educational guidance received, but the evidence of a desire for more vocational guidance in 91.8 per cent of the responses was in line with the evidence provided by the studies of Fogelman (1972) and King et al. (1974).

Again, a lack of interest in personal guidance emerged and the writer felt that the introduction of a programme for personal development such as that suggested by Hamblin (1978) would provide some answer. Such a programme would assist sixth formers to assess their behaviour and their methods of problem-solving more realistically and aid the development of their personal autonomy. At the same time sixth formers would be aware of sources of support within the school and could use them if they so desired.

Where such guidance programmes are introduced, pupil reactions to the various elements in the programme should be sought. If the reaction is a negative one, and the prevailing feeling is that the activity was of little practical use in helping them cope with a discontinuity within school or a wider developmental task, then staff surely should pause and consider carefully their justification for continuing to include it in the programme.

However the emphasis in the study was not all on pupil perceptions of pastoral activity – the information from the questionnaires was set in a wider context within which cross-checking of findings could take place. For example, interviews with form tutors had made clear that many felt they were being bypassed with heads of year spending a considerable amount of their time dealing with individual pupils. The questionnaires backed this up. Section Six of the questionnaire, which asked pupils to give their perceptions of the work of form tutors and heads of year, revealed that more pupils saw the head of year, not the form tutor, as the member of staff to whom one goes if a problem has to be resolved. Other sections of the questionnaire which related to the work of tutors and year heads reinforced these findings.

From the outset it has been clear that the illuminative approach commits its users to find out the reactions of those directly involved in the programme being evaluated, whether they are staff or pupils, but the practical evidence of this study made it abundantly clear than any evaluation which ignores the pupil dimension is very much the poorer.

FINAL JUSTIFICATION

In this final section the contribution that evaluation can make in the total life of the school will be emphasized and in particular, the value of the illuminative approach used in the study described will be underlined.

Latterly educationalists have become aware of the approaches in management which can provide guidelines for decision-making in schools, and from this it has emerged that evaluation must be a tool of the efficient school management team. Admittedly, the illuminative approach concentrates more on the information-gathering than the decision-making component of evaluation, and the knowledge gained does not automatically determine the decisions the management team will make about pastoral provision, but it is clear that sound decision-making does require adequate relevant information.

For all its lack of quantitative data, comparatively speaking, such a study as that described above does not simply produce opinions and impressions – indeed if this were all that emerged teachers might well be justified in being sceptical. In fact it was possible to pinpoint vital areas of concern within the school:

1. The need for clear job specifications for form tutors and heads of year.
2. The need to introduce such a development in a way which would build upon the good work being done by pastoral staff.

Furthermore the study raised a number of fundamental questions lying at the heart of pastoral care work. Is pastoral care concerned with the development of every child, and therefore, is it seen as a means of support to the school in the achieving of its objectives? In what direction is 'pastoral energy' expended? Is most energy expended on remedial work of some kind with pupils who have found themselves in difficulty or is there a realization that pastoral care is also concerned with the anticipation of difficulties, with the result that pastoral endeavour becomes transformed into an active educative programme for all pupils within the school?

In this study, the aim was to evaluate the pastoral system in its entirety. However in many schools, the time available may suggest that evaluation begins on a smaller scale. Certainly one area which seems to demand closer scrutiny concerns the educational guidance given to third-form pupils making subject choices, a point borne out by the findings of Reid et al. (1974). Falling school rolls and a reduction in the number of teaching staff will of course compound the difficulties here.

In the research carried out by Reid et al. (1974) the basis of the evaluation was an approach which combined the pupil's subjective view of his choices and the more objective assessments of the teachers, although they did admit that an illuminative approach would have been helpful since it would have taken account of the complexities of the school environment.

Certainly, pupil views of their subject choices can be investigated by means of questionnaires, followed up perhaps by small-group discussion. Any difficulties being experienced in the study of these subjects can then emerge, and appropriate action can then be taken.

I recently investigated how fourth formers in my present school viewed the subject choices they had made. The questionnaire was issued to them after they had studied the subjects for more than a term and had taken internal school examinations. They were asked:

1. Which subjects did you choose from the groups available last year?
2. Do you now regret choosing any of these subjects? – if so which?
3. If your answer to question 2 was *Yes* explain why you regret choosing the subject(s). (If you had no other choice because of the grouping of subjects make this clear.)
4. Do you consider that you had enough guidance in school when making your choices? If not, please give suggestions as to ways in which the guidance could be improved?
5. What have you found to be the main difference (if any) between work in third and fourth form?

This basic questionnaire provided some useful information – in particular, the answers to question 5 revealed a need for more help to be given to fourth formers in organizing their work, making good notes and revising for examinations. Answers to question 4 were generally favourable but answers to question 3 suggested that not enough information had been given on the way in which subjects change at fourth-form level. As a result more emphasis was placed on this in the guidance programme devised for third formers this year.

As Reid *et al.* (1974) found, teachers' objective assessments of pupil choices can be helpful but the scope of the investigation could be much wider than this. Interviews with appropriate staff could focus on the objectives of the guidance given. Is there agreement on these? What is the relationship between those objectives and the actual procedures carried out? At the same time attention should be paid to the total school environment which is having an influence on what is being offered to those third-form pupils.

It may well be that one of the objectives is to help pupils make subject choices which are linked to future career choices. In practice, however, how much opportunity is given to pupils to consider the demands of individual subjects and to keep in mind the vocational implications of their choices? Are they just given one brief talk or is there a guidance programme being offered which gives them a chance to engage in self-assessment, allows them greater insights into differing life-styles and the need to match personal qualities with those required in jobs, and attempts to inculcate decision-making ability?

Another objective may be to involve parents in the process of choosing subjects, but it may well be that parents are only drawn in at the end to give some kind of 'imprimatur' to what has already been decided. It could be argued indeed that many parents must find traditional parents' meetings somewhat frustrating – at one level the school may be saying that parental contact is important, yet parents may go away feeling that they have been 'talked at' and have had to stand in long queues to speak to teachers for even a few minutes.

Secondly, interviews with staff could also investigate the current functioning of the guidance system for third formers. Attention could be focused on the boundaries that may exist between the academic and pastoral sub-systems in the school and the boundaries between the sub-systems in the school which are associated with ability. These may be bands or streams within each year-group.

In order to investigate these areas a number of vital questions must be asked. Who in fact selects the third-form options and who administers them to the pupils? How much is left to form tutors and how far are subject teachers involved? Information on these points will give a clear indication of how wide the academic/pastoral split in the school may be.

Are all the pupils actually given a choice, or does the school make a decision about a suitable curriculum for some of its pupils? If the latter is the case it would seem that certain pupils are being denied decision-making experience and it may also suggest that some type of 'labelling' process is at work. What messages are being sent to certain pupils about the school's view of their ability, and perhaps too, their behaviour? The allocation of staff to particular groups is one way in which the message can be conveyed. Could changes be made in the teaching methods adopted in certain subjects in order to leave them open to more pupils and thus create more job possibilities for them?

A FRAMEWORK FOR EVALUATING A FIRST YEAR INDUCTION PROGRAMME

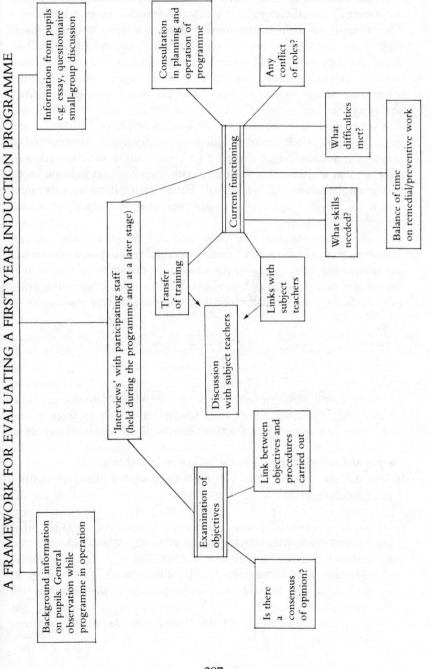

Background information on pupils. General observation while programme in operation

Information from pupils e.g. essay, questionnaire small-group discussion

'Interviews' with participating staff (held during the programme and at a later stage)

Examination of objectives

Link between objectives and procedures carried out

Is there a consensus of opinion?

Discussion with subject teachers

Transfer of training

Links with subject teachers

Current functioning

Consultation in planning and operation of programme

Any conflict of roles?

What difficulties met?

What skills needed?

Balance of time on remedial/preventive work

As for those directly involved in the guidance of the pupils, what are their role specifications? Is there any confusion or overlap here? The attitudes of form tutors may well require close scrutiny since they could find themselves in a position where much is expected of them, yet they may feel ill-equipped for the task. It may be that the communication system does not provide them with all the information they require or they may be aware of a lack of the necessary training.

It seems clear that whether the evaluation of pastoral provision is on a large or small scale the illuminative approach is singularly suitable. It acknowledges the need to bear in mind the total school environment and this is in harmony with the view that pastoral care is a central activity of the school. Furthermore it is an approach which is flexible and readily adaptable to the needs of each individual school.

In the end, however, the plea must be for evaluation, using whatever methods the school deems suitable, so long as it results in an increased understanding of the basis and practice of pastoral care, encourages decisions which are based on sound judgements and safeguards the professional integrity of the participating staff.

APPENDIX 13.1. PUPIL QUESTIONNAIRE

Section One

Please answer *YES* or *NO* to the following questions:
In the last six months have you discussed with a member of the school teaching staff:

Answers

(a) A personal matter which worried you? e.g. difficulties at home, having too few friends at school.

(b) Difficulties you have had with school work? e.g. difficulties with homework, choosing subject options.

(c) Your future career?

(d) A problem that does not fall clearly into (a), (b) or (c)?

Section Two

If *any* answer to section one was *YES* think of the person with whom you had the discussion. Then write down their *position* within the school – not their name.

Some examples of positions are: form tutor, English teacher, school counsellor, careers teacher.

```
┌─────────────────────┐
│                     │
│                     │
└─────────────────────┘
```

Section Three

If *any* answer to section one was *NO*, during the past six months, have you discussed with someone outside school:

Answers

(a) A personal matter which worried you?

(b) Difficulties which you have had with school work?

(c) Your future career?

(d) A problem that does not fall clearly into (a), (b) or (c)?

Section Four

If *any* answer to section three was *YES*, then think of the person with whom you had the discussion and then write down their *position* not their name, in the box below.

Some examples of positions outside school are: parent, relative, parent of a friend, clergyman, youth club leader.

```
┌─────────────────────┐
│                     │
│                     │
└─────────────────────┘
```

Section Five

If you were worried about any of the following matters and you wanted to discuss them with someone, who would it be? In each

289

case give the *position*, not their name. It may be someone in school or someone outside school.

(a) If worried about a personal matter.

(b) If worried about school work.

(c) If worried about your future career.

Section Six

Please write a brief description of what the job of the following people seems to be:

1. *A form tutor*

2. *A head of year*

Section Seven

Please complete each of the following sentences.

1. Every form has a tutor so that ....
....

2. If I was sent to my head of year, it would be because ....
   ....

3. The counsellor sees pupils who ....
   ....

4. If my form tutor sends for me I feel ....
   ....

5. ....
   .... in our registration period.

6. Pupils who get into serious trouble are sent to ....
   ....

7. If only my form tutor would ....
   ....

8. I think the school counsellor should ....
   ....

9. If I felt really worried about anything in school I would ....
   ....

10. The form tutor ....
    ....

11. Registration period is a good time to ....
    ....

12. I would like the careers teacher to ....
    ....

13. Finding time to talk to my form tutor is ....
    ....

14. I would go to see my head of year if ....
    ....

15. ....
    .... care about their pupils.

Section Eight

Listed below are four situations in which pupils might find themselves. If you were the pupil involved, what action would you take? – would you discuss the problem with someone?

Please say what you would do in the boxes below.

SITUATION A

There are problems at home making it difficult to concentrate on school work. Exams are approaching and you have got behind with studies and revision.

    (a) What would you do?
    (b) Who would you ask for help?

(a)
(b)

SITUATION B

You feel very confused – you do not know whether to leave school at sixteen or to stay on to take more exams which you think you need for a job that interests you.

    (a) What would you do?
    (b) Who would you ask for help?

(a)
(b)

You do not seem to be making any progress with one of your school subjects. You hate going to the classes and you wish you could give it up.

(a) What would you do?
(b) Who would you ask for help?

(a)
(b)

SITUATION D

You find it hard to make friends and to make matters worse, a group in your class are making your life a misery.

(a) What would you do?
(b) Who would you ask for help?

(a)
(b)

Section Nine

Have you any suggestions about how the pastoral care system in this school could be improved?

Please put your ideas in the box below.

```



```

Questions to be answered by sixth formers only

How much information or guidance have you received at school on:

(a) Employment opportunities?
(b) Educational matters? e.g. subject choices, future educational opportunities.
(c) Personal matters?

Please put a *ring* around the number which is under the appropriate answer.

	A lot	Some	Hardly any	None at all
Employment opportunities	1	2	3	4
Educational matters	1	2	3	4
Personal matters	1	2	3	4

How helpful have you found the information or guidance you have received at school?

	Very helpful	Fairly helpful	Not really helpful	Not at all helpful	Question does not apply
Employment opportunities	1	2	3	4	5
Educational matters	1	2	3	4	5
Personal matters	1	2	3	4	5

294

How much more information and guidance would you like to receive at school?

	Much more	A little more	Neither more nor less	A little less	Much less
Employment opportunities	1	2	3	4	5
Educational matters	1	2	3	4	5
Personal matters	1	2	3	4	5

References

Allport, C. W. (1955) *Becoming*, New Haven: Yale University Press.

Anderson, E. M. (1973) *The Disabled Schoolchild*, London: Methuen.

Bandura, A. (1962) Social learning through imitation. In: Jones, M. R. (Ed.) *Nebraska Symposium on Motivation*, Lincoln: University of Nebraska Press.

Banks, O. and Finlayson, D. (1973) *Success and Failure in the Secondary School*, London: Methuen.

Bernstein, B. (1971) *Class, Codes and Control*, London: Routledge & Kegan Paul.

Best, R. (1980) (ed.) *Perspectives in Pastoral Care*, London: Heinemann.

Blackburn, K. (1975) *The Tutor*, London: Heinemann.

Bolam, R. (1978) School-focused inset and consultancy, *Educational Change and Development*, 1 April.

Boocock, S. (1972) *An Introduction to the Sociology of Learning*, Boston: Houghton Mifflin.

Boocock, S. and Schild, E. O. (eds) (1968) *Simulation Games in Learning*, Beverley Hills: Sage.

Bowley, A. H. and Gardener, L. (1972) *The Handicapped Child*, Churchill Livingstone: London.

Burgoyne, J. (1973) *The Evaluation of Managerial Development Programmes with Special Reference to the Manchester Business School*, unpublished Ph.D thesis: University of Manchester.

Buzan, T. (1974) *Use Your Head*, London: BBC.

Caspari, I. (1976) *Troublesome Children in Class*, London: Routledge and Kegan Paul.

Chapman, H. L. (1977) *The Self-concept and Social Competence of the Physically Handicapped Adolescent*, unpublished M.Ed. Dissertation, University College of Swansea.

Chesler, M. and Fox, R. (1966) *Role-playing Methods in the Classroom*, Chicago: Science Research Associates.

Cope, C. and Anderson, E. M. (1977) *Special Units in Ordinary Schools*, University of London: Institute of Education.

Cosin, B. (1972) 'Ideologies and Education' in Seaman, P., Esland, G., Cosin, B., *Innovation and Ideology*, Bletchley: The Open University Press.

Cowley, J., Caruana, S. and Rutherford, D. (1978) *Teaching about Alcohol and Drinking*, Manchester: TACADE Press.

Csikszentmihalyi, M., Larson, R. and Prescott, S. (1977) 'The Ecology of Adolescent Activity and Experience', *Journal of Youth and Adolescence*, Vol. 6: No. 3, pp. 281–294.

Dahl, P. R. (1978) A Practical Guide to Mainstreaming, *School Shop*, Vol. 37, April 1978.

Daunt, P. (1975) *Comprehensive Values*, London: Heinemann.

David, K. and Cowley, J. (1979) *Counselling and Pastoral Care in Schools*, London: Edward Arnold.

Davies, I. K. (1976) *Objectives in Curriculum Design*, London: McGraw-Hill.

Davies, J. and Stacey, B. (1972) *Teenagers and Alcohol – A Developmental Study in Glasgow*, Vol. 2, London: HMSO.

Davison, A. and Gordon, P. (1978) *Games and Simulations in Action*, London: Woburn Press.

Department of Education and Science. (1965) *The Education of Maladjusted Children*, Pamphlet No. 47.

Department of Education and Science. (1973) *Education Survey 18*, London: HMSO.

Department of Education and Science. (1979) *Design note 18: Access for the Physically Disabled to Educational Buildings*, London: HMSO.

Dorn, N. (1976) Self-fulfilling prophecy, *Drug Link*, Summer Vol. 2, Issue 1–2, London: ISDD.

Dorn, N. (1978) *Teaching Decision-Making Skills about Legal and Illegal Drugs*, London: HEC and ISDD.

Fogelman, K. P. (1972) *Leaving the Sixth Form*, Slough: NFER.

Furneaux, B. (1969) *The Special Child*, Harmondsworth: Penguin.

Garnett, J. (1976) Special Children in the Comprehensive School, *Special Education*, Vol. 3, No. i, March 1976.

Gaudry, E. and Spielberger, C. (1971) *Anxiety and Educational Achievement*, Sydney: Wiley.

Gibbs, E. I. (1974) *Handbook of Games and Simulation Exercises*, London: E & F. N. Spon Ltd.

Gibbs, I. and Wilcox, J. (1977) *Perspectives on academic gaming and simulation*, Loughborough: SAGSET.

Glandon, N. (1978) 'The Hidden Curriculum In Simulations: Some Implications of Our Applications' in McAleese, R. (Ed.) *Perspectives on Academic Gaming and Simulation*, Vol. 3, Training and Professional Education, London: Kogan Page (SAGSET).*

Gloucestershire Scheme, Third Report (1971): Gloucestershire LEA.

Gross, N., Giacquinta, J. and Bernstein, M. (1971) *Implementing Organizational Innovations*, New York: Harper and Row.

Gulliford, R. (1971) *Special Educational Needs*, London: Routledge and Kegan Paul.

Halliwell, M. and Spain, B. (1977) Integrating Pupils with Spina Bifida, *Special Education*, Vol. 4, Dec. 1977, pp. 15–17.

Hamblin, A. (1970) 'Evaluation of training', Supplement to *Industrial Training International*, Vol. 5, No. 11.

Hamblin, A. (1974) *Evaluation and Control of Training*, London: McGraw Hill.

Hamblin, D. (1974) *The Teacher and Counselling*, Oxford: Blackwell.

Hamblin, D. (1975) *Unpublished lecture notes*, Swansea University: Department of Education.

Hamblin, D. (1975) The counsellor and strategies for the treatment of disturbed children in secondary school, *British Journal of Guidance and Counselling*, Vol. 3, No. 2, July.

Hamblin, D. (1977) *Sixth Form Study Skills*, Mimeograph, Swansea University: Department of Education.

Hamblin, D. (1978) *The Teacher and Pastoral Care*, Oxford: Blackwell.

Hargreaves, D. H. (1972) *Interpersonal Relationships and Education*, London: Routledge and Kegan Paul.

Hassall, C. (1968) A controlled study of the children of young male alcoholics, *British Journal of Addiction*, Vol. 63, p. 193.

*SAGSET, the Society for Academic Gaming and Simulation in Education and Training, acts as a clearing-house for simulation material, runs conferences and publishes a journal. Details from Centre for Extension Studies, University of Technology, Loughborough, Leics. LE11 3TU.

Hawker, A. (1978) *Adolescents and Alcohol*, London: Edsall.

Heim, A. (1975) *AH 2*, Slough, NFER.

Heron, T. E. (1978) Maintaining the Mainstreamed child in the Regular Classroom, *Journal of Learning Disabilities*, Vol. II, No. 4, April 1978.

HMSO (1976) *Departmental Committee on Drinking and Driving – Blennerhassett Report*, London: Department of the Environment.

Jackson, R. and Juniper, K. (1971) *A Manual of Educational Guidance*, London: Holt, Rinehart and Winston.

Jahoda, G. (1972) *Children and Alcohol – A Developmental Study in Glasgow*, Vol. 1, London: HMSO.

Jamieson, M., Parlett, M. and Pocklington, K. (1977) *Towards Integration*, Slough, NFER.

Jones, K. (1975) *Nine graded simulations*. ILEA Learning Materials Service, London: Publishing Centre, Highbury Station Road.

Katz, D. (1967) 'The Functional Approach to the Study of Attitudes' in Fishbein, H. (Ed.), *Readings in Attitude Theory and Measurement*, New York: John Wiley.

Kellmer-Pringle, M. L. and Fiddes, D. O. (1970) *The Challenge of Thalidomide*, London: Longman.

Kershaw, J. (1974) Handicapped Children in the Ordinary School. In *The Handicapped Person in the Community*, Boswell and Wingrove, London: Tavistock.

Kessel, N. and Walton, H. (1969) *Alcoholism*, Harmondsworth: Penguin.

King, E., Moor, C. and Mundy, J. (1974) *Post Compulsory Education*, Vol. 1. *A New Analysis in Western Europe*, London: Sage.

Kohl, H. R. (1974) *Writing Maths and Games in the Open Classroom*, London: Methuen.

Krupar, K. R. (1973) *Communication Games: Partcipant's Manual*, London: Collier Macmillan.

Lancashire, E. A. (1979) *Active Tutorial Work*, (the First and Second Years), Oxford: Blackwell.

Large, P. (1978) Integration: will Warnock cause more delay? *Where?*, No. 139, June 1978.

Long, N., Morse, W. and Newman, R. (eds) (1965) *Conflict in the Classroom: The Education of Emotionally Disturbed Children*, Belmont: Wadsworth.

Manpower Services Commission (1978) *Services for Disabled People*, An MSC programme.

Marland, M. (1974) *Pastoral Care*, London: Heinemann.

Marshall, J. (1979) Pre-tops in Practice, *NATFHE Journal*, No. 3, April 1979.

McPhail, P. (1967) 'Adolescence: The Age of Social Experiment', Paper to BPS conference *reprinted in* Open University Personality Growth and Learning Course (1972): *Social Relationships Unit 10: The Self Concept*.

McPhail, P. (1972) 'Building a role-play exercise: "the after the party scene"', *in* Longley, C. (Ed.) *Games and Simulations*, London: BBC.

Megarry, J. (1976) The further mistakes made by simulation and game designers, *SAGSET Journal*, Vol. 6, pp. 87–92.

Megarry, J. (1977) *Aspects of Simulation and Gaming*, Kogan Page.

Ministry of Education (1954) Circular No. 276.

Morgan, G. (1977) Integration v. Segregation in Ontario, *Special Education Forward Trends*, Vol. 4, No. i, March 1977, pp. 18–21.

Morgan, M. (1974) Like Other School Leavers? In: Boswell and Wingrove, *The Handicapped Person in the Community*, London: Tavistock.

'*Objectives in Health Education Workshop – Alcohol Case Study*' (1979) In Press. To be published by TACADE.

Parlett, M. and Hamilton, D. (1972) *Evaluation as illumination* Occ. Paper 9. Edinburgh: Centre for Research Education Sciences.

Pastoral Care and Education for Personal Relationships in Lancashire Secondary Schools, (1978) Lancashire LEA.

Peddar, R. (1975) The Multihandicapped Child in a Boarding School for Cerebral Palsy. In: *The Integration of Handicapped Children in Society*, Loring, J. and Burn, G., London: Routledge and Kegan Paul.

Phillips, B. (1978) *School Stress and Anxiety*, New York: Human Sciences Press.

Poster, C. (1976) *School Decision-Making*, London: Heinemann.

Reid, M., Barnett, B. and Rosenberg, H. (1974) *A Matter of Choice*, Slough: NFER.

Report of theAdvisory Committee on Handicapped Children (1972) *Children with Specific Reading Difficulties*, London: HMSO.

Richardson, E. (1973) *The Teacher, the School and the Task of Management*, London: Heinemann.

Rutter, M., Maugham, B., Mortimore, P. and Ouston, J. (1979) *Fifteen Thousand Hours*, London: Open Books.

Salmon, P. (1979) The Role of The Peer Group. In: Coleman, J. C. (Ed.) *The School Years*, London: Methuen.

Sex Education in Perspective Chapter 7, (1979) NMGC.

Shaftel, F. and Shaftel, G. (1967) *Role Playing For Social Values*, Engelwood Cliffs: Prentice Hall.

Shipman, M. (1979) *In-school Evaluation*, London: Heinemann.

Slade, P. (1971) *Child Drama*, London: University of London Press.

Stadsklev, R. (Ed.) (1974) *Handbook of Simulation Gaming in Social Education part 1*: Textbook, University of Alabama: Institute of Higher Education Research and Services (distributed by SAGSET).

Stanford, G. (1977) *Developing Effective Classroom Groups: a Practical Guide for Teachers*, New York: Hart Publishing Co.

Stenhouse, L. (1975) *Introduction to Curriculum Research and Development*, London: Heinemann.

Student Counselling in Lancashire (1979): Lancashire LEA.

Taylor, J. and Walford, R. (1972) *Simulation in the Classroom*, Harmondsworth: Penguin.

Taylor, J. and Walford, R. (1978) *Learning and the Simulation Game*, Milton Keynes: The Open University Press.

Vandenberghe, R. (1978) Meaning of the demand of a practice-centred in-service training, *British Journal of In-Service Education*, Vol. 5, No. 1.

Wall, W. (1948) *The Adolescent Child*, London: Methuen.

Wall, W. D. (1968) *Adolescents in School and Society*, Slough: NFER.

Wall, W. D. (1977) *Constructive Education For Adolescents*, London: UNESCO/Harrap.

Warnock, H. M. (1978) (Chairman) *Special Educational Needs: Report of the Committee of Enquiry into the Education of Handicapped Children and Young People*, London: HMSO.

Watts, M. (1979) 'School Reports to Parents' in Goacher, B. and Weindling, D., *School Reports Newsletter No. 1*, Slough: NFER.

Wright, B. (1960) *Physical Disability: A Psychological Approach*, New York: Harper and Row.

Index

305